THE COMPLETE BOOK OF **TAPAS** AND
SPANISH COOKING

THE COMPLETE BOOK OF **TAPAS** AND
SPANISH COOKING

discover the authentic sun-drenched dishes of a rich
traditional cuisine in 150 recipes and 700 photographs

PEPITA ARIS

JG
PRESS

Published by World Publications Group, Inc.
140 Laurel Street East Bridgewater, MA 02333
www.wrldpub.net

Produced by Anness Publishing Ltd
Hermes House 88–89 Blackfriars Road London SE1 8HA
tel. 020 7401 2077; fax 020 7633 9499; www.annesspublishing.com

If you like the images in this book and would like to investigate using them for publishing, promotions or advertising, please visit our website www.practicalpictures.com for more information.

Publisher: Joanna Lorenz
Managing Editor: Linda Fraser
Editor: Susannah Blake
Photographer: Nicki Dowey
Home Economist: Lucy McKelvie
Assistant Home Economists: Emma McKintosh
Stylist: Helen Trent
Designer: Nigel Partridge
Copy-editor: Rosie Hankin

ETHICAL TRADING POLICY
Because of our ongoing ecological investment programme, you, as our customer, can have the pleasure and reassurance of knowing that a tree is being cultivated on your behalf to naturally replace the materials used to make the book you are holding. For further information about this scheme, go to www.annesspublishing.com/trees

ISBN-10: 1-57215-535-3
ISBN-13: 978-1-57215-535-0

Printed and bound in China

Previously published as *Spanish*

PUBLISHER'S NOTE
Although the advice and information in this book are believed to be accurate and true at the time of going to press, neither the authors nor the publisher can accept any legal responsibility or liability for any errors or omissions that may be made nor for any inaccuracies nor for any harm or injury that comes about from following instructions or advice in this book.

NOTES

Bracketed terms are intended for American readers.
For all recipes, quantities are given in both metric and imperial measures and, where appropriate, measures are also given in standard cups and spoons. Follow one set, but not a mixture, because they are not interchangeable.
Standard spoon and cup measures are level. 1 tsp = 5ml, 1 tbsp = 15ml, 1 cup = 250ml/8fl oz.
Australian standard tablespoons are 20ml. Australian readers should use 3 tsp in place of 1 tbsp for measuring small quantities of gelatine, flour, salt, etc.
American pints are 16fl oz/2 cups. American readers should use 20fl oz/2.5 cups in place of 1 pint when measuring liquids.
Electric oven temperatures in this book are for conventional ovens. When using a fan oven, the temperature will probably need to be reduced by about 10–20°C/20–40°F. Since ovens vary, you should check with your manufacturer's instruction book for guidance.
Medium (US large) eggs are used unless otherwise stated.

CONTENTS

THE BARNYARD   57

GAME   58

FRUIT AND DESSERTS   60

BREAD AND CAKES   62

WINE   64

ALCOHOLIC AND OTHER DRINKS   66

TAPAS   68

EGGS AND SOUP   92

SALADS AND VEGETABLES   112

RICE AND PASTA   136

FISH AND SHELLFISH   154

POULTRY AND GAME BIRDS   180

MEAT AND FURRED GAME   202

DESSERTS AND BAKING   226

SHOPPING AND FURTHER INFORMATION   252

INDEX   253

INTRODUCTION   6

THE SPANISH CUISINE   6

THE REGIONS OF SPAIN   10

THE SOCIAL CONTEXT   20

TAPAS   22

FEAST DAYS AND FIESTAS   24

COOKING IN SPAIN   28

THE SPANISH KITCHEN   30

THE OLIVE TREE   32

CHEESE AND DAIRY PRODUCE   34

VEGETABLES OF THE OLD WORLD   36

VEGETABLES FROM AMERICA   38

SPICES, HERBS AND FLAVOURINGS   40

RICE AND PASTA   42

ATLANTIC AND MEDITERRANEAN FISH   44

PRESERVED FISH   46

SHELLFISH   48

BEEF, VEAL, LAMB AND KID   50

PORK   52

SAUSAGES   54

HAMS   56

THE SPANISH CUISINE

The history and religion of Spain are visible on the plate. It is always true, to some extent, that what we eat says who we are. But in no country is it more obvious than in Spain. Ingredients, cooking methods and many recipes all have an easy-to-trace and fascinating past. And Spain's most famous foods – chorizo, cocido, gazpacho, bacalao, paella – have an encoded history.

MOORISH INFLUENCES

"A land which hovers between Europe and Africa, between the hat and the turban" was Richard Ford's description of Spain in 1845. The Moors invaded Spain from North Africa, in AD711, and stayed for nearly 800 years. The Moorish influence is still evident today. To start with, a huge number of food words are derived from the Arabic: *aceite* (oil), *arroz* (rice), *albóndigas* (meatballs), *almendras* (almonds), *almirez* (the mortar) and *almuerzo* itself, the word for lunch.

In the mosques of and palaces of Cordoba, irrigation systems were planned, making possible wonderful gardens such as the Generalife in Granada, as well as Valencia's rice fields. The valleys of the Guadalquiver

Above (left and right): Many classic desserts such as fritters drenched in honey and rich fruit syrups show the Moorish origins of much Spanish food.

and Granada bloomed. The grey-green olive and the newly introduced almond transformed the landscape, while orange and lemon trees filled courtyards and surrounded buildings. New crops were planted, including sugar, spinach, aubergines (eggplant) and mint.

From the Moorish cuisine came new culinary methods – cooking in sealed clay pots and wood-burning ovens were introduced. The meat skewer and kebabs arrived, and *churrasco* (pieces of meat cooked on the barbecue) is still

a Spanish favourite. Frying with olive oil and preserving in vinegar (*escabeche*) were both Arab practices, the latter eagerly adopted by the locals for preserving surplus fish for a little longer. The mortar and pestle could grind nuts to a smooth cream, used to thicken chilled soups such as the almond *ajo blanco* (white garlic soup) or *salmorejo* (a cream of garlic, bread and vinegar). Both were forerunners of the classic chilled soup, gazpacho.

Many things that are now considered typically Spanish come from this era: almond pastries, fritters in honey, milk puddings, quince paste, peaches in syrup, iced sorbets (sherbets), raisins and pine nuts used together in sauces, and the "caviar", botargo.

The spices brought by the Moors included cinnamon, cumin and nutmeg, served with chicken the way they are now, and the magnificent golden saffron. They enjoyed sour-and-sweet (*agridulce*) mixtures and anise bread. Look around in Spain now and you will find all these things still on the menu.

Left: The Spanish love to cook and eat outdoors and cooking pieces of meat on skewers over a barbecue comes from the Moorish tradition.

Right: The slow-cooked stew of meats and chickpeas, cocido, *was inspired by the Jewish sabbath stew,* adafina.

CATHOLICISM CONQUERS

The *Reyes Católics* – the Catholic kings, Isabella and Ferdinand – conquered Granada, the last Moorish stronghold, in 1492. They threw out the Moors and the Jews, who were the Moorish managerial class, to make one united Catholic kingdom. The Jews, who had been in Spain for many centuries, left several imprints on Spanish cuisine, including *cocido* (meat and chickpea stew). The Christmas *roscón* has common features with the sticky braided *challah*, the Jewish Sabbath loaf.

The new foods enjoyed in this era were spectacularly different, favoured almost entirely for their religious orthodoxy. *Bacalao* (salt cod) was for Church fast days, of which there were some 200, when abstinence from meat – and sex – were required. Pork, which neither displaced peoples would touch, became an integral part of Spanish religion, and therefore everyday life. Eating sausages became a statement of loyalty and proof, if required, of conversion to the Catholic church.

Below: Of all the spices that the Moors brought with them to Spain, rich golden saffron is the one most distinctively associated with Spanish cooking.

Cocido, the national dish

It is ironic that the *cocido*, that pot of long-cooked meats with chickpeas, is the legacy of a people whom the Spanish rejected. Its origins lie in the Jewish *adafina*, the Sabbath casserole, cooked the night before, and also served in three courses. *Pelotas* are

Below: Since the days of the Catholic kings, pork sausages such as spicy red chorizo have become the main meat eaten in Spain.

still added to *cocido* on big occasions. These are balls of minced (ground) meat or chicken livers, bread and pine nuts that echo the hamine eggs that the Jews added to *adafina*.

Adopted by the Catholic Spaniards, pork and sausages were added to the other meats in the *cocido*, as proof that the eaters were neither Jewish nor Muslim. Made almost entirely with meat, it was at first a thoroughly aristocratic dish. Then, as more chickpeas and potatoes were added, so it slipped down the social scale. Every region adds its own vegetables, and the further from Madrid, the more of a rural *puchero* (bean and sausage or meat stew) it becomes.

The Sephardim

This was the name given to the Spanish Jews; it is the Hebrew word for Spanish. When the Jews fled from Spain, they took with them many of its vegetables and dishes, including lentils, citron, fried fish, the boiling chicken with the bird's unshed eggs still inside, chicken with olives, and chicken soup with almonds.

HOLY SWEETMEATS

At one time, the church employed one tenth of the population, many of them women. In Old Castile and the south, nuns turned to cookie- and sweetmeat-making for charity. Egg whites were used in sherry-making and the left-over yolks given to the convents. The nuns combined these with cheap sugar from the New World to make little *natillas* (custards) and sweetmeats.

Today, you can still go to closed convents and place your order through the grille or put money on the shelf in a *tornador* (revolving door) and receive back goodies.

The best-known of these are *yemas de San Leandro* (egg yolk balls). Christmas brings red quince jellies, coconut truffles, *mantecados*, *polvorones* and potato cakes called *cubilitos* (little cubes). Other delicacies include the almond and cinnamon cream known as *bien me sabe* (it tastes good to me).

Below: Dried salt cod has been enjoyed in Spain for centuries. In times past, the dried fish was carried across the country by muleteers.

FOOD ON THE ROAD

Spain is a country of mountains, and of fierce regionalism. Nevertheless, it has always had its travellers. The muleteers of León were the equivalent of modern-day lorry drivers, criss-crossing Spain with their load of salt cod and news. They had their own recipe, *bacalao ajo arriero* (dry, hard fish rehydrated in a pot with oil and garlic), which is now often transformed into a Christmas *brandade* or into a tomato-based dish.

Tourism is not a new phenomenon in Spain either. Santiago de Compostella has been a major shrine for pilgrims for a millenium. In the 1550s, at the height of its popularity, up to two million people a year, from all over Europe, walked there south of the mountains on the *camino frances*, or along the coast. Scallop shells were their badge, but in their bags they carried bread and smoked sausage. At the pilgrim monasteries, crowds of up to 1,500 were fed on chickpeas and chard.

Another transient people, the gypsies (with a background in Egypt and India) arrived in the 1450s. They settled in Andalusia where they took up the jobs left vacant by the Moors and Jews. They also annexed the folklore of the south and became the smugglers and bandits of the 19th century. Their contribution to the Spanish cuisine was an element of improvisation in food, instead of traditional long-cooked stews.

Above (left and right): The tradition of sweet cookies and custard desserts was once the province of Spanish nuns, who made and sold them for charity.

FOODS FROM NEW LANDS

The introduction of new foods from America after 1492 changed the Mediterranean diet for ever. Spain was transformed from being a bean, grain and meat-eating country, into a place where vegetables were widely enjoyed. An increase in population followed in Spain and Europe.

Chocolate and chilli peppers quickly became firm favourites in the Spanish kitchen: chocolate as a drink, and chillies as a condiment. Tomatoes were adopted and used in sauces, and beans became a firm fixture at the heart of the Spanish cuisine. Potatoes, however, never displaced the great popularity of chickpeas, and corn was adopted only in Spain's fringes. (Could the reason for this be that tobacco was discovered on the same day – and the Spanish preferred the latter?)

From the opposite direction, the Portuguese returning from China in the early 1500s, brought with them sweet oranges. To this day, oranges are still known as *chinas*. The resulting orange trees, which now grow in such abundance all over Spain, have dramatically altered the landscape of the east and south coast.

Right and far right: Spain boasts the longest coastline in Europe and from two oceans come a vast array of fresh seafood, including scampi and sardines.

BETWEEN TWO OCEANS

Spain's longest frontiers are water so it is no wonder the Spanish are seafarers. Spain has always looked outward to the Atlantic as well as inward to the Mediterranean. First came shipping salt, whaling and fishing. Later Cádiz and Sevilla provided the ships and stores for "the Empire on which the sun never sets" – a phrase used to describe Spain before it was borrowed by the British Empire. In Spain, *América* refers to Latin America, which was open territory for the *conquistadores* (adventurers) to make their fortune.

Mediterranean links

Since the Phoenicians first arrived and planted olive trees, Spain has long had links with its Eastern neighbours. In terms of food influences, Spain has given much more than it has received.

The Romans imported Spanish olive oil and adopted Spanish chickpeas to feed their armies. Under the Borgias, Spain introduced beans to Tuscany –

and possibly *sofrito* (fried onion-based dishes). When the kings of Aragón ruled Italy, saffron and short-grained rice were planted, which were to become the base of the classic Italian dish, risotto.

France adopted mayonnaise, *aioli*, iced soups, chocolate, haricots and tomatoes, plus the beans and spices that transformed their *cassoulet*. With France's culinary reputation, you might expect to find French dishes in Spain, but there are actually more Spanish dishes to be found in France.

Thanks to the Moorish legacy, a huge range of kitchen skills travelled from Spain to other countries. In return, the best gift to Spain came from France in the form of wine-making skills. These included the technique of maturing wine in oak barrels.

Below: Chillies came from America and became a widely used condiment in Spanish food and cooking.

Below: Lemons were brought to Spain by the Moors, while sweet oranges were brought from China by the Portuguese.

Below: Spanish olives owe their legacy to the Phoenicians who first planted the trees there hundreds of years ago.

THE REGIONS OF SPAIN

The Spanish regions are divided by many mountain ranges. This separates them geographically, but has also led to cultural differences as well. The climate, too, varies enormously, both across the regions and from winter to summer. Both these factors have contributed to the creation of distinctive local food traditions.

THE SOUTH

Typical images of Spain are of the south: blinding sunshine and a cool arch into a Moorish patio where a guitarist is quietly practising; white walls, covered with pots of bright geraniums; horses parading and girls in polka-dot flounced skirts. The great black bull silhouette that advertises Veterano brandy stands proudly on the rims of the brown *sierras* and leaves a lasting impression.

Andalusia

This region encompasses the whole of the south coast, looking east on the Mediterranean from Almeria province, south to Africa from Málaga and out on to the Atlantic beyond Gibraltar. It embraces two sunlit worlds – that of the tourist beaches and another of fishing, farming and flamenco.

Water splashing from fountains, running in rills through gardens, or poured from cans at night on the green

plants in every doorway, is the key to the country. For it was these fertile valleys that brought the Moors across the narrow straights from Africa. Now wonderful crops of asparagus and strawberries grow in the Guadalquiver delta and the *vega* of Granada. Valleys of tropical fruit face the sea, ripening in the glorious sunshine. Almería, with the help of irrigation, supplies all of Europe with tomatoes and (bell) peppers. The grey-green olive grows where nothing else will, and orange and lemon trees, loaded with fruit, surround the hamlets.

The province is mountainous with many *sierras*: the Sierra Morena north of Seville and the Sierra Nevada south east of Granada, where the Mulhacén rises 3,482m/11,420ft, its icy diamond piercing the sky beyond Granada. The *pueblos blancos*, white villages, cascade down the brown hillsides. This is the land where tapas were created – a little drink, a little food – as an unwinder at the end of a scorching day.

Andalusia's greatest foods are green olives and the scarlet, dried hams of the *sierras* – hence the name *jamón serrano*. A wide variety of shellfish are found in abundance in the warm Mediterranean, and from the Atlantic come big fish such as sharks and tuna.

In this corner of the province are the sherry *bodegas*, cathedrals where oak barrels, stacked in dark tiers, mature the precious liquid. Sherry flies through the air when the *venecia* (a sampling can fixed on a long rod) dips into the butt and is poured in a graceful arc into a row of glasses held between the fingers of a master.

Splendid church processions and pilgrimages with ox carts, bull fighting and fiestas celebrating horses or sherry, all punctuate the year. They lend formality as well as colour to a region deeply committed to its folklore. Gypsies, especially in Seville and Granada, have created the rhythms of flamenco. They also have a reputation for improvising quick and delicious dishes.

Left: Sun and shade, blinding white walls and pots filled with geraniums are typical of Andalusia's many villages.

Murcia

To the east of Andalusia lies Murcia, another Moorish province; indeed, they ruled here, unnoticed, until 1609. This is another market garden area, with the *Huerta de Murcia* growing seas of bright green parsley and broad (fava) beans so tender they are cooked in the pod. It is said you breakfast twice here, once on chocolate and once on (bell) peppers. Stuffed peppers, tomato salad with cumin and an *escabeche* of aubergines (eggplant) with vinegar are popular. But the region is famous for lemons and for Calasparra rice, Spain's best and ideal for paella, as well as for pickled capers.

Moorish dishes include *pastel murciano*, a pigeon pie with elaborate pastry that mimics the *b'stilla* of Morocco, desserts such as *arrope* and *jarabes* (fruit syrups), and *pan de higo* (pressed fig cake). The region also has a connection with Cuba, with dishes such as *arroz cubana* (Cuban rice).

In the salt lagoons of the Mar Menor, grey mullet are reared to eat and for caviar. *Lubina* (sea bass) baked in salt, is an internationally acclaimed dish.

Below: Water was the key to the Moors' success in Andalusia and the fountains of the Genaralife in Granada irrigate one of their greatest gardens.

Above: Murcia's hot climate and lush plains produce nearly half of Spain's lemons each year.

Andalusia is said to be the "zone of frying"; certainly it is done superbly. But in the villages, old-fashioned stews of beans or chickpeas are just as common. *Gazpacho*, once the only daytime meal of poor labourers (who ate it again hot at night) is these days a chilled tomato and cucumber soup, wonderfully refreshing in the midday heat. There are many different versions of *gazpacho*, but all contain garlic, vinegar and oil.

Sangría, the chilled mixture of wine and citrus juice made in a jug (pitcher), is another summer cooler. It belongs to a world of the *siesta* – afternoons of pure peace, when jobs can be put off until *mañana* (tomorrow).

CENTRAL SPAIN

At 700m/2,300ft, the *Meseta* is the high heart of Spain and comprises nearly half the country. This is *Castilla* (of the castles), a great plain with Madrid in the middle, which divides into two rather different halves.

Northern Castile and León

Tierra de pan y vino (land of bread and wine) is one description of the Duero valley. Bread has mystical significance in the great grain plains of Old Castile. The bread basket of Spain produces round *hogazas*, big close-grained loaves, and houses retain their circular ovens, even when they no longer work.

Legumes are daily fare, well-flavoured with garlic. Chickpeas and lentils grow here, and white *alubias* that are used to make bean stews with oxtail or pigs' ears and sausage. The northern fringe, El Bierzo, is very wild, but known for *empanada de batallón*, a pie that gathers all the good produce of the region together – chicken, rabbit, frogs, chorizos and (bell) peppers. The old kingdom of León is deeply influenced by the French pilgrim route passing through it, which shows in foodstuffs such as sausages. Best known are Burgos's *morcilla*, a black pudding (blood sausage) with rice, and Cantimpalo's *chorizo*, Madrid's choice for their traditional stew-pot, *cocido*.

In the north-east, sheep graze happily in the summer, but winter is icy here and woollen blankets sell well. Soría and Burgos are important centres in this region. Sheep's milk is used to make cheeses – soft, white Burgos and the celebrated *manchego*.

Above: Painted wall tiles in a Madrid restaurant advertise the wood-oven that is used to make notable roast meats.

The region is famous for its wood-fired ovens. In Sepúlvedra they roast *lechazo*, milk-fed lamb, while further west in Arévalo and Segovia, *tostones*, tiny 15–20-day-old suckling pigs are roasted to perfection. The best calves in the country are reared in Ávila.

Fritters, punch cakes and Tordesilla pastries appear in cake shops, while the many convents specialize in *repostería* (confectionery), including *rosquillas fritas* (fried rings), *pastas de té* (tea cakes) and *cocos* (coconut balls).

Madrid

Everyone in Madrid belongs to the country, so they say, and patronizes a regional restaurant. The city's dish is *cocido*, but *callos* (tripe) is so popular that it has moved from the home to become bar fare. Madrid's many restaurants introduced short-order cooking to Spain – *madrileño* used to indicate quicker dishes. The city is spoiled for fish and delicatessens. In May, San Isidro is celebrated with mixed salads and puff pastries.

Left: The fairytale Alcázar *(fortress) of Segovia is one of the many medieval castles scattering central Spain – giving the region its name, Castile.*

New Castile and La Mancha

La Mancha, Don Quixote country, means parched. No wonder Cervantes chose it for his poor knight. The great plains are covered with low vines, with odd corners of saffron planted by the Moors. The intense heat of the summer fuels a preference for strong, robust flavours. *Sopa de ajo* (garlic and bread soup) and dishes with cumin are typical fare. Huge quantities of thyme are mixed with pig's liver, paprika and pine nuts, or go into meatballs and one-pot stews.

The food is simple yet quite delicious – glistening tomato salads, luscious *el asadilla* (baked sweet red peppers) and fabulous marinated vegetables such as aubergines (eggplant) pickled in Almalgro in the Moorish fashion. Genuine *pisto* is simply made using (bell) peppers, tomatoes and courgettes (zucchini). Paprika, for red sausages, is made here and in the neighbouring La Vera valley from *choricero* chillies. *Morteruelo* is a liver pâté with game. Best-known of all, however, is *tortilla* – the thick, solid potato and onion omelette. This classic was originally prepared, it is said, by a peasant for a hungry king. Valdepeñas make the best wines, good enough for a *chateo* (a walk round the bars) in Madrid.

Above: Wild black ibérico pigs forage under the holm oaks of Extremadura, where acorns give their hams special flavour. The region is famous for its pork consumption and its sausages.

Below: In Castile, sheep are valued for their wool and milk, which is turned into cheese. Their meat is eaten while the animals are still young and tender.

Extremadura

The rolling plains are called the *charro* – a land of holm oak and corks, knee-deep in flowers in spring, with more pigs and sheep than people. The explorers Cortes and Pizarro were born here – and left to find something better. Extramadura is poor and there is a good deal of hunting for free food: birds, rabbits, frogs, freshwater fish and summer truffles. Rich tomato sauces are favoured for many of these foods.

Montanchez and Guijelo are famous for *pata negra* (black foot) hams. The black pigs run wild under the oaks, fattening up on acorns. The locals are great consumers of pork. The seasoning of the mince (ground pork) for sausage-making is tested in *prueba* (meatballs). *Pringada* is anything fried in bacon fat. Everything from the pig that can be is made into sausages, and the rest is either pickled, stewed or minced in some manner. The region produces half the pork pâté eaten in Spain.

Migas (fried breadcrumbs) are served with fry-ups, or combined with bacon and chillies. Local hospitality demands that the plates are always piled high. Local paprika colours *el frito* (fried lamb) red; *caldereta extremeña* is lamb stewed with its liver.

THE NORTH COAST

Isolated from the rest of Spain, the wet north has a rugged coast and a Celtic tradition that links it closely to its northern neighbours.

Galicia

Europe's western corner is green and misty, the cabbages rocked by the wind that blows on two coasts. *Hórreos* (stone-roofed storehouses), which are used for storing maize (corn), potatoes and local cheeses, stand guard outside every house.

Below: Vineyards above the Miño River around the village of San Esteban in Galicia produce white wines.

Galicia grows innovative produce for the Madrid markets, including *padrón* peppers, watercress and kiwi fruit. The favourites at home are a special white potato (*cachelo*), which is indispensable for any traditional meal, turnips and, more particularly, *grelos* – the turnip leaves just coming into bud.

The poorer south is covered with chestnut trees, whose nuts were long a basic food but which are now eaten at festivals. Three-quarters of the land provides pasture for dairy cows, whose milk is used to make the famous Galician cheeses such as *tetilla*. Here you will also find the blond breed *rubio gallego*, which supplies much of the country's best meat. Unemployment is rife, however, and the region is called "the goodbye lands" because people leave in the hope of finding a better future in Latin America.

Maize grows on the north coast, and the local breads, heavy in texture, are made with corn meal, barley and rye. Raisins are sometimes added to the corn bread for Christmas.

The Moors never conquered these Celtic lands, which have more in common with Normandy and Wales than they have with provinces further south. Oil and garlic are seldom used in the kitchens of this region and cooking tends to be simple. Fat pigs are prized; the native dish is *lacón*, the salted front leg. Markets sell rolls of back fat for cooking, as well as tripe and numerous types of sausage. Barnyard poultry produce red-yolked eggs, and fat ginger hens are sold with unshed eggs inside.

Cape Finisterre – the world's end and the last stop before America – is known as the Cape of Death, because of the number of ships wrecked there. It provides the best choice and quality of seafood in the world. Half of the mussels eaten in the world grow here.

Windy, westward Santiago de Compostela cathedral, with its cliff-face façade, is a place of world pilgrimage, famous for the grave of St James. The pilgrims' badge is a scallop shell, and even those who do not wear it must surely eat them. Vigo is the biggest fishing port in Europe.

New wineries of gleaming steel make wine from grapes that grow on the south-facing seaside slopes. The white *alberiño* is said to come from a Riesling grape brought by German monks. Its "green" wine is often sparkling – the perfect partner for shellfish.

Galicia has over 200 food festivals a year, celebrated with bagpipes, tambourines and simple dances. An ancient pre-Christian culture lies just beneath the surface, with herbalism and a touch of witchcraft. In the magic ritual of the *queimada*, which is used for divination, a rough brandy (*orujo*) and sugar are flamed. The chief witch, in his straw cape, sets fire to the pot. The lights go down and the flames shoot up.

Above: The stone hórreos *that are used for storing corn cobs and local cheeses can be seen all over Galicia.*

Asturias and Cantabria

The range of mountains that run east to west along the north coast stretch 500km/300 miles, with many peaks at 2,500m/8,000ft. Oak and beechwoods support spectacular wild life – bears, wolves and wild cats, as well as deer, boar and capercaillie. Civilization here dates back to the Bronze Age.

This is "green Spain", with some 250 varieties of apple, and where cider-drinking is a serious sport. Clogs are worn against the frequent drizzle, while cauldrons of stew offer a different form of protection against the cold in this mining country. *Pote asturiana* combines cabbage, beans, salt foreleg, pig fat and ribs. Great melt-in-the-mouth white kidney beans go into *fabada*. In the hinterland of Santander, known as *la montaña*, you will find stews of mutton and beans, as well as the bullet cabbage. There are also bean stews with clams and other shellfish.

All four northern regions are famous for their smoke-cured sausages. The *morcillas* (blood sausages) are dried out, then reydrated in stews. *Botiello* (ribs and tail) are served at carnival.

High up, flower-strewn dairy pastures provide the milk for half of Spain's cheeses. The Picos de Europa have 27 varieties, including the famed *cabrales*. This is a dairy culture, which sends milk and yogurt across Spain; at home the milk and butter are used in rice puddings, apple batter cake and butter sponges for breakfast. The Val de Liébana produces wonderful cheese; it is also an enclave of Mediterranean agriculture, growing tiny, delicious chickpeas as well as fruit.

Oviedo, a centre of coal and iron mining, is a wealthy and fast-living city. It has fabulous seafood such as the *changurro* (spider crab) and many modern creations by talented chefs. This is the largest salmon-producing region in the country. Classically the fish is soaked in milk, salt and lemon, then grilled (broiled) – *a la parrilla*.

Cantabria, the corridor west from the Basque country, is a coast of small bays and little fishing harbours, with the flag-flying casino city of Santander. Sardines are found in abundance and the very popular hake is cooked *a la sidra* (in cider), with mussels and brandy. Squid (*rabas*) are breaded and fried.

Above: Scallop shells are the symbol of St James at Santiago de Compostela. These are painted with his sword.

Below: The Asturias is milk country and the rich pastures that cover the hillsides offer excellent grazing.

ALONG THE PYRENEES

Three very different provinces border France. The successful Basque Country, smaller Navarra and large, poor Aragon.

The Basque country

Snuggled into the Pyrenees by France, el País Vasco has many Michelin-starred restaurants. The lucky Basques have it all; well-hung beef, wild mushrooms, fish and vegetables. Long recognized as Spain's finest cooks, they do things the French way, using butter and cream (unusual for Spain), and take their food very seriously. Basque chefs embraced *la nueva cocina* a quarter of a century ago, seeking a profile that extended beyond Spain.

Eating is thoroughly social, with an eatery per every 1,000 people. The Basques adopted the *pincho* (a *tapa* on a stick) and are sophisticated tapas crawlers. In the *cofradías* (men's clubs), cooking is done by the members, who create dishes with *angulas* (elvers) and *kokotxas* (the tasty part of hake throat).

Basques are nationalists through and through, with their own exotic language. The "TX" of the Basque language can prove tricky. The small glass used for

Below: The Pyrenees offer grazing for Basque sheep, whose milk is made into the richly flavoured cheese, Idiazábal.

local wine, *txiquito*, is pronounced *chiquito*. The perfumed spider crab is called *txangurro*, pronounced *changurro*. "TX" over a restaurant door anywhere in Spain means that the chef is Basque, which is usually a good sign.

The Basques have a long connection with the sea, with some of the biggest fleets in the world. Cod is mainly fished off the coast of Iceland, to be sold, salted, in *bacalao* shops. Salt fish goes

Above: Basque fishermen unload their catch at Getaria. The Basques have the largest fishing fleet in Spain.

into *zurraputuna*, a soup with bread and chilli, and *porrusaldo*, soup with leeks, which is eaten mid-morning as the workmen's breakfast.

Biscay is our name for the waters of Viscaya, whose fish are cooked *a la brasa*, over charcoal. Perfectionists say that fish is only worth eating if it has been line-caught rather than netted.

Basque cuisine boasts four main sauces to serve with fish. White sauce, *pil-pil*, is an emulsion of olive oil and garlic; green *salsa verde* combines wine and parsley and is usually served with hake; *vizcaína* (Biscay) is tomato-based; and the fourth sauce is black, made with the ink of the cuttle fish, and often served with it, *en su tinta*.

Spring brings new peas (*tarvillas*) and beans, eaten with other new shoots in *coussinat*, and fungi stalls at markets. In this maize region, corn meal cakes are made on the griddle. But the locals prefer beans – red, black and all shades between – and sausages.

For dessert there are apples (*reinettas*) and *cañutillas* (cream horns), and this is also Spain's main

chocolate centre. Firm cheeses revolve around Idiazábal, which are slightly caramelized when smoked.

Rioja is known for its style of wine, which is flavoured from storage in oak casks. It is the best known of Spain's wine and most widely drunk abroad.

Navarra

This tiny region is relatively isolated, with one highway, the great Valley of Roncesvalles, passed through by so many millions of pilgrims. These travellers are remembered with *bacalao al arriero*, now often a cream of salt cod and garlic, and a hank of *chistorra* sausage. The cheese of Roncal is firm and widely enjoyed in France. Mountain dishes include mushrooms with herbs, roast quail in fig leaves in September and brown trout. Lamb is fried in *cochifrito* or stewed with red (bell) peppers as *chilindrón*.

The fashionable, fruity wines are red or rosé. The vineyards face those of Rioja across the Ebro, Spain's greatest river. Peppers, asparagus and lettuces also grow well here. The many almonds grown in the region are ground for cake-making and marzipan, which is extremely popular.

Below: Vineyards in Navarra produce strong but very fruity wines.

Above: Bright yellow sunflowers are grown for their seeds, which are often served as a tapa*, or crushed to make margarine or cooking oil.*

Aragón

Huge Aragón boasts soaring mountains, with many chamois and boar. Game is a speciality, especially the birds that skim over the mountain passes. Pigeons are served in *salmorejo* (garlic and vinegar sauce) and partridges with chocolate, an idea that has caught on across the country. The hams of Teruel, one of the three best in the country, are eaten as *magras con tomate* locally, where slices of ham are served in tomato sauce.

Aragón is sometimes mocked for the simplicity of its cooking – the locals like grills, such as goat on a spit, served with *allioli*. Stews with vegetables, baked dough rounds with sardines and red (bell) peppers, and *migas* (fried breadcrumbs) with chocolate are all popular dishes.

Downwards to the dusty plain, Zaragoza is a large grower of maize (corn), sunflowers and many herbs. Borage is still cultivated and used in the same way as spinach. *Boliches* are white beans of great quality.

Groves of almond trees date from Moorish times, with apple, cherry and peach orchards stretching from Zaragoza to Teruel. Here they make *vi rancios* (fortified dessert wine) and cystallized fruit and candied peels. Delicious almond sweetmeats are a reminder of the long Moorish rule.

THE EAST COAST AND THE ISLANDS

As with the other regions of Spain, the east coast and the islands that lie off the mainland have their own specific culture, flavour and traditions.

Catalonia

The French discovered the excellent fish on the Costa Brava, and named the place the Wild Coast. Ever since then people have crossed Spain's borders to eat *zarzuela* (fish stew studded with shellfish) and *susquet*, with tomato and potatoes. Gerona is famous for its sea bass, and Barcelona for its monkfish in a dark cream of toasted garlic.

Catalunya, the small province next to France, has Spain's business brains and earns one fifth of the national income. The cuisine here leans towards the French tradition of fine cooking mixed with a little Italian spontaneity – and less towards Africa. Sauces are thickened with yolks in the French style and béchamel is used. Ducks are reared, and confit and magrets (breast fillets) are on the menu.

Catalans have long had a tradition of good restaurants – and are now thought of as Spain's best cooks. (French chefs voted *El Bulli* to be the world's top restaurant.) Barcelona is a city of 10,000 eateries, and its market, *la Boquería*, is one of the world's greatest.

Catalan cooking is eclectic. *Allioli* was invented here and first recorded in AD100. Saffron and the tradition of combining meat with fruit go back to the Roman times. Sweet-and-sour is a Moorish taste, while lobster with chocolate came later. Other dishes are inspired by local ingredients – *mar i muntanya* (sea and mountain) refers to dishes that combine seafood and meat such as clams with partridge. Black rice with squid ink is a modern speciality.

Above: A shop window in Catalonia, displays a wonderful selection of foods, including sausages, hams and cheeses.

Almonds, onions, spinach and aubergines (eggplant) remain popular, while the provincial dish is the chickpea *escudella* with pork dumpling, served in two courses. White beans are called *mongetes* here and are cooked with *botifarro*, the local sausage. Vic, a sausage capital, produces a black-and-white speciality, as well as the carmine drumstick, *fuet*.

Quality shows in simple foods such as *pa amb tomàquet* (bread rubbed with garlic, oiled and rubbed with the ripest tomato). There is also the *rovelló* mushroom of autumn (fall), and rich, tangy tomato sauce flavoured with bitter orange peel.

Unlike many homes in Spain, Catalan houses have ovens, and cakes for dessert means puff pastries, sweet *cocas* (like pizzas) and little almond and pine nut cookies. The region is the centre of creative wine-making – and *champán's* biggest house in the world, Cordoníu. There is even a non-drip bottle, in the *porrón*, to drink from.

Left: The Boqueria market in the centre of Barcelona sells the freshest seasonal foods such as rovellones *(bleeding milk cap mushrooms).*

The Levante

The east coast includes Alicante and Valencia and a good many of Spain's sunshine beaches. Paella was invented here by picnicking men, and it is still customary to have a *tío* (uncle) in charge. Lake Albufera has freshwater eels, eaten with pepper (*alli-pebre*). Rice dishes often include special runner (green) beans, or *garrafones* (huge flat dried white beans). These are described as "paving stones across rice" in the dish *arros empedrat*.

Alicante's paella contains chicken and rabbit, rather than seafood. Alternatively, it may be made with pasta instead of rice to make *fideuá*. Fresh sausages, *blancs*, are popular, as is the black *poltrona* sausage.

It was a priest who had the brilliant idea of planting oranges commercially here in the 1780s. Now they are on the trees year-round. There are lemons and dates, too, and muscat grapes that survive the heat until after Christmas. *Horchata*, a cool milky drink made from *chufas* (tiger nuts) is a local speciality. It is also a region of festival cakes and Christmas *turrón* (nougat).

Below: The Forn de Teatre bakery in Mallorca is famous for its ensaimadas – coils of exquisite pastry.

The Balearic Islands

Mallorca, Menorca and Ibiza are islands with good lobsters and fish, and gulleys full of herbs. The British fleet, which was stationed in Menorca for 150 years, left gin, clover and dairy cows that now provide the milk for the cheese *mahón*. The French discovered *mahonesa* (mayonnaise) here in the 1750s and instantly adopted it.

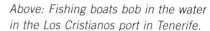

Above: Fishing boats bob in the water in the Los Cristianos port in Tenerife.

Food tends to be solid, as in the layered-vegetable *tumbet*, along with rich soups, and snails from the earthenware *greixonera*. Pigs take centre stage, the high point being the exquisite, spreadable, bright orange *sobrasada* sausage, which is widely available outside the Balearics.

An overlay of cultures has left Moorish-influenced *sucrerías* (sweet shops), which sell jams, pastries and an exquisite cheesecake (*flao*).

The Canary Islands

Las Canarias specialize in local fish, which are beautiful in their varying colours, such as the yellow-purple *vieja*, and cooked simply. They are served with unusual wrinkled potatoes (*papas arrugadas*), which are cooked in sea water and served unpeeled. With them comes *mojo*, a green sauce of blended garlic, coriander (cilantro) and vinegar. A climate of eternal spring produces a wealth of vegetables, including corn. The islands are known for small, sweet aromatic bananas, which are a good partner for the rich, amber *malvasía*, a local dessert wine.

THE SOCIAL CONTEXT

The Spanish are a gregarious people and much of their social life revolves around food. Many people breakfast in a bar before going to work; others go out mid-morning.

They can enjoy *café con leche, zumo* (juice) and *tostadas* (toast) or, if they are lucky, a sophisticated roll such as *ensaimada* or *sobao*. For anyone in no hurry, there is always hot chocolate served with *churros* – long strips of deep fried batter for dunking in the thick chocolate drink.

Lunch is a big affair, typically starting at around two o'clock but later on feast days. The old pattern, in middle-class households, was to eat meat at lunch, then fish at night, with vegetables as a first course. Now it is one or the other. Children have a *merienda* (drink and snack) at about five o'clock. Women often meet friends for a *merienda* after work. Whole families go for the *paseo* – a seven o'clock promenade. Men might go for an *aperativo*. Supper is late, and is a light meal, often vegetable-based.

Large cities never seem to sleep. Dinner bookings are made for ten o'clock at night, and in Madrid there is a rush hour at three in the morning as everyone goes home to sleep before starting work at eight that morning. And the famous siesta? The lunch hour, for office workers, is two hours long and is mainly spent talking.

MENUS

Salad is universal as a first course in summer. Placed in the centre of the table, everyone uses their own fork to eat from it. A restaurant will offer ham or several cold meats, egg dishes, shellfish and soups. The latter are often heavy, and would be regarded as stews elsewhere. Rice and pasta are listed separately, but are a first course in Spain. Then there is a fish or meat course, perhaps offered *a la brasa* or from the *barbacoa* (cooked over charcoal). Restaurants offer desserts, but at home these are usually reserved for saints' days and fiestas.

COOKING AT HOME

The Spanish tradition is for slow-cooking, which can go on all day. The *puchero*, a pot of mixed pulses and meats or sausage, was made most days and left on the stove, wafting rich aromas around the house. Mothers were kept busy in the kitchen but life is different now, and many women work. The delicatessen round the corner stays open until late and supermarkets, with their ready meals, are open all hours.

Left: Cafés provide drinks throughout the day, offering a place to pause and relax or to meet friends and family.

Table manners
Good children keep their hands on the table throughout a meal, so nothing can go on "underneath the counter". It is thought very bad manners to leave any food on your plate, and anyone not mopping up with bread is considered *mal educado*.

SPANISH CUISINE

The strength of Spanish cooking lies in careful selection of ingredients, then finding perfect ways of cooking them. What does it matter that a recipe goes back 400 years, or even 800 years? If it tastes good, why change it?

Today freezers and imports may have improved choice somewhat, but essentially Spanish cooking is regional, devoted to *la patria chica* (my home town and the things it does well). The big 1970s influx of tourists coincided with *la nueva cocina* and its message to use locally produced ingredients. The *Denominación de Origen* (D.O.) system, introduced to protect locally distinctive quality food and drink, is broadly extended and covers hams, cheese and peppers as well as wine. The *Paradores* (state-run hotels), also encourage menus that feature local dishes.

The bride's cookbook
The *Manual de Cocina* is the cookbook given to brides. It dates from the 1930s, when Pilar Prima de Rivera, daughter of dictator Miguél, ran the *Sección Feminina*, a politicized women's group. The organization collected simple, classic recipes from across the country. The book has now run to some 30 editions and is as popular as ever.

THE GREAT OUTDOORS

Eating outdoors is part of the Spanish psyche and houses have balconies and patios, and perhaps a little outdoor summerhouse called a *comedor* (eating place) because it is often too hot to sit in the sun. Built-in charcoal barbecues grace many gardens.

The Spanish are great picnickers. On casual occasions, family groups may go for a happy day out in the *campo* (fields), or for a harvest picnic. For more formal gatherings such as pilgrimages and fairs, makeshift booths or houses (*casetas*) are put up for entertainment. They offer dining, dance floors and kitchens with gas tripods over which paella is cooked. As many as 2,000 people may be accommodated for the night at unpublicized local events, in tents that are put up and taken down in a single weekend.

Above: Outdoor cooking is a big part of Spanish life and many homes have a built-in fire or barbecue in the garden.

RESTAURANT CULTURE

Families eat out together at weekends, with all the generations present. This is one of the reasons why restaurants are so numerous and prices remain so affordable. Hospitality is offered in restaurants rather than at home and many eating establishments advertise catering for large numbers. Jokingly called a *palacio de boda* (wedding palaces), big parties celebrate not just weddings but First Communions and golden weddings. Spectacularly tiered cakes may appear at any of the celebrations. These large parties are paid for by the guests, who come with large cash rolls: the bill is paid, then the rest forms the bridal gift.

TAPAS

Tapas are Spain's greatest food invention. "Eat when you drink, drink when you eat" is the philosophy. Spanish men traditionally drink outside the home and rarely alone. Tapas are not meant to be a meal (although a *ración* is a substantial portion). One *tapa* per person and a different one with each drink is the idea, then everyone enjoys tasting and sharing. Tapas food is real food – good local ingredients presented with flair.

The idea comes from Andalusia. It started, so they say, with a piece of bread, soon topped with ham or cheese, balanced over a glass, to keep out the flies – the word *tapa* means a cover. Tapas were once free snacks included in the price of the drink. Now this is a way of life in the south. In dim caverns, where the sherry barrels are stacked high, men revolve the wine in their *copitas*, gently sipping, then select a new wine from a different cask. To compare and contrast is part of the tapas ritual. An old man may sit by the door, with a bucket of *conchas finas*, opening clams slowly and to order. It is a life less hectic than our own.

Below: An old Seville tapas bar sign advertises food to help sell its drinks.

CLASSIC TAPAS

Tapas dishes revolve around shellfish. In the southern triangle of sherry towns – between Jerez de la Frontera, El Puerto de Santa Maria and Sanlúcar de Barrameda – you may eat amazing shellfish, including squid eggs, whelks (*cañadillas*) and fritters of minute shrimps. The south is also famous for fried fish, *cazón* (a type of shark) marinated in saffron, and *frita malagueña* (mixed battered seafood).

Charcuterie is an important part of the tradition. Hams hang over every bar, with little upturned paper umbrellas underneath to catch dissolving fat: the incomparable scarlet *jamón serrano*.

Above: Hams hang behind the bar in a traditional tapas bar in Madrid, while bulls' heads adorn the walls.

SOCIAL AMBIENCE

Tapas bars were once the preserve of men. Now they attract women too but they are still a great place to discuss sport, particularly bullfighting. In this macho atmosphere old foods survive, for example squares of blood (set with vinegar) "to give men strength at night". Tapas also fuel Spain's many fiestas. After all, how could one follow an all-night procession without a little bite to eat? A café terrace is also an ideal place from which to watch the spectacle.

Above: A bartender in Madrid pulls a caño, *a beer drawn from the pump.*

Right: This smart tapas bar in Bilbao, decorated with ornate gilt, entices a sophisticated and loyal clientele.

Pepitas ...

Think "pippy", for *pepitas* are seeds – little nibbles to pick up in handfuls. Toasted chickpeas, soaked *chufas* (tiger nuts), pistachios and large, soaked yellow lupin seeds, *altramuz*. *Pepitas* themselves are creamy-flavoured pumpkin seeds, but also common are *pipas de girasol* (sunflower seeds).

... and pepitos

A *pepito* is a long soft roll (like a bridge roll), often filled with succulent roast veal. A *montadito* (which literally means mounted) is a piece of bread with a topping such as chorizo or (bell) peppers, perhaps speared with a cocktail stick (wooden toothpick). Though the name *bocadillo* translates as mouthful, it is in fact a substantial sandwich of crusty bread, often with ham and cheese.

People go to bars for the company, but stay for the temptations. A range of flavours is offered in tiny portions, from the sophisticated and exotic to the bland and soothing. They are laid out on the counter, like jewels in a shop window: yolk-yellow *tortilla*, kidneys in sherry, red-hot potatoes, Russian salad (*ensaladilla*) and stuffed baby squid.

CITY SPECIALITIES

Madrid favours tripe, *boquerones en vinagre* (fresh anchovy fillets cured in vinegar) and, of course, shellfish. The old tradition was to throw prawn and shrimp heads on the floor of the bar to show how popular the place was. In Barcelona, designer bars are all the rage and people go there to see and be seen. Basque bars in cities reflect a much more bourgeois clientele. The phrase *ir de pinchos* means to go for a tapas crawl, which can be a popular way to spend an evening.

Fried tapas in the north evoke an era of nostalgia, with bechamel-based *croquetas* (croquettes), and *gambas en gabardinas* (prawns/shrimp in batter).

Bars are also the place to find local food specialities such as spider crab in San Sebastián, and elvers and hake throats in Bilbao. The morsels can often be very elaborate, high cuisine presented in miniature. Tapas bars are also a wonderful way to sample Spain's best dishes such as *rabo de toro* (bull's tail) and the delicious *escabeche de perdiz* (vinegared partridge).

FEAST DAYS AND FIESTAS

In Spain, almost every event involves food. There are special foods for feast days – and feast days solely to celebrate food. Every town, and nearly every village, has its fiesta – over 3,000 occur annually. All are occasions for dressing up, parading the children and drinking with the neighbours.

Holy week is an occasion of high drama but the local saint's day, or an incident in a town's history, will be celebrated with processions and street crowds. The seasons of the year are also greeted with affection.

CHRISTMAS AND NEW YEAR

The Christmas lights go up, and there are *belenes* in shop windows, manger scenes often with a huge cast of characters. On Christmas Eve, *Noche Buena*, it is elvers if you are Basque, or perhaps a salt cod cream (*bacalao al arriero*) after midnight mass in Aragón. The Madrid choice is baked *lubina* (sea bream) and red cabbage; the Catalans eat roast turkey. There are gifts of almond *turrón* and marzipan on the table. Twelfth night is a magical day for children; it is the day they receive gifts.

The three kings' arrival in Bethlehem is remembered in the *roscon de reyes*, a crown of rich yeast bread.

On *Noche Vieja* (New Year's Eve), it is grapes at midnight at the Puerta de Sol in Madrid, with costume parties and street festivals in the warmer south. For good luck, people eat one grape for each toll of the midnight bell.

SPRING CARNIVALS

Jueves lardero (Mardi Gras) sees a big carnival in Tenerife, the largest of the Canary Islands. In Andalusia the day is marked with a feast of all good things from the pig, before the start of the 40 meatless days of Lent.

In Valencia, *La Fiesta de Las Fallas* culminates on the saint's day of San José, 19 March. Some 400 huge caricature creations are set alight in one vast bonfire and all-night party. Further south in Alcoy every April, San Jorge is celebrated with a battle reenactment. The saint appears on a white horse to lift the Muslim seige. Black beans with white rice (*moros y cristianos*) are eaten as a reminder.

For Seville's *Feria de Abril*, streets of *casetas* are erected, and days are given over to drinking and dancing. The close is followed by *lunes de la resaca* (hangover Monday).

HOLY WEEK

Semana Santa, the days from Palm Sunday to Easter, is the big festival, particularly in the south. The heavy *pasos* (scenes of Christ's death) and the weeping virgins banked by scented lilies and tall candles are paraded night after night, later and later, before packed crowds and to a constant reverberating noise of drumming.

The Easter foods are few: *torijillos* (fried toast), cheesecake, and perhaps lamb for *Resurreción* day. However, it is *carajillos* (brandy and black coffee) that you will need to cope with the drama and exhaustion of the festival.

Left: The Virgin and Child are paraded around Valencia for the patronal festival. The special relationship of each town to its patron makes her "our" virgin.

Above: The sinister costumes of the penitentes *were adopted in the past to hide the identity of the genuine* penitentes. *Today, they are a traditional part of Holy Week in the south.*

CELEBRATING THE NEW SEASON

Food coming into season is joyfully greeted – the reappearance of freshwater crayfish, the first salmon of the year, a *caracolada* (feast of river snails) in Lerida. Tarragona people wear bibs when they suck the *calçots* (spring onions/scallions) from the barbecued black leaves. In Valls and Cambrils, the celebrations include human towers.

In Murcia, the end of Lent is marked with floats and a parade for the "Burial of the Sardine". The return of sardines to Spanish waters marks the coming of summer. In Malaga, the fish are roasted over beach fires for *la moraga*. Fishermen give thanks on San Pedro and the Virgen de Carmen on 15 July with a flotilla of decorated boats, followed by fish suppers.

For the children
Many festivals start with a carriage procession and a *chupinaza* – pelting children with candy. *Chupa* is a ball of candy on a stick.

SAINTS' DAYS AND PATRONAL FESTIVALS

Spaniards don't have birthdays but instead celebrate their saint's day. For example, if your name is José everyone will remember you on 19 March, with congratulations, flowers and sweets (candy) for the children. It is "your day". Towns, and districts within them, also seek the protection of a saint, whose image is paraded annually. These days are a frenzy of baking.

In Badajoz, people celebrate with little Moorish fritters, and in Logroño they eat yeast buns called *bollas* for San Marco. A topsy-turvy day in Segovia on Santa Agatha, when the men are replaced by "mayoresses", is celebrated by women with moscatel-soaked cake (*ponche segoviana*).

To celebrate San José on 19 March, everyone eats *buñuelos de viento*, little choux puffs that "just blow away". In Madrid these airy pastries are made with lard and *coñac*, and have a special filling of rich, sweet, creamy custard to celebrate San Isidro.

Local cookies come out for fiestas such as the Valencia *Fallas*: baked nut *almendrados*, little *glorias* (pyramids of marzipan and meringue), and sweet pastry *rollets* and *fartons* (fingers of sweet rolled dough, baked and sugared). Santa Clara, patroness of so many nuns, is celebrated in August with *rosquillas* (iced ring doughnuts) and, in the summer, street crowds on the east coast and islands eat *cocas* (flat buns) with candied fruit for St John and St James.

Below: Brightly coloured costumes with a team theme add to the fun at many festivals such as carnaval *in Cádiz.*

SUMMER IN THE SUN

Summer brings the perfect weather for celebrations. Spain's biggest picnic is *El Rocío* when a million people traipse with wagons, drawn by face-fringed oxen, to the shrine of the *Virgen de Rocío* in Andalusia. The Assumption of the Virgin on 15 August is celebrated with days of street fairs, table tennis, dancing, flirting and flamenco, and is a bigger festival than Christmas. Madrid and Barcelona have year-round festivals, including San Isidro each May in Madrid and Festa de la Mercè every September in Barcelona. All of them serve typical local dishes. Pamplona has the most challenging festival of all from 6–14 July to celebrate San Firmín. Called the *encierro* (bull penning), each day, the bulls chase any who are brave enough to participate across the town.

ST JAMES' DAY – SANTIAGO

Spain's National Day on 25 July means fiesta time in Santiago de Compostela. Jostling crowds of people, many of whom have walked the last few kilometres into town, pack the streets around the cathedral. There are balloons, pavement stalls, music, dancing, fireworks and beauty queens. No one is drunk, just happy. *Gigantes y cabezas* amuse the crowds. The giants (men on stilts) represent figures from the past – Queen Isabel or a Moor. They have comic papier-mâché heads and costumes that go down to the shoes.

To feast on, bars serve octopus *a la feria*, gently stewed with paprika. There is also lobster followed by *tarta de Santiago*, a cinnamon almond tart, with a stencil of St James' great two-handed sword outlined in powdered sugar.

Above: Gigantes *feature in many traditional festivals. Valencia is famous for its papier-mâché figures, which are balanced on the shoulders.*

HARVESTS

In the days when grapes were crushed by men dancing in the vats with bare feet, there was close physical contact to the harvest. Today, abundance is celebrated in a different fashion. *La tomatina*, held in Bunyol in Valencia at the end of August, is the messiest of all these festivals. It starts with trying to get a ham off the top of a greasy pole and is followed by 15 minutes of mayhem as thousands of people pelt each other with ripe tomatoes.

Haro, in La Rioja, celebrates San Pedro at the end of June with a "war of the wines". Neighbours dress up in white and bombard each other with wine squirted from a leather bottle. In the Asturian town of Nava, the cider apple harvest is celebrated by a chain of celebrants pouring cider from pitcher to pitcher down the street. There are plenty of free drinks along the way.

Left: Oxen wearing Cleopatra-style headdresses pull the gilded cart that carries the Virgin of El Rocío on Spain's biggest pilgrimage.

MATANZA – PIG KILLING TIME

The *matanza* is the greatest social festival of the year. The proverb goes: "every pig has his St Martin" (pride comes before a fall), and traditionally 10–11 November is the time for pig killing. If you don't have a pig, then you muscle in on someone else's, because it needs a team for sausage-making. The annual event brings families together and lasts for two or more days. The pig's liver, cooked with onions, is served for lunch on the first day, and the kidneys with rice or potatoes is served on the second.

If you can't find a pig, then you can party at a *matanza* feast in a restaurant, accompanied by oboes, drums and dancing of the *paso doble*. Over 30 courses, the skilled chefs demonstrate just what you can do with a pig. Brains and ears, hot and cold, salad and soup make up the delicious first courses. Hot courses follow: roasts, stews of tail, trotters, marinated loin, roast ham, *solomillo* (tenderloin) with occasional garnishes of vegetables, and tiny roast pigs too. All is accompanied by hunting horns, singing and *olé* to everything.

Above: Dancers skip around a maypole at a local festival in Belunchón, Toledo.

Below: Flamenco dancers at the Fiera de Abril in Seville wear the flounced skirts usually associated with Andalusia. Here, they are known as sevillanas.

THE DAY OF THE DEAD

All Saints, on 1 November, is celebrated by families all over Spain, carrying flowers to the graveyards. *Huesos de santos* (saint's bones), made of almond pastry, sweet potato or batter, are eaten. Sometimes they are fried around a piece of bamboo cane, which makes them ghoulishly hollow. Catalans bake little nut *panellets*. In Galicia, there are all-night vigils by candlelight, with chestnuts roasting on braziers and the mists drifting in from the sea.

CELEBRATION EATING

Huge outdoor meals are a typically Spanish event, but crowd cooking from a single pot is a challenge that only the Spanish would accept. In the town square of Valencia, a vast paella pan 4m/4yds across and set over charcoal was used to cook yellow rice for 1,000 people. The ingredients were stirred with wooden oars.

Vast cauldrons, to dance around as well as to eat from, bubble on fires in the middle of public squares in many places. Arévalo, in Castile, celebrates St John of the Cross in December with a *cocido de San Juan* (plates of beans and chorizo). Benifairó de Les Valls, in Valencia, has its *calderete* of everything porcine, with rice and many vegetables.

COOKING IN SPAIN

*The wonderful ingredients of Spain — olives, rice, wine,
Mediterranean vegetables, cheeses and sausages, and fish and shellfish
from the longest coastline in Europe — have shaped the country's
individual style of cooking. These ingredients are matched by
cooking methods and recipes that best display their virtues.*

The Spanish Kitchen

Spanish cooking methods have stayed mainly unchanged over the centuries. Although modern kitchen appliances have taken away some of the labour of food preparation, the pots, pans and techniques remain the same.

COOKING OVER CHARCOAL

This is very much a Spanish tradition. Wood and charcoal fires are still used in homes and many restaurants today. The fire is built on a brick shelf and a metal plate (*la plancha*) sits over the fire at cooking height, with holes for the pots to sit in. It is also used for grilling.

Small terracotta stoves may also be used, heated with charcoal from the main fire in winter, and an outdoor fire in summer. These stoves feature in the 16th-century paintings of Velásquez, and have not changed since that time.

ABOUT THE HOUSE

Spanish winters are chilly, so a *brasero* (two-handled brass tray of hot charcoal) sits under the sitting-room table; a cloth over the table holds in heat, keeping the feet warm. The *brasero* is not actually used for cooking, but is handy for toasting bread.

The cellar (*bodega*) is also of great importance. In the big country *cortijo* (farmhouse complex) the cold cellar stones near the well were often the only cold place. This is where gazpacho was chilled overnight.

Below: The shallow paella pan and the deep-frying pan are widely used in the Spanish kitchen.

Above: Classic earthenware cazuelas are used for both cooking and serving.

POTS AND PANS

All over the world the paella pan is identified with Spain. The real Valencian *paellera* has green handles, a dimpled base and is quite thin. They range in size from small to enormous – big enough for a party. The other traditional frying pan is deep and two-handled, used for stews and for deep-frying fish.

The *puchero* (or *olla*) is the pot that has given its name to many Spanish stews. In central Spain it may be earthenware with a bulbous body, narrow neck and two handles but in other areas it is more frequently an upright, loop-handled, metal or copper pot. The witches' kettle (a round-bellied metal *caldereta* with three legs) is used for fish dishes and the rice dish, *arroz caldoso*. A bigger version of this is *un caulderón*, which is used for cooking large stews in public squares at fiestas. It is the classic vessel carried around to Galician fairs by itinerant octopus cookers.

EARTHENWARE DISHES

The earthenware *cazuela* is a splendid invention. Glazed inside, it comes in all sizes from small to very large, and may be rectangular as well as round. In Castile they are used for roasting, and in Catalonia and Levante for oven-baked dishes. Flameproof, when used with a heat diffuser (except over charcoal), the virtue of the *cazuela* is that it retains heat for a long time, but also remains cold, which was crucial in the days before refrigeration.

BOWLS, JARS AND JUGS

There are many traditional bowls and vessels that are still used in kitchens today. *Lebrillos* are earthenware mixing bowls. The *cuenco*, with a small base and straight sides rising to a wide rim, is characteristic, and the large bowl is used in the south. The wooden *artesa* is a trough used for kneading bread and salting hams. Traditional gazpacho bowls are made of olive wood and in the north the saucers used for serving octopus are also wooden.

Storage jars come in many wonderful shapes and sizes and may be lidded or unlidded. Some jars are glazed and painted, while others are simply glazed on the inside. The unglazed *tinaja* is a handleless urn of Moorish origin that is used for storing wine and grain or, in Catalonia, oil. You will see huge ones sitting by the roadside driving south into Valdepeñas.

Below: Small brown casserole dishes cook individual servings.

Above: This earthenware apothecary's jar is a typical type of storage container.

Many modern kitchens have two oil jugs (pitchers) labelled *aceite de pescado* and *aceite de carne* each with its own strainer. The former is used for cooking fish, and the latter for cooking meat. Oil is stored in these jugs after frying for reuse. A popular wedding present is a matching set of oil jugs on a tray, with china vinaigrette bottles and cruets, and a jar for toothpicks.

Below: Traditional gazpacho bowls are made of olive wood.

Traditional drinking jugs

In the Andalusian countryside men go to work carrying a *botijo*, a round pot with a handle and two spouts – one for filling and the other, narrower, one for drinking.

The more elegant Catalan equivalent is the glass *porrón*, which is used for passing hand-to-hand indoors. Its long, thin spout tips into the mouth, but the body of the jug slopes backwards, to prevent spillages.

KITCHEN EQUIPMENT

There are many gadgets in the Spanish kitchen, some for general use and others that are used for a specific dish. Originally, the mortar and pestle were used for the tasks that are now carried out using a food processor or blender. The Spanish *almirez* (mortar), which comes in varying sizes, has four "ears", one of which has a pouring channel. It was introduced to Spain by the Moors and had a huge impact on Spanish cuisine. Dishes such as *salmorejo* (a smooth garlic and tomato soup) became possible, eventually leading to the creation of gazpacho. Purists still press gazpacho through a hair sieve but the mixture can also be pounded or finely chopped. Today, most people chop the vegetables in a *cuenco* (earthenware bowl) using a hand-held blender.

La quemadora is the tool used for caramelizing sugar on *crema catalana* – the metal disc attached to a wooden handle is heated, then held close to the sugared surface to give a caramel finish.

A ridged rolling pin is used to make striped pastry for sweet *empanadillas* (the savoury ones are unstriped) and dariole moulds are used to make *flan* (baked custard). Traditional kitchens also have a box on the wall covered with a cloth, or a drawer in the dresser, for storing stale bread. Bread is bought daily, and eaten with meals. Leftover bread is pounded and used to thicken soups and sauces.

THE OLIVE TREE

One of the oldest cultivated trees, and one of the oldest Mediterranean crops, the olive tree is thought to have been spread throughout Spain by the Phoenicians before 1000BC. Spain is now the largest producer and exporter of olive oil, most of it from the south. These oils are typically rich and fruity, with an olive aroma.

GROWING OLIVES

The Mediterranean basin is defined by where olives will grow. Three-quarters of olive oil comes from the south of Spain, but olives also grow to the west as far north as Madrid and to the Pyrenees at Huesca in the east, with a corridor through La Mancha to Valencia.

Olive trees grow on flat or hilly land, but need winter cold as well as warmth to flourish. They blossom in May in an explosion of white flowers. Half of Spain's olives are the *picual* variety, which turn black on the trees before being picked for oil at the end of November. About 4–5kg/8¾–11lb olives are needed to make a litre of oil.

In Catalonia, oil-making dates back to Roman times, when Spanish oil was a luxury product. The region's favourite tree, the *arbequina*, is small and not particularly vigorous, producing large amounts of small olives that never turn black, even when fully ripe. The oil is smooth and low in astringency with, some say, a slight banana flavour. Catalonia has three *Denominación de Origen* (D.O.) areas (although these represent just 4 per cent of production): Borjas Blancas in Lérida, Siurana west of Tarragona, and Las Garrigues in the southern part of Lérida.

Andalusia has a different oil tradition that dates back to Moorish times. The oil is very fruity, with high astringency. It is made from *picual* with *hojiblanca* (the white-leaf variety of olive). It has a lower oil yield but a fresh taste and strong aroma. The D.O. areas are Córdoba and Jaén: Baena and Priego de Córdoba in the former, and the Sierra de Segura and Sierra Magina in the latter. The Montes de Toledo, Murcia and Aragón also have D.O. areas.

OLIVE OIL

The health benefits of the Mediterranean diet are owed, in part, to olive oil. The oil is rich in oleic acid, which can help to reduce levels of bad cholesterol and raise levels of good cholesterol. It contains vitamin E, a natural oxidant that helps bone formation in the young and old. It also helps reduce blood pressure and may even be an aphrodisiac for women, for it is high in the female hormone oestrogen.

However, it is for its kitchen virtues that the olive has been cultivated. A simple dressing of virgin oil brings out the flavour of food, cold or hot. Olive oil is also the best choice for frying, as the subtle bitterness of Spanish oil counters the rich effect of frying. It can also be used to preserve food – the Moors used

Left: Unfiltered single-olive oils such as this one are new in Spain.

Left: An unfiltered (opalino) extra virgin green olive oil

it for storing fresh beans. The high acidity of Spanish oil makes it ideal for making sauces and emulsions such as mayonnaise, which was first made in Spain.

Once exposed to air, oil deteriorates and should be used within three months, though top-quality oils may keep well for up to a year.

OIL CATEGORIES

Flor de aceite is top of the range – the "flower" of the oil that seeps from the crushed olive paste as it revolves in the barrel. Spain's best oil is clear, golden Nuñez de Prado from Baena. Extra virgin (or cold pressed) is the oil that drips from olives crushed on mats. The difference between extra virgin and virgin is the acidity. Top-quality oils must have less than 0.8 per cent acidity. Spanish oils are always labelled with the acidity and the average is 0.4 to 0.8 per cent (virgin oils may be higher). Unfiltered oils deteriorate more quickly. *Aceite de orujo* is oil extracted chemically from the leftover paste. Branded olive oils (formerly labelled "pure") have about 15 per cent virgin oil added for the flavour. Two well-known Spanish brands are Carbonel and Ybarra.

> **Denominación de Origen**
> As with the system for wine, the best olive-producing areas are given D.O. status, and the quality of their products is carefully regulated.

BELAZU

EARLY HARVEST
EXTRA VIRGIN
OLIVE OIL
UNFILTERED ARBEQUINA

1 Litre ℮
PRODUCT OF
SPAIN

OLIVE OIL SAUCES

Aliñada Virgin oil is often used as a dressing for cooked food. The name literally means embellished.

Ajada This is north coast food. Fish is fried in the oil, then vinegar and paprika are added to make a sauce.

Allioli Garlic and oil are blended to make a thick, white emulsion, which is served with vegetables. The Catalan *allioli amb ous* is allioli with egg yolk, which is served with fish and rice.

Mahonesa Spanish "mayonnaise" takes its name from Mahón in Menorca. It is a rich emulsion of egg yolk and oil and is more subtle than allioli from which it is probably derived. It is the perfect partner for shellfish.

Pil pil Like allioli, this is an emulsified sauce. It combines the gelatine in fish skin with oil. The fish is cooked in the oil, and the oil is then swirled in the hot casserole dish until it thickens.

Making Mahonesa

Put 2 egg yolks in a bowl with a good pinch of salt. Using a hand-held blender, beat well, then add 30ml/2 tbsp vinegar and beat again. Work in up to 250ml/8fl oz/ 1 cup ordinary (not virgin) olive oil, drizzling very slowly at first, until it becomes thick and creamy. Flavour with lemon juice, extra virgin olive oil and pepper to taste.

Above: Negras perlas are fruity black olives with a mild flavour.

TABLE OLIVES

Lawrence Durrell said that the taste of olives is "older than meat, older than wine, a taste as old as cold water". Spain is the world's chief olive producer, with half the crop being exported. The vast majority of these olives grow on unirrigated land within range of Seville.

Spanish cured olives are mainly picked when they are bright green and unripe. At this point, they are low in oil, being made up of only acid and sugars. In this state, the olives will keep their colour and grassy tang for several months after brining. Left on the tree they turn a mottled purple, and finally black, with a softer, fuller flavour. The *muerta* (dead) just drop from the tree, black and wrinkled.

To remove their bitterness, green olives are washed in several changes of water and then stored for a few days in brine (known as the Seville way) with flavourings, to make *aceitunas aliñadas* (seasoned olives). In Andalusia garlic, oregano and herbs are used; in the Balearics wild fennel and lemon leaves. Pitted olives stuffed with little pieces of cooked pimiento, slivers of almond, anchovy or roasted garlic are also sold, and popularly exported.

Left: Allioli made with egg yolks is a powerful garlic mayonnaise with a history dating back over 2,000 years.

Above: Pimiento-stuffed olives were originally filled by hand.

Above: Manzanillas are the best-known and most popular of Spanish olives.

Types of olive

There are many different varieties of olive, each with their own individual appearance and character.

Arbequina comes from the village of La Arbeca in Lérida. It is very small, greenish-brown and has a high oil content and pleasant bitter-to-aromatic flavour. It is *the* Catalan appetizer.

Cornezuelo is horn-shaped, green and with a white tip. It has a strong flavour with a hint of bitterness.

Cuquillo is round, small, and blue-black. It is often prepared with chopped onion and hot spices, and is good as a partner to beer.

Gordal or **reina** (queen) are trade names for the largest, dark green, fleshy olive, often called *sevilles* in Spain.

Hojiblanco is slightly rectangular in shape. One of the main types of olives, it is more fibrous and less tasty than other varieties.

Manzanilla is apple- or pear-shaped, the best-known and most popular olive. It is suitable for stuffing.

Pelotín from Andalusia, is small, round and green.

Negra is black, spiced or dried and pickled, and perfect with red wine. Large negras are called *negras perlas*.

CHEESE AND DAIRY PRODUCE

Spain produces about 200 varieties of cheese (*queso*), most of them in farmhouse dairies and with limited distribution. A considerable number are exported, with the hard cheeses being the most successful.

Cheeses are shaped according to local tradition. Muslin (cheesecloth) is used to shape the Galician *tetilla* and also *Mahón*, producing very different results. *Camerano* is a ball-shaped cheese, moulded in a basket. Sycamore or maple leaves are pressed on to the wet rind of northern blue cheeses. Esparto grass hoops give Manchego cheese a welt, which becomes broader on the rind of the *Ronda*.

Although goat's, cow's and ewe's milk all produce distinct cheeses with their own unique character, some generic cheeses are made with milk blends. The semi-hard *Aragón* is made with ewe's and goat's milk, as is *Gamonedo*. Some cheese is smoked – most notably the versions of *San Simón*, *Gamonedo* and *Idiazábal*. *Quesucos* (part of the Liébana D.O.) is a mild, smoked, mixed-milk cheese from Santander, pale yellow inside, with "eyes".

Hard cheeses are often served as a tapas dish, while soft ones are served with honey and nuts as dessert. There is little in the way of cheese cooking – only fried hard-cheese cubes, and *flamenquines* (ham and cheese rolls that are breadcrumbed and deep-fried).

Below: Menorcan Mahón is made using cow's milk. Its bright orange rind is produced by rubbing the rind with butter, paprika and oil.

Right: San Simón is a semi-soft cow's milk cheese from Galicia. It has a supple texture and is often smoked.

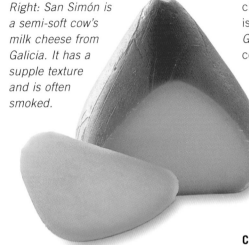

FRESH AND SOFT CHEESES

Fresh curd cheese (*requesón*) is much liked and made all over Spain. Ewe's milk is normally used to make matured cheese, but there are some soft ones, which include the white *Anso*, from the valley of Huesca; and the mild *Cervera* and *Puzol*, both from Valencia. Two are widely available and typical: *Queso de Burgos* is rindless, often with mould markings, and soft. It is made from scalded curd, which is moulded then salted in brine for 24 hours. *Villalón* or *pata de mulo*, from the Valladolid region, is an elongated cylinder.

GOAT'S MILK CHEESES

In the south, cheeses are predominantly made with goat's milk. Often pressed, their flavour is distinct and clean. They are not pungent like many of the French varieties, and they have a light, crumbly texture. Unaged goat's milk cheeses include *Alicante*, *Camerano* from the Rioja area, and the slightly aromatic *Málaga*, with its buff rind, lightly pressed into an esparto grass mould. Southern goat's cheeses include: *Cádiz*, which is medium-pressed, full of holes, and with a rind marked with esparto; and *Añejo de cabra* from the *Sierra de Huelva*, whose ripened paste is dark orange, with a rough rind. The Canary Islands make only goat's

cheese, the best being *Majorero*, which is matured for two months. In the east, *Garroxta* is made all over Catalonia. In central Spain, *Ibores* from Extremadura, is made from *retinto* goat's milk. It is aromatic, slightly sour, with a soft oiled rind coated with paprika. *Soría* has a firm white skin and is lightly salted. *Cabra de Tiétar,* from Ávila, is lightly pressed and briefly matured. *Valdeteja*, from León, has a sharp, goaty smell. It is shaped into a cylinder, has some holes and a crusty rind.

COW'S MILK CHEESES

In the north, the cheeses are made with cow's milk. They are generally eaten quite young and are creamy and soft.

Tetilla, from Pontevedra in Galicia, is white inside, moulded with a cloth and sometimes has a golden rind. Its name literally means teat or nipple, reflecting the shape of the cheese. *Cebrero* (*Piedrafita*), from the mountains of Lugo, looks like a chef's hat; it is tangy and white inside. The mild, yellow *Gallego* (*Ulloa*) is a slightly flattened ball. *León* is a yellow drum, with a close texture and rough yellow rind. The dry, astringent *afuega el pitu*, from Asturias, is shaped in a small cone. *Pasiego prensado*, which is made south-west of Santander, is white and creamy with small holes and a distinctive flavour.

Eggs

Spain is a country of poultry breeders and the use of eggs (*huevos*) in cooking reflects this. Galician free-range (farm-fresh) eggs are famous for the red albumen in their yolks – they are used in Madrid for making tortillas.

Menus still have an egg course and proper attention is given to egg cooking. *Revuelta*, soft scrambled eggs, is the way to display such luxuries as summer truffles and caviars. Eggs make everyday meals with a good deal of spontaneity, such as flamenco eggs and other gypsy recipes.

Above:
Idiazábal D.O. has been
made for centuries by shepherds
in the Urbia and Alara mountains.

San Simón, from the Lugo province in Galicia, is large, shiny, brown and pear-shaped; it is oiled on the outside then smoked, but remains creamy inside.

Extremadura produces two soft-rind, creamy cheeses that are unusual for Spain. *La Serena* D.O., made in Cáceres, and *torta de Casar* are spring cheeses – the latter set with cardoon, which makes it pleasantly bitter. It is very creamy and is usually spooned out of its pink rind.

In the Balearics *Mahón* D.O., from Menorca, owes its existence to the British, who brought Friesian cows to the island, where the salty grazing affects the cheese's taste. It is hand-pressed into rectangles.

BLUE CHEESES

Cabrales D.O. is a real gourmet cheese made from cow's milk (or sometimes a blend) in 25 × 20cm/10 × 8in drums. A worthy competitor to Roquefort, the paste is off-white with blue veins, slightly stonger and more acidic than the French cheese. It is moulded, dry-salted, then matured for about six months in natural limestone caves in the Asturias, then wrapped in plane tree leaves. Related cheeses are *Picón* (part of the *Liébana* D.O.) and *Tresviso*. *Gamonedo*, another Asturian blue made from blended milk, which is unusual both for being smoked for ten to twelve days before maturing, and for its wrapping of fern leaves. The white flesh is blue-veined with oval eyes.

EWE'S MILK CHEESES

In central-north Spain, Castile and León produce most of the ewe's milk. This is the home of hard, pressed cheeses with dark rinds. Made in big drums, they are well-matured, strong, dense and grainy. *Roncal* was Spain's first D.O. cheese. The ivory paste has tiny holes. *Idiazábal* D.O., from the Basque Provinces, is a classic, holey, often smoked cheese. *Zamorano* D.O., from western Castile, is unpasteurized, made from the best milk in Spain.

Other firm cheeses include *Grazalema* from Cadiz, *Orduña* from Navarra, the *Oropesa* from Toledo and Basque *Gorbea*, with a dark shiny rind, flat base and rounded top. *Pedroches* from Córdoba is piquant and salty, which is brought out by storing it in oil.

MILK

Spain's dairy region is the Cantabrian range, along the north coast. Here cows move up to summer pastures in the high mountains. The Spanish drink milk at breakfast time, mixed half and half with coffee. Fresh milk is drunk by children and the elderly or made into *cuajada* (a sort of junket) and yogurt. Milk puddings have always been popular, and whipped cream (*nata*) is often piped over desserts.

BUTTER

Called *mantequilla*, butter is used for frying in the Basque country. This is one important way Basque cooking can be distinguished from the rest of Spain. Their sauces and cakes contain butter, as they now do in Catalonia. Elsewhere, oil and pork fat still dominate.

All about Manchego

Spain's premier cheese is made from the milk of Manchega ewes from the centre of the country. It is made in 3kg/6½lb drums, or occasionally smaller. Sometimes pasteurized, the curds are heated and pressed into esparto grass moulds, which pattern the outside of the cheese. Golden inside, Manchego becomes stronger as it ages and is sold as *semi-curado* (under 13 weeks), *curado* (up to six months), *viejo* (over six months), and also packed in oil. Mature (sharp) cheeses are similar to Parmesan. Exported cheeses, called *ibéricos* are often made using blended milk.

Below: Manchego, from left, aged for 4 months, 6 months and 10 months

VEGETABLES OF THE OLD WORLD

The Spanish really appreciate fresh vegetables. In spring, fresh peas, the first asparagus and shoots of young crops such as garlic are all gathered and served in egg dishes and *menestras* (vegetable stews), where their virtues can shine. New small artichokes (*alcachofas*) are grilled on the first barbecues of summer.

Growing delicate green asparagus (*espárragos*) is a big industry in the south, in the valleys around Granada, while white asparagus, fat like rich men's fingers, are grown in the valley of the Ebro, in Navarre, and canned for sale all over Europe. Other excellent food crops grow there too, including *cogollos* (Little Gem, or Bibb, lettuces). Unusual vegetables such as borage, blue-flowered and hairy stemmed, are still stewed in Aragón. Carrots are another ancient vegetable and flourish in the Spanish sunshine.

Spinach was introduced by the Moors and their *espinacas a la catalana*, with pine nuts and raisins, is still made today. In the south, spinach is replaced by the prolific chard (*acelga*) with similar but coarser leaves. The pearly stalks can be battered and fried.

The true vegetable of the Islamic lands is *berenjena*, the aubergine or eggplant (*albergenies* in Catalan). Many recipes using aubergine go back 800 years. *Almodrote* combines aubergine with garlic, cumin, pine nuts and cheese; *alboronia* is similar to ratatouille, but with no tomatoes.

Above: Large Spanish onions are sweet and mild enough to eat raw.

ONIONS AND GARLIC

The Moors loved onions, especially raw, which is one reason why the Spanish onion is so big and mild. *Sofrito* is the combination of onion and garlic fried together to form the base of numerous sauces. *Cebollones* (*calçots* in Catalan) are oversized spring onions (scallions), with the mild flavour of shallots. Young garlic shoots, plucked when green, are similar and these *ajetes* have a spring cuisine of their own, usually cooked with eggs and seafood. Leeks are popular with the Basques and are used in soups such as *purrusalda*.

Garlic is as old as the Pyramids and in Spain many sauces contain this pungent vegetable. *Ajo-pollo*, which means "the sort of sauce used for chicken", combines crushed garlic with ground almonds and breadcrumbs. Valencian *alli-pebre* is a mixture of garlic and paprika, and *alli oli* is simply a mixture of garlic and oil – the names say it all.

Left: Leafy green spinach has been eaten in Spain for centuries and is used in many Catalan dishes.

All about garlic

Fundamental to Spanish cooking, garlic is often mistakenly thought to dominate it. Its role in the kitchen is reflected in the saying, *estar en el ajo* (to be in the know). Garlic is more than a flavouring – it is good for you too. It lowers cholesterol levels and acts as an antiseptic on cuts. It is said in Spain that garlic gives you guts. After the San Fermín bull running at Pamplona, young men take home strings of garlic to build up their courage for the next year.

Used raw or cooked, garlic has two quite different flavours, the first pungent, the second more suggestive. Any dish *al ajillo* is flavoured with chopped garlic, while *con ajo* means "with whole cloves", which are made sweet and mild with long cooking.

In Spanish cooking, garlic is often the first ingredient into the frying pan. It is used to flavour the oil, but is then discarded before the rest of the ingredients are added. Before adding garlic to an uncooked sauce, make a paste by crushing it with a little salt using the flat side of a knife.

Below: Garlic is widely used in Spanish cooking, adding a distinctive flavour.

Above: Chickpeas, with their lovely, nutty flavour, are the basic carbohydrate of Spanish cuisine.

DRIED BEANS, LENTILS AND PEAS

Dried broad (fava) beans were used widely in Spanish dishes in years past, and are still used in a few dishes today, such as the Valencian *micherones* (stewed with garlic). Dried peas and lentils (*lentejas*) are still weekly fare, partnered with the inevitable chorizo, particularly north of Madrid.

Chickpeas (*garbanzos*) are the potatoes of Spain, growing well through the hot summers. In ancient times, the Romans mocked the chickpea-eating Spanish, suggesting that their enormous consumption of the legume not only indicated stupidity but also induced it. Chickpeas are the least easy of dried beans and peas to spoil, but do not absorb flavour from accompanying ingredients in the way that beans do. Although they need soaking and take up to 2 hours to cook, chickpeas keep their shape well, even when reheated. *Garbanzos con chorizos* (chickpeas with chorizo) is a classic, while chickpeas, chard and salt cod are combined to make a traditional Lenten dish.

Right: Today, fresh broad beans are far more widely used than dried ones, and are celebrated in a national dish, habas con jamón, *with ham.*

CABBAGES, TURNIPS AND CARDOONS

Galician cabbages are huge, but every province likes this vegetable. There are more words for cabbage in Spanish than in English, and more varieties. *Lombardo* (red cabbage) is popular in Madrid and is used to garnish sea bream on Christmas Eve; a *cocido de berza* will contain cabbage. However, it is turnips that Galicians really love, both the root and the green tops (*grelos*) when they just start budding. Cardoon (*cardo*) is the artichoke's bigger cousin and comes into season at the end of the year.

WILD FOOD

Much produce is gathered from the countryside, especially in poorer areas. Lupin seed is a yellow tapas bar nibble, and is sold at fairs as a snack. Wild asparagus is a speciality, picked in April and again before winter. *Targina* is a thistle with short side stems that are eaten in the same way as cardoon or with beans or eggs. Dandelion leaves go into salads, chicory root is dug to make coffee, and fennel is used to season fish. Chestnuts grow in the south of Galicia and were a basic foodstuff until potatoes arrived.

Capers originally grew wild all over the southern coasts. But they are now a huge industry. Both the buds and the plump berries are pickled, the latter eaten in the same way as olives.

Above: Fresh young turnips and their leafy green tops are Galicia's pride.

WILD MUSHROOMS

The Spanish in general are not great mushrooms pickers, and the Galicians are positively against it. However, the Basques and Catalans make up for this. About 50 kinds of mushroom are gathered throughout the year. They are cooked simply, with garlic or eggs, and are used in game casseroles. Ceps (*bolets*) are grilled (broiled) whole.

Setas (wild mushrooms) and *hongos* (fungi) are much in demand, as are *setas de cardo* (oyster mushrooms). In Catalonia, picking the golden yellow *rovolló* is almost an obsession. Called *níscalo* in the rest of Spain, the bleeding milk cap oozes red drops from the stem when it is cut.

The Basque favourite is the tiny yellowish white spring St George's mushroom with its penetrating perfume. Called *zizak* locally, it is *moixernons* elsewhere. Truffles also grow in Spain, and the common *criadillas de tierra* are served in tapas bars in Extremadura during the summer months.

VEGETABLES FROM AMERICA

The colour, sweetness and piquancy of American vegetables, brought home by Christopher Columbus, revolutionized Spanish cooking – and with it, Europe. The Mediterranean climate is ideal for tomatoes, peppers, courgettes (zucchini) and pumpkins. Maize (corn) was adopted in northern Spain, for fattening poultry and as corn meal for bread, and potatoes had their biggest Spanish success fried as *patatas fritas*.

TOMATOES

Today, tomatoes are a great success story in Spain. Three or even four crops a year are produced in the *invernadores* (plastic tunnels) of Almería, and they are loaded into lorries that roar north from southern Spain.

The name *tomate* comes from the Aztec *tomatl*, meaning something plump. The tomato was not an instant success when it was introduced to Spain and was, at first, used simply as the liquid for serving chilli. Tomato sauce was still a novelty as late as the 1820s – and regarded by outsiders as a Spanish curiosity. A *sauce espagnole* in a restaurant in France is a classic meat-stock sauce with tomato in it.

Today tomatoes are combined with sweet (bell) peppers in a huge number of dishes: *gazpacho, pisto, bacalo a la viscaína* (salt cod baked with tomato) and all the dishes called *samfaína*. Tomatoes are sold in two classes: ripest and ripe. The first are for sauces, the second for salads. There are even salads where one tomato is dressed with the juice of another – *ajotomate*.

FRESH PEPPERS

Morrones (bell) peppers, are often two-fist size, fleshy with tough skin, green or the sweeter red. There are other sweet varieties and a long, thin, green one with a thin skin. When soft and baked, red pepper has become an ingredient in its own right, called *pimiento*.

The red *piquillo*, grown in Navarra and Rioja, is the gourmet's pepper. Smaller, stocky and with a point at one end, it is crisper and distinctly piquant. It is often stuffed with cod and baked. It is also wonderful canned, after being roasted over beechwood.

Below: Tomatoes are used subtlely in Spanish cuisine, partnering but never dominating other flavours.

Above: Sweet pimientos *peppers go into many dishes. Little* padróns *are a Galician speciality, popular everywhere.*

The green Galician pepper, *padrón*, is part of a popular joke. As long as a thumb, they are deep-fried and served with a little salt as an appetizer, about twenty to a plate. Though normally sweet, one in that number will be fiery hot, and there is no knowing which.

DRIED CHILLIES

Columbus' mission was to look for the spice, black pepper. He discovered spicy red peppers instead. Towards winter, chilli peppers are hung up all over Spain to dry, particularly in Rioja, in red *ristras* (strings).

The general rule for these chillies is the larger, the milder. Cooking, in particular roasting, makes them sweeter, as the bitterness is in the skin. The flavour of chillies is made more concentrated and robust by drying or toasting. Including vinegar in the recipe gives the same intensified effect.

Choricero This chilli has given its name, colour and piquancy to the red Spanish frying sausage. The chilli is larger than a fist, elongated but rounded, red, and extremely sweet and mild – 1/10 on the Mexican chilli-heat scale. It can be crumbled into dishes or reconstituted in liquid, then the flesh scraped out. One or two per person go into dishes such

Below: Romesco or ñora chillies are usually hung up to dry in long, decorative strings.

Right: Red kidney beans are a Basque favourite stewed with ham bone, red chorizo sausage and black morcilla.

as *chilindrón*, (lamb with chilli).

Ñora This is called *romesco* in Catalonia and is a walnut-sized chilli; red and cherry-round. It has a sweet fruit flavour, with a hint of a biting finish – 2/10 on the Mexican chilli-heat scale. It was adopted by the Catalans in the 16th century and is common in Alicante and Murcia. It has very little flesh but the colour and flavour are concentrated, hence its use in salsas, *romescos* of fish, rice and paella. Ancho or jalapeño chillies may be used as substitutes.

Guindilla As long as a finger, this is Spain's hot chilli – 3/10 on the Mexican chilli-heat scale – but it is also medium sweet. It adds zip to dishes such as *gambas pil pil* (prawns with chilli).

BEANS

Large American kidney beans were considered much more elegant and tasty than old, brown beans. *Judías* are green beans (pods) and *alubias* are dried ones. The latter come in all sizes – from the tiniest *arroncini* (rice-sized) to the big *judiones* of El Barco de Ávila and the *garrafones* (carboys) of Valencia – and in all colours: white, to mottled red or green, to purple with green eyes. Spain is the bean capital of the world.

Every province soon adopted and grew their own beans, in fierce regional competition, cooking them with their own sausages. The Basques once specialized in red beans, but now theirs is the "black" bean of Tolosa. The finest beans grown are *fabes de la granja* from Asturias, used to make *fabada*.

They are very expensive and sold in numbered cotton bags.

Fresh beans make one national dish, eaten with ham, while *pochas* (kidney beans fresh from the pod) are a little October speciality, stewed with quail. A Spanish type that is just becoming known elsewhere is *ferraura*. Bred from runner beans, they are "flat beans", long, soft-surfaced, stringless green pods – and one of the original ingredients of paella.

POTATOES AND SQUASH

While potatoes were ignored in northern Europe, they were a success in Seville. They found their true home in Galicia, which now grows *cachelos*, a large white tuber of exceptional quality, near the sea, where it absorbs salt from the soil. They accompany the local *lacón* (cured pork shoulder) or sardines, and are often layered into fish stews.

Sweet potatoes are *batata* (yellow-fleshed; the US yam) and *boniato* (white-fleshed). They are made into little cakes or served in honey.

The *calabaza* (marrow/large zucchini, summer squash or pumpkins) goes into stewpots like *calabazote* (with potatoes and beans). But *calabacín* (courgette/ zucchini) was little known until the 1980s, and more of a success in Italy.

Below: In the south, squash are added to gypsy vegetable and bean stews.

SPICES, HERBS AND FLAVOURINGS

The Spanish cuisine has its own range of spices, herbs, condiments and nuts, all of which contribute to the unique and characteristic taste of Spanish food.

SAFFRON

With its aromatic scent and golden colour, *azafrán* is a quintessentially Moorish spice. For paella and fish and shellfish stews, there is no substitute. For chicken, all *pepitorias* (nut sauces), creams, buns and ices, saffron is king.

The purple crocuses from which saffron is obtained flower quite suddenly in mid-October in parched La Mancha, creating purple carpets around the vines. The flowers are plucked by hand, then three orange stamens are pulled from each flower, toasted over charcoal and dried to bring out the flavour. A hard day's work produces only about 50g/2oz saffron.

Mancha selecto is the world's best saffron; it is deep red, with long threads and a high oil content. Spain produces 70 per cent of the world's saffron. Although very expensive, a tiny amount flavours a dish for two to three people.

Spanish saffron is rarely powdered, as this is too easy to adulterate with cheap yellow dyes such as safflower (*cártamo*), colouring (*colorante*), and the chemical tartrazine.

Below: Top quality saffron all comes from Spain, grown in La Mancha.

Above: Warm, spicy, aromatic cumin is a legacy of the Moors and is widely used in southern cooking.

OTHER SPICES

The Moors introduced cumin (*comino*) to Spain and it is widely used with vegetables and tomatoes, and with skewered meats. Coriander seeds (*cilantro*) also came from North Africa, and are often partnered with cumin and used to flavour skewered meat cooked on the barbecue. Coloured yellow with turmeric, pork cubes are sold ready-spiced in many southern butchers. Other popular spice flavourings include turmeric (*cúrcuma*), cloves (*clavos*), cardamom (*cardamoma*) and – to a lesser extent – ginger (*jengibre*).

The Catalans are generous users of black pepper (*pimienta*), whereas the rest of Spain uses paprika (*pimentón*).

There is no clear division between sweet and savoury spices in Spain – another Moorish legacy. Nutmeg (*nuez moscada*) goes into *morcillas* (black pudding) – along with cumin, cinnamon (*canela*) and aniseed (*matalhuva*) – and is also used to flavour custards. Cinnamon is the obligatory flavouring used in rice milk puddings and the ice cream that accompanies fruit. It is also commonly used with poultry and in stews, which also often contain saffron.

Aniseed (*anís*) is a key flavour in Spanish food and drink. It is basic to many liqueurs and its seeds are ground and used in many pastries, doughs and sausages. Another very Spanish flavour is dried orange peel (*cachorreña*), which is pounded and added to shellfish and fish soups.

SALT

Intimately tied to Spain's commercial history, the salt trade is an old one, and grew up around the Mediterranean salt pans. Cadiz supplied salt beef for the ships journeying to the Americas, and the Basques have been shipping home salt cod since the 17th century.

Today salt has changed from being a preservative to being a preference. The Spanish seek out foods that contain salt, especially cured foods such as *mohama*, *cecina*, *anchoas* and *botargo* (tuna, beef, anchovies and grey mullet caviar). Salt adds interest to beans, while eating salt fish on Fridays is a 500-year-old tradition.

Paprika

Pimentón is a basic flavouring in Spanish cooking, used like black pepper, and not just sprinkled for decoration. It is made from a sweet red (bell) pepper with a round body and pointed end. There are three grades of paprika used in Spain: *dulce* (mild), *picante* (which contains a little *guindilla* chilli), and *agridulce* (bittersweet). You can substitute cayenne pepper for *picante*. The main centre of production is the Vera valley, where peppers are smoked before being ground.

Below: Sweet paprika is Spain's most commonly used pepper.

HERBS

Bay leaves (*hojas de laurel*) Partnered with rosemary and thyme, aromatic bay leaves make up Spain's herbal trinity. The leaves are added to stews and thrown on the barbecue. Fresh leaves are battered, fried and sugared to make sweet *paparejotes*.

Coriander (*cilantro*) Pungent fresh coriander leaves are thought of as the Portuguese herb and only used in Extremadura and the Canary Islands, where the herb is crushed to make the green *mojo verde* sauce for fish. It is also excellent rubbed over pork to flavour the meat before roasting.

Fennel (*hinojo*) This beautiful herb has a slight flavour of aniseed and grows wild everywhere. It is used to flavour the cooking water for shellfish and its tiny aromatic seeds are sometimes added to home-cured olives.

Lemon verbena (*hierba luisa*) Used to make a delicious fragrant tea, this popular herb can be found growing in many Spanish gardens.

Mint (*menta*) Known as *hierba buena*, the good herb, Moroccan mint is a favourite garden plant. It goes into *morcilla* (black pudding) and is used with offal. *Poleo* is Pennyroyal mint (*Mentha pulegium*), which is used for tea – and also in a soup for hangovers.

Oregano (*origano*) This is the sausage herb, and also goes into meat stews and marinades. Its essential oil doesn't deteriorate with long cooking, so it is one of the few herbs that can be added early on in cooking. The related English herb, marjoram (*mejorana*), is thought of as a medicinal herb in Spain.

Left: Many varieties of thyme grow in the Spanish sierras.

Parsley (*perejil*, or *julivert* in Catalan) The Spanish grow flat leaf parsley, which is milder than curly parsley. It is a popular herb and is used lavishly in Murcia.

Rosemary (*romero*) Snails eat rosemary, so they are used as "rosemary cubes" to flavour rabbit stews and paella. Big old bushes of the wild herb are also used to fuel bread ovens and wood-burning stoves. Rosemary with thyme and chilli are traditionally used to flavour dried bean dishes.

Thyme (*tomillo*) There are several varieties of thyme with small white flowers, which are used for cooking. *Tomillo salsero* (sauce thyme) is picked in April to give to friends at Christmas. The herb is much used to flavour rabbit and, with summer savory (*ajedrea blanca*), to flavour dried bean dishes.

NUTS

Almonds (*almendras*) These are second only to oranges as a major crop. There are two types. The first is the smaller, bitter almond, which is grown only for almond oil and essence (extract), as it is poisonous if eaten raw. The second type is the sweet *Jordan* almond. Of Spanish origin, its name is a corruption of *jardín* meaning garden. Grown in the south-east, they are long, flat and slender, and the best cocktail almonds in the world. *Marcona* almonds are used to make turrón (*nougat*).

Ground almonds are used in place of flour to thicken sauces in Spain. They are the base of *picada*, which thickens sauces instead of a roux, and any dish called a *pepitoria*. Almonds are also pounded for soups, used in biscuits (cookies) and coated with sugar to make festival *almendras garipinadas* and Catalan *ametlles*.

Hazelnuts (*avellanas*) These nuts grow in mountain regions and were farmed in Tarragona, where they are made into a soup. The Basques use them to thicken stews, and they are added to meringues as far apart as Granada and Asturias.

Sherry vinegar
With its stunning tobacco aromas, sherry vinegar is used in salad dressings and gives a superior finish to sauces. Young sherries, reserved because of their high acidity, are matured in wood and concentrated to intensify their flavour. Aged up to 25 years, a really good sherry vinegar far surpasses a cheap *balsámico*. One of the best is Emilio Lustau $^{1}/_{24}$ solera, or look for Xerés.

Pine nuts (*piñones*) These come from the cones of the stone pine, one of the West's ancient fertility symbols. The cones are gathered in winter and are then dried through the next summer. The tiny creamy nuts have a slightly astringent taste and are improved by toasting, which brings out and enhances their flavour. They are good used in salads and sauces, or baked in little cakes, such as festival *paneletts* and nut-covered *piñonates*.

Below: Pine nuts have a distinctive taste and are frequently toasted before being added to dishes.

Below: Hazelnuts are used to flavour sweet dishes such as desserts, cakes and cookies, as well as savoury sauces.

RICE AND PASTA

These two staples are at the heart of both everyday family meals and classic celebration dishes in Spain.

RICE

Valencia is forever linked with rice. The Moors planted rice there and it was the only crop that could be grown on the hot Mediterranean littoral in summer.

Rice is eaten on a daily basis in the east and south of Spain. It is eaten plain, added to soupy stews, and combined with beans to make stuffings for vegetables. Many *morcillas* (black puddings) contain rice, especially those made in Burgos, Aragón, Rioja and the Levante. *Arroz con leche* (rice pudding) rivals *flan* (baked custard) as Spain's national dessert.

It is the quality and flavour of rice that matters, so flavourings tend to be simple – a pinch of saffron, perhaps with a little bacon and *morcilla* (black pudding). Alicante *arros amb costra*, a Catalan oven-baked dish, comes with a rice crust concealing the chickpea and sausage stew. *Arros perdiu* (partridge rice) is "trick dish" made for Lent – instead of partridge, it has a whole baked garlic bulb in the centre. Valencian restaurants feature a different rice every day, but the popular choice for Sundays is rice with salt cod.

Below: Bomba is the most readily available variety of paella rice.

Above: Paella, originally from Valencia, is probably Spain's most famous dish. It is eaten for celebrations but is also an incredibly popular dish for tourists.

Short grain rice

The short, fat Spanish grain originates from Japanese round rice, rather than the Indian long grain, and it has a slight bite, like risotto rice. Spain became Europe's largest rice producer because it was the first country to try to find a suitable grain for the Mediterranean climate. A large amount of rice is grown in the Seville area but the best type of rice is *Calasparra*, which grows in Murcia. The grains swell dramatically when cooked in stock, absorbing three or four times their volume of liquid.

Below: The prized Calasparra rice is sold in numbered cotton bags.

Rice pans and dishes

When cooking rice, there are different types of pan for cooking specific dishes. Paella is cooked in the shallow *paellera*. The Valencian model is thin with a dimpled base. The finished dish should be "dry" (but moist), with every grain separate. Strictly speaking, paella is the Valencian name for the dish, and similar dishes elsewhere should simply be called *arroz* (*arros* in Catalan).

"Wet" rice dishes are soupy and eaten with a spoon. They are often fish dishes, cooked in a round-based cooking pot known as a *caldereta*. The pot gives its name to some of the classic wet rice dishes, including *el caldero* (rice with fish). *Arroz a banda* is rice cooked in fish stock, but separately from the fish (which makes another course). It is the perfect dish to reveal just how good plain rice can be, done the Spanish way. These soupy dishes used to be considered far too provincial to appear on restaurant menus, but one exception is the winter *arros amb fesol i naps* (rice with yellow swede/rutabaga and turnip). Another substantial dish is *el perrol*, a cauldron of rice stewed with meat and a large quantity of vegetables.

Paella

The birthplace of paella is the marshland outside the city of Valencia, round Lake Albufera. The area is still a place of ducks and eels. Bamboo groves standing in water separate lake from lake and little bridges carry small roads from village to village. El Palmar, one of the best-known villages, is surrounded by water.

Paella was invented here some 200 years ago. It is a summer dish, intended for picnics, and generally cooked by men in a flat pan set over a charcoal fire. Originally, paella used ingredients from the surrounding area – rice, garlic and parsley, either eels or snails, plus good beans, either flat green beans that look like runner beans or big flat kidney beans called *garrafones*. The seasoning was Spain's best – saffron – while the snails added a hint of rosemary. The rice is cooked very slowly, then covered with newspaper for the last 10 minutes, until all liquid has been absorbed. The paella is allowed to crisp slightly underneath before serving.

Saffron-yellow *paella valenciana*, decorated with mussels and strips of red (bell) pepper, prawns (shrimp) and chicken pieces like buried treasure, is eaten in Spain on every festive occasion. In Valencia, however, it is more of a tourist dish. Locals are more likely to opt for just shellfish or chicken; on the south coast, the usual choice is rabbit.

PASTA

Pasta has been eaten in Spain for longer than it has in north Italy. (There is even a recipe for a noodle soup in Catalonia's first printed cook book, by Rupert de Nolan, in 1477.) Pasta became everyday food in Spain and Italy at the same time, in the late 18th century. Durum wheat, used to make pasta, was planted in Catalonia in the 1950s. Today pasta is made in Andalusia and Extremadura.

The Catalan favourite is *fideos*, a thin, short spaghetti used in soups or served with sauces and sausage. South of paella country is Gandía (home of the

Above: Macaroni is a popular pasta, usually served with grated cheese.

Borgias, the family of Pope Alexander VI) where they have a *fideuá* (noodle) festival every year. The big pasta dish these days is shellfish with *fideos* instead of rice, which is a great deal easier to make than paella. It was invented in the 1970s and now features along the entire coast from Málaga to the Costa Brava, including one version where the pasta is dry-fried first.

Canelones (cannelloni) were introduced to Spain by the many Italian chefs who came to work in Barcelona in the 19th century. Flat dry squares, *obleas* (thin wafers), are now sold for making lasagne or for rolling into *canelones*. Home-made pasta was originally made by poor shepherds. They added simple flour-and-water paste squares (Manchego wafers) to stews such as *andrajos*.

Below: Fideos is a thin and short Spanish pasta – about 5cm/2in long.

Ten tips to good paella

Good paella is not difficult to make, but there are a few simple steps to ensure perfect results.

• Use a wide pan – 20cm/8in is right for two people. A deep pizza pan can be substituted for a paella pan.

• Use paella (or risotto) rice. Use 50–75g/2–3oz/generous ¼–scant ½ cup per person. (Don't stint on the rice.)

• Don't overdo the extras; they are there to flavour the rice. Choose a theme such as rabbit or shellfish.

• Don't be mean with the saffron, and use threads not powder. 0.1g is sufficient for two to three people and for six you will need 0.3g.

• Start with double the amount of stock to the volume of rice – some rices take more. Taste and warm the stock before adding it to the pan, making sure it is deeply flavoured. If the stock is insipid, so will be the paella.

• Don't overfill the pan; a depth of 2cm/¾in is about right.

• Use a wide heat source. Ideally the heat source should equal the diameter of the pan. The Spanish have special wide gas rings for making paella. Cooking over charcoal works well and solid fuel cookers are also suitable.

• If the heat source is smaller than the base of the pan, move the pan every 2–3 minutes, to prevent the middle cooking while the outside remains uncooked.

• The shape and size of the pan and the heat source are the main problems outside Spain. If in doubt, cover the pan with foil and bake in the oven for the second half of the cooking time.

• Let the paella stand, covered, off the heat for 10 minutes at the end of the cooking time, to absorb the last of the liquid. Paella should be a "dry" rice dish.

ATLANTIC AND MEDITERRANEAN FISH

Spain is second only to Japan in fish consumption, with over 500g/1lb eaten per head per week. Madrid has been called "the biggest port in Europe".

The two coasts of Spain are very different. The roaring, scourging Atlantic breaks on Cape Finisterre, where the finest fish in the world are caught. The Mediterranean, lazy and warm, is better for shellfish than fish, the best being caught outside Gibraltar.

Farming fish for salting goes back to Roman times, and today fish from salt flats such as Murcia's *Mar Menor* are prized for their extra flavour. The *salinas* off Cadiz raise gilthead bream, and sea bass and turbot are bred in El Grove on the Galician coast.

Cadiz is probably home to the original take-away (take-out) fried fish shop. Frying is something the Spanish do superbly well, although battered fried fish, called *a la romana*, is credited to the Italians. Málaga is famed for its mixed *pescaito frito*.

Spain shares the general Mediterranean love of fish stews and some say that the Spanish *bulla baissa* was the origin of French *bouillabaisse*. *Romesco de peix* (mixed fish with Catalan chilli), *zarzuela*, and the similar *suquet*, are incontestably Spanish. On the north coast, and in Galicia, the great *caldieras* layer mixed fish with potatoes. The east coast has *calderos* with rice, which include *cabracho* (the rascasse or large-scaled scorpion fish), the indispensable fish for soups and for making the broth of rice dishes.

Below: Delicately flavoured hake is one of Spain's best-loved fish.

Above (from front): Gilthead bream, red bream and blackhead bream

LUXURY FISH

Sea bass (*lubina*), turbot (*rodaballo*) and monkfish (*rape*, or *pixin* as it is known in Asturias) are cooked in wine and shellfish sauces, or with cider and potatoes. Really good fish needs no disguise and *ajada* (a simple mixture of oil, garlic and paprika) frequently partners fish in the north, in the same way that lemons do in the south. A typical dish is *besugo a la espalda*, in which red bream is spatchcocked on the grill and finished with garlic, hot chilli and a few drops of vinegar.

Dorada, the gilthead bream is the finest Mediterranean bream. Like the related *urta*, the sea bream lives on a diet of shellfish, which scents the flesh. Sea bream is most famously cooked with brandy and tomatoes.

Hake (*merluza*), with its delicate flavour and flaky texture, is extremely popular in Spain. It is often partnered with green sauces of asparagus or parsley. The back of the neck may be roasted, and *kokotas* (triangles cut from the lower throat) are a true speciality,

EVERYDAY FISH

The most popular everyday fish is salt cod (*bacalao*), then *pescadilla* – a small hake which is fried in a ring, with its tail in its mouth – and many small flat fish such as *gallo* (a type of plaice).

Sardines have an honoured place in Spanish cuisine, with festivals in Bilbao and elsewhere dedicated to the fish. They are enjoyed as an outdoor food and the *moraga*, on the Málaga coast, marks the beginning of summer: fish are skewered on to bamboo sticks, like sails on a tall mast, and are cooked beside the fires on the beaches. Mackerel, *caballo* and *melva* (from warm water) are other popular fish.

Left: Sardines are popular all over Spain and the freshly caught fish are often cooked on the beach, on the south and north coasts.

often served in *pil pil* (a hot emulsion of garlic and oil). The *lenguado* (Dover or Channel sole) has a major fishing ground in the Bay of Biscay, while grey mullet (*mújol* or *lisa*) is popular in the Levante. Red mullet (*salmonetes*) are beloved by everyone in Spain.

Tiny *chanquetes* (whitebait) now have to be protected to retain stocks, but little anchovies (*boquerones*) are popular everywhere, though they are mainly fished in the Bay of Biscay. Anchovies are one of the best fish for frying and may be presented Málaga-style, fried in a fan pattern. More often they are marinated for tapas because they deteriorate so fast.

Elvers

Angulas, tiny baby eels, are a speciality of the *cofradías*, the Basque all-male gastronomic societies. Once considered only good enough to be fed to pigs, elvers are now an expensive delicacy, eaten around Christmas.

European eels spawn in the Sargasso Sea, between the West Indies and the Azores. The spawn set off for home and, amazingly, they head for the rivers from which their parents came, for example the Nervión, near Bilbao. The elvers of Aguinaga (west of San Sebastián) are the most highly prized. After a three-year journey back across the Atlantic, the elvers grow to 10cm/2in. They are washed ten times, then dipped in a cold tobacco solution to kill them. Sold cooked, they are then tossed in a hot earthenware bowl with oil and garlic. Once cooked, they look rather like spaghetti with only their eyes indicating that they are fish.

Elvers are also bred in Northern Ireland and France for sale in the Spanish market. These are softer and whiter than their wild cousins.

Above: Swordfish is a delicious, meaty fish that is very pink when raw but turns a greyish colour when cooked.

Above: Shark loin is good marinated with aromatic saffron and grilled.

TUNA, SWORDFISH AND SHARK

Tuna are landed at Vigo, from ships that trawl the world. They are also fished off Zahara de los Atunes (outside Gibraltar) with nets in the *alamadraba* – a bloody ritual that goes back as far as Roman times, where men fight the fish.

Tuna steaks are meaty and nutritious, and may be fried, grilled (broiled) or cooked on the barbecue. *Bonito del norte*, white tuna, is cooked in stews with (bell) peppers and potatoes. In Tarragona it is eaten *all cremat* (pot-roast with caramelized garlic).

Swordfish (*pez espada*) is ideal for grilling. Dogfish (*cazón*) and sharks such as *cailón* (porbeagle/mackerel shark) are good marinated and grilled.

FRESHWATER FISH

Spain has many fast-flowing rivers in its mountainous regions. Trout catches in some Pyrenees rivers run at 1,500 a day. León has about 3,000km/1,800 miles of trout rivers, as well as lakes. Brown trout abound in the rivers of western Asturias; *truchas del Bierzo* are well known. *Rea* (sea trout or salmon trout) run up the Galician *rías* (coastal inlets). Brown trout with *jamón serrano* is a famous combination, but otherwise cooking is simple, with fish being poached in cider or the Basque wine, *txacoli*.

Salmon teem in the rivers of Galicia and swim up into the Picos de Europa, south of Santander. Arriondas is the salmon capital of Spain. The same story is told here, as in Scotland, of labourers refusing to eat salmon more than three times a week. The classic salmon recipe is to salt them for one hour, then fry in pork fat. *Lamprea* (lamprey) follow the salmon, especially in the river Miño, while other fish, such as tench, carp and barbel are very much in evidence in Extremadura in summer.

Below: Brown and rainbow trout flourish in the rivers and lakes of Spain.

PRESERVED FISH

The Spanish adore preserved fish, and it is still weekly fare across the country. *Bacalao* is salt cod, which has been used in dishes for centuries. Other fish are salted too, including sardines and anchovies. Numerous fish and shellfish are canned – sometimes simply in brine, in rich, fruity olive oil, or in a spicy marinade such as *escabeche*. Fish caviars are a speciality.

BACALAO

It is ironic that the most commonly eaten fish in Spain – cod – is one that swims on neither of her shores. The Basques fished cod more than a millennium ago off the Gulf of St Lawrence, in the North Atlantic, and brought it back to Spain in salt. With the discovery of the Americas, the Basques were driven away by other fleets and a new fishing ground was established around Iceland and Norway.

Bacalao was called the inland fish, and was sold as stiff kite-shaped boards. With Catholic Spain imposing a Friday fast and a fast for the 40 days of

Below: Salt cod, known as bacalao, *is immensely popular and has remained weekly fare in Spain for centuries.*

Lent, it became a fixture in the Spanish diet. In these less religious days, where refrigeration is commonplace, *bacalao* has remained popular – probably due to the exquisite balance of salt and fish. In warmer climes, the flavour appears to deepen and salt tastes better in the south than it does in the colder north.

In Madrid, Bilbao and Barcelona, whole shops (*bacalao* boutiques) are devoted to the one product. The fish is sold like meat, ready cut and labelled with the place of origin and the dishes for which the cut is suitable. You can buy loin, strips and cheaper, thinner tail ends. The fatter, whiter Norwegian cuts are preferred for fillet dishes such as the Catalan *a la llauna*. Scottish *bacalao* is yellower and stronger tasting, and should be cooked with rice or potatoes. There are modern cures such as *bacalao inglés* that require less soaking.

There are over 100 classic *bacalao* dishes and many books devoted to *bacalao*. There is even a competition held at Guernika for the best new dish. *Bacalao* dishes are classed as red or white, according to whether they are made with, or without, tomatoes. *Bacalao al ajo arriero* contains tomato and red (bell) peppers. Best of the

white dishes is *bacalao pil-pil*. In this dish, the fish is cooked with garlic in oil in an earthenware dish (which retains heat) and is then swung for 15 or so minutes, until the gelatine in the fish skin combines with the oil to make a light, mayonnaise-like sauce.

Salt cod can be eaten at any time of the day. The fishermen in the north eat it for breakfast as *zurruputuna* (salt cod prepared with garlic, chillies and soaked bread). *Purrusaldo* is a robust soup made with salt cod, leek and potato. *Potaje de cuaresma*, made with salt cod, chickpeas and chard, is thought to have come from the monastery of Yuste and is eaten during Holy Week. The Cuenca area has a brandade-style dish, a purée of fish, potato and pine nuts. One of the best-known tapas dishes is *soldaditos de Pavia*, named after the Hussars in their yellow coats – sticks of salt cod are battered, then deep-fried until crisp and golden.

Raw salt cod salads are also very popular. *Rinrán* is a dish of salt cod with potato, olives and (bell) peppers. The Andalusian version of *remojón* pairs salt cod with sliced orange, and in Catalan *esqueixada* it is accompanied by red (bell) peppers and tomatoes.

Buying and soaking bacalao

The thinner cuts of salt cod are fin and tail pieces and are used to make puréed dishes such as salt cod fritters and soup. The fish doubles in weight during soaking, but half of this will be lost when the skin and bone are removed and discarded. The thickest pieces come from the loin and are used to make dishes such as *pil pil*.

Salt cod requires a minimum of 24 hours soaking, with 2–3 changes of water (more often in summer, because the soaking fish can smell pretty bad). The fish needs to retain some salt to maintain the interest of flavour and texture, but how long to soak the fish is a matter of personal judgement and depends on the dish being prepared.

In Andalusia the custom is to toast the fish first, break it up and then soak it. This has produced a range of dishes called *tiznao* that taste faintly of the fire.

CURED AND PRESERVED FISH

Mahogany-coloured *mojama* is the salted, wind-dried back flesh of the bluefin tuna (*atún*) and is a speciality of Seville and Cadiz. *Mojama* used to be street food, but it is becoming less common. It is similar to dried beef and, at its best, the thin ruby-coloured slices are almost transparent.

Canned tuna is Spain's second fish and is eaten weekly by most Spanish families. White albacore *atún blanco* (or *bonito del norte*), the long-finned tuna, is the world's best canned fish – and widely believed to be better canned than fresh. The most common of the tunas, *atún claro*, the yellow fin, is caught off the Cantabrian coast. It has darker and less dense meat – *ventresca* (belly) being the best.

Larger sardines are salted, both in the north and in Huelva in the south, where they are packed in large barrels. Sardine canning is also a major industry throughout Galicia.

Anchovies are also salted, and are called *anchoas* when canned in oil. In the north, some anchovies are brine-pickled before being packed in

Below: Fine Spanish anchoas are canned in olive oil.

Above: White albacore is the finest type of canned tuna.

Left: Canned sardines are widely eaten in Spain and are offered in many ways.

oil, and may also be smoked. Catalan La Escala, in the bay of Las Rosas, has a D.O. rating and here anchovies are salt-cured for a year – a process known as tanning – before being packed in oil in glass jars.

Some 140 varieties of fish and shellfish are canned in Galicia. The range of canned shellfish is enormous – from plump clams to scallops and mussels in spicy sauces such as *escabeche*. Tiny squid are canned in their ink, octopus in a variety of sauces, and there are also less familiar delights such as "crab thumbs" (the thickest part of the claw).

FISH CAVIARS

Luxurious caviars are a speciality of the Mediterranean. *Huevas de marucca*, from ling, are among the most common; the tiny salty eggs are sold in blocks cut from the pressed roe. The best caviar comes from the Murcian salt lagoons, from the grey mullet and is called *huevas de mújol de Mar Menor*. Before sturgeon caviar reached

Europe, this was used to make the great *botargo* (dark shavings cut from the pressed salted roe). Mixed and single moist roes packed into small jars are also sold and exported. These fish roes are particularly good served with eggs. Golden-brown *huevas de atún* come from the bluefin tuna, and have a sharp, faintly metallic taste. Other roes include the poorest cod (*capelán*), black herring roe and huge red salmon eggs, while restaurants offer caviars from sea bream, hake and anchovy.

Above: Black herring roe (back left) and grey mullet mújol, *or* shikrán, *(front left and right) are both good moist caviars.*

Below: Pressed huevas de marucca *(salted ling roe) is a delicacy but is widely available throughout the country.*

SHELLFISH

Atlantic currents, sweeping on to Cape Finisterre, bring food to an incredible range of shellfish on Europe's most westerly corner, to the Galician *rías* (coastal inlets) and the Spanish north coast. In these waters shellfish grow at great speed. In the Mediterranean the continental shelf is perfect for shellfish. The Spanish are really spoilt for choice.

Spanish shellfish are cooked to demonstrate their superb quality, usually either simply boiled or cooked *a la parrilla* (on the barbecue). Sea salt, and perhaps lemon wedges, are the common accompaniments.

SCALLOPS AND MUSSELS

Santiago de Compostela in Galicia is famous for scallops, and the pilgrims have chosen their shell for their badge. Today scallops are farmed in the quiet bays to the west. Large ones, *vieras*, and little *zamburiñas* (queens or bay scallops) are cooked with their orange roe curled round them. Scallops may be breadcrumbed and fried, cooked with wine and chilli, or with tomato sauce (in St James' style). They feature in the flat Galician pie that is prepared for special occasions.

The mussel beds of Galicia are famous, and Tarragona in the east is also an important mussel area. The bivalves are grown on ropes secured

to platforms, out in the western bays. In Galicia, 2.5 million mussels are canned per day, and there are plenty of fresh ones for the whole of Spain, too. It is their sheer size and tenderness that astounds. They are large enough to be breadcrumbed and fried, although wine and parsley mixtures, sometimes with bacon, are more usual. They are also added to many fish dishes and stews. A favourite tapas dish in Madrid is *tigres* – mussels in béchamel sauce with a little chopped (bell) pepper, breadcrumbed then grilled.

CLAMS AND COCKLES

In Spain clams are common fare. They are boiled for tapas, added to soups and pasta, and used to garnish grander dishes. They are fished on both coasts, but the northern ones are plumper, and a regional speciality. There are many varieties; one of the best is the *almeja fina* (the carpetshell). Most magnificent is the *concha fina* (Venus), which measures about 8cm/3in across, with orange flesh inside. It is opened to order in the sherry bars of the south.

Other bivalves include common cockles, the dog cockle, *almendra de mar*, razor shells and *ostíon*, the Portuguese oyster, found on the Cantabrian coast.

Left: Carpetshell clams are very popular and are most often served in sauces.

PRAWNS AND SHRIMPS

Saltwater varieties are fished on both coasts. In size order:

Camarones These are the tiniest Spanish shrimps and are caught around Cadiz. They turn white, rather than pink, when cooked, and are made into delicious little fritters.

Quisquilla This term covers all the smaller varieties of prawn (shrimp) that are caught in their thousands off the Spanish coasts. They are added to scrambled eggs and stuffings, or used to add interest to *ensaladilla* (diced vegetable salad) and various sauces.

Gamba These have a good colour and are fished reasonably deep, giving them a good flavour. They are used in some of Spain's most famous dishes. *Gambas en gabardinas* (in overcoats) are battered then fried, while the southern dish *gambas pil pil* (which is quite different from northern *pil pil*) is based on chilli, and is very hot.

Langostino These are the longest Mediterranean prawn, fished from deep water. Sometimes they are called tiger prawns, as some varieties are striped. They are served simply to show off their true flavour – for example in salads.

Below: Cigalas (scampi) have a fabulous flavour and are fished on every coast.

Percebes

One of the world's most expensive shellfish, *percebes* are known in English as goose barnacles. You understand why if you see them crowded on the storm-washed rocks. Fixed at the foot, reaching perhaps 5cm/2in high, blackish or mottled, they look like a gaggle of geese with outstretched necks, particularly so because the tips are pointed and white, like a beak.

Percebes are either left raw or briefly boiled. Their orange flesh is squeezed from its casing and served with vinaigrette. Their taste is "essence of seawater".

Carabinero These prawns grow to 20cm/8in long and are a deep scarlet colour with a violet head. (They are named after the red coats worn by the military.) They lack the flavour of *langostinos* but are excellent in northern matured bean dishes, where the prawn heads add flavour, and in display salads, because the bodies retain their delightful red markings after shelling.

LOBSTERS

Bogavante, the true lobster, is party fare, while *langosta* (in Castilian), the spiny lobster (saltwater crayfish) is eaten to celebrate Spain's national day. Squat (or slipper) lobsters, called *cigarra* in Spain, make cricket-like noises under water. They have insignificant claws, but stocky little tails. St James even has his own lobster, the *santiaguiño*, with a cross on its head.

Scampi (*cigala* or *escarmarlan grande* in Catalan) are "false lobsters". They are a luxury, and four or five make a good portion. Their splendid heads have beady eyes, their long straight claws are pink and scarlet even when raw. They go very well with mayonnaise.

Right: Gambas are probably the best of all prawns and have a wonderful flavour and lovely texture.

Freshwater crustaceans

Crayfish (*cangrejos*) are found in the Duero and Tago rivers. There are festivals to celebrate them in Herrera del Pisuergo and at Palencia where the locals eat them in great numbers.

Tiny crayfish also flourish in freshwater reservoirs all over Spain. These crustaceans are sold as *embalsadores* (behind the dam) and are used to make a range of good sauces and soups.

Right: The spider crab is known as centollo *or* txangurro *in Spain.*

CRABS

Small shore crabs, such as *necoras*, which have red knees, are served simply boiled, and picked to pieces at the table. They make ideal beach food. *Buey de mar* (ox of the sea) is the large-clawed crab, but the favourite, particularly on the north coast, is the spider crab (*centollo* in Castilian), great beasts on akimbo legs, with stronger and sweeter meat. The classic Basque dish is *txangurro* (dressed meat in the shell); there is one crab per person.

SQUID, CUTTLEFISH AND OCTOPUS

Common to both oceans, squid are universal and a popular food. Few travellers have visited a Spanish beach and not eaten *calamares* (fried squid rings in batter). There are many varieties of squid, and they can vary considerably in size. Their pink skin turns grey after a time on shore, so choose fresh pink ones when buying. They are also commonly sold cut into rings for stews and should be cooked fast or very slowly, otherwise they will become rubbery. On the north coast, where they are known as *raba*, breaded squid are popular.

Cuttlefish, called *jibia* or *sepia*, and *chocos* and *chiperones* if tiny, are very similar to squid but rounder in shape. They are often sold without the skin when their colour is milky white. When cleaning, be very careful to remove the ink sacs intact because the ink stains. Slit the body open to remove the broad white cuttle bone.

The flesh of the cuttlefish is thick and sweeter than squid. It is ideal for slow simmering or cooking stuffed. The black ink is also used in cooking and classic dishes include *sepia en su tinto* (cuttlefish in their ink) and *arroz negro* (black rice). Ink also features in many signature dishes in top restaurants from Arzak to El Bullí.

Octopus are particularly popular in the north. All the bars in Santiago de Compostela have one sitting like a great wig on a hat-stand. They are mainly cooked with paprika, as in *pulpo de feria*, or they are stewed. Octopus are tough, so traditionally wine corks are added to stews, which are thought to help tenderize the flesh.

Below: Squid are popularly fried in rings, grilled or stuffed and braised.

BEEF, VEAL, LAMB AND KID

The varieties of meat (*carne*) available in Spain are far wider than elsewhere. The middle classes eat a great deal of meat, while the working classes eat comparatively little; there is virtually no vegetarian cooking. Pulse and vegetable dishes are invariably flavoured with sausages and pork fat.

BEEF AND VEAL

The Spanish have never been great beef eaters. Richard Ford, a century ago, remarked that "bulls are bred for baiting and oxen for the plough, not the spit".

High temperatures elsewhere mean the best beef comes from the north, and Galicia produces about two-thirds of Spanish beef. However, new breeding programmes, and the modern practice of moving cattle indoors, means more beef is now being produced in Catalonia, Aragón and the cereal plains of Castile. Only the Basques will eat "bloody" meat, and red meat is exported in return for veal cattle. The native breed is mahogany-red *retinto. Morucho* and *avilana* are work animals.

Spain has at least three sorts of beef. Hung beef is a northern taste, and vast *chuletones* (chops) are enjoyed in this region. Cattle are slaughtered at between two and five years old to produce *carne de buey* (ox) or *vaca* (cow). This lesser quality beef is stewed, famously with chocolate, or with vegetables as in the Catalan *estofat*. Meatballs are sold in every bar and are loved by children, too. Cuts such as salt brisket go into stews.

Younger beef is the popular choice; *añojo* means yearling although, in fact, the cattle are slaughtered at between 10 and 18 months. Joints of meat are frequently labelled with their age and diet. For example, *lomo cebón* is loin fattened on barley.

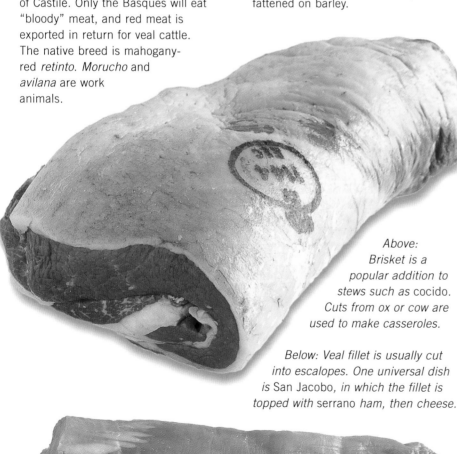

Above: Ox tail, or bull's tail, benefits from long, slow cooking and is a very popular choice when stewed.

Ternera translates as veal, but it is pink or grey veal, not white. Veal calves are never intensively reared in Spain, and they are often four times the age of Dutch or Italian calves when they are slaughtered. Only in Ávila are calves killed very young. One veal of note is the northern *ternera gallega*, D.O., which comes from the honey-blond *rubio* cattle.

Veal escalopes may be braised with vegetables or fried. *Filetitos* are small escalopes fried with lemon juice, and six or seven make up a single portion. Veal is wonderful with artichokes and sherry, and can be made into excellent stews with young vegetables.

Above: Brisket is a popular addition to stews such as cocido. *Cuts from ox or cow are used to make casseroles.*

Below: Veal fillet is usually cut into escalopes. One universal dish is San Jacobo, *in which the fillet is topped with* serrano *ham, then cheese.*

The Moorish oven
Domed ovens built of *adobe* (roofing bricks), which hold the heat, rather than firebricks, are prized for roasting tiny lambs and piglets particularly in Castile, in places such as Aranda de Duero and Haro. These ovens are part of the restaurant structure, and are about 2m/6ft in diameter inside. They are wood-fired, and cooking only takes place when the glowing charcoal subsides. The burned-out coals are pushed to the side, the dishes are put into the oven using long paddles, then the door is sealed. In the hot south, similar ovens are built outside houses for domestic use.

THE FIGHTING BULL

The fighting bull is either slaughtered at the age of one, and the meat is minced (ground), or it lives a life of luxury until it comes to the ring at the age of three or four. The meat from these bulls (*toro de lidia*) is sold in specialist shops. Ex-matadors frequently buy restaurants, and a number of these source beef from the local bullring. The meat is deep black-red (though not tough) and is eaten as steaks in sherry in Jerez, or minced or stewed. The *rabo* (tail) is a popular choice for hotpots, while the testicles – the matadors' titbit – may be breadcrumbed and fried. Valencia produces a special bull ham.

LAMB AND KID

Lamb is very expensive, but it is still the traditional meat in the grazing regions of central and western Spain, and up into the mountains of Aragón and Murcia. Elsewhere, it is an Easter or wedding treat. Spain has 24 million sheep – the same number as when Napoleon marched there during the Peninsular War (1808–14) – which dominate the Meseta, the high heart of Spain. They spend the winter in Extremadura and southern Castile, and once walked north in vast flocks (the *transhumance*) to summer pastures in Cantabria. However, today sheep are transported by train, with Burgos as the commercial sheep centre.

Thyme is used to flavour roast lamb. Lamb chops are popular, and tiny legs of lamb provide an exquisite eating experience. Stews can consist of a whole animal, chopped. *Cochifrito* is flavoured with lemon or vinegar and paprika; *chilindrones*, around Logroño traditionally feature a mild red chilli pepper. *Menestra* are spring stews cooked with young vegetables.

Mutton is used in a few dishes in Aragón and Extremadura, and some of the classic stews such as *chilindrón* and *caldereta* originally used mutton.

Kid (*cabrito* or *choto*) is another luxury meat, either cooked on a spit or in traditional stews such as *tumbet* in Valencia or *caldereta extremeña*, which is thickened with the kid's puréed liver.

Spanish stews

Olla puchero Both these words mean cooking pot, the large vessel used to make the daily stew cooked by many families in Spain.

Olla podrida Literally meaning rotten pot, the name of this stew actually means hotchpotch – a mixed stew of beef, bacon, ham and vegetables, simmered so long the ingredients become very soft-textured.

Cocido Meaning boiled or simmered, *cocido* is shorthand for mixed stew.

Cocido madrileño This is the national dish, where several different meats are cooked with chickpeas and fresh vegetables. It makes a three-course feast. Made all over the country, the meat content is reduced the further from the capital you get; every region includes its own sausages and other produce. The Basques like to add red beans, and in Seville both rice and chickpeas are included, with garlic, sweet potatoes and *morcilla* sausage. In the south pears and pumpkins are often used, and in the Canaries, sweet potatoes and fresh corn are added.

Escudella This is the Catalan word for *cocido* or stew. *Escudella i carn d'olla* is a big dish, with the *carn* (pork) as one large dumpling, or it may contain a selection of ham, chicken, veal and *botifarra* sausage, with chickpeas and noodles, plus vegetables. The liquid is served first as soup, the rest follows. *Escudella de pagès* is a country-style stew, with carrots, potatoes and cabbage.

Fabada This is the Asturian stew of dried beans, salt pork and ham, with oak-smoked *morcilla* and *chorizo*.

Caldereta Meaning witch's cauldron, this is the name of the lamb, goat or fish stew that is cooked in it.

Estofado *Estofat* in Catalan, this is meat that is slow-cooked, usually in its fat and juice.

Guiso Also known as *guisado*, this is simply a stew with sauce.

Cochifrito Pieces of lamb or goat are fried, and seasoned with vinegar or lemon and paprika.

Fricandó Small veal pieces are stewed with vegetables such as carrots. The Catalan version contains onions and tomatoes.

Above: In Spain, legs of lamb may be very small – with one leg per person.

Above: Kid is a luxury meat that often replaces lamb in traditional stews.

PORK

The pig represents Spain's history and religion on the plate. To eat pork and sausages became, after the unification of the country at the end of the fifteenth century, a way of demonstrating nationality. (The Muslim Moors and the Jews were forbidden to eat pork.) In a poor, mountainous country, the pig provided the major source of nutrition, and it is still Spain's most widely eaten meat.

Almost every family would once have owned a pig. People in the villages would throw their rubbish into local gullies and streams, and this waste sustained foraging pigs. People who live in apartments in Madrid will still tell you about the family porker in Galicia. The *matanza* (pig killing), when families gather to make sausages and celebrate, is the greatest non-religious festival of the year.

Although cured meat is eaten more often than fresh, pork chops and loin of pork remain Spain's most familiar meat. *Solomillo*, which means fillet of beef in the north, becomes pork in the south; it is delicious *a la trianera* (roasted with sherry). *Magro* is a pork steak, commonly served with a tomato sauce or potatoes. *El frite*, or *cochefrito*, is chopped fried meat flavoured with

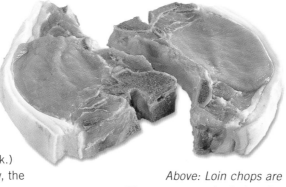

Above: Loin chops are popular in beach bars.

Above: Chump chops are great cooked on la plancha, *the iron grill sheet.*

vinegar and paprika; it is traditionally prepared to test the meat of a newly killed pig. Minced (ground) pork is used in dishes such as *pringa* and *prueba*, which were both devised as a way to test the spicing mix, before stuffing the meat into sausage casings. *Gazpacho manchego* is a delicious coarse pork pâté, and is quite different from the well-known southern gazpacho.

Other cuts of pork are cured, as well as the ubiquitous ham. In the north, the famous cured meat is *lacón*, a front-leg ham. Among the *salazones* (salted meats), there is coarse-salted belly, and also *panceta* (streaky bacon), which is sometimes marinated before being cured and/or smoked. *Torreznos* are pork slices, fried like bacon and served with eggs, a popular dish in the centre of the country and Extremadura.

However, their social status is indicated by their name in Cervantes novel, *Don Quixote, duelos y quebrantes*, which means sorrow and suffering.

Below: In Spain, pork loin is trimmed to the meat eye only.

THE BLACK WILD PIG

The native *ibérico* pig is known by its black trotter (*pata negra*). (The phrase *pata negra* is also a slang term used to describe anything good.) There are actually four dark-skinned breeds, the main two having black or red hair. The pigs are trim and graceful, with long legs. They run wild in small groups, in the *sierras* of Andalusia and particularly in Extremadura, in the flower pastures under the holm oaks, called the *dehesa*.

Their numbers are decreasing as their fame rises. Their final food is acorns, which give the meat its full flavour and an old golden tinge. If meat is labelled *bellota*, it means the pig fed entirely on acorns and will therefore have excellent flavour.

Wild pigs are slaughtered at 18 months, weighing about 160kg/352lb – the domestic hog reaches that weight at nine months. Highly prized for ham, they now make up only five per cent of Spanish *serrano* (compared with 25 per cent in the 1950s) 90 per cent of which is taken up by restaurants. Another restaurant speciality is fresh steaks of *cerdo ibérico*; it is dark like beef and tastes like game.

Below: Spanish panceta *is fresh or cured belly. If it is unavailable, Italian pancetta makes an excellent substitute.*

Cooking with pork fat

Pork fat (*manteca*) adds a very characteristic flavour to many Spanish dishes. *Manteca colorada* is fat coloured with paprika. It is delicious spread on bread for breakfast in the south. The fat is also made into *rillettes* (fat packed around cooked, shredded pork).

Tocino is solid fat, fresh or salted, back or belly, for cubing and frying. Like *panceta* (fresh or cured pork belly), it adds flavour and goodness to pulse dishes. Dry or poor-quality *serrano* ham is chopped and used for cooking.

SUCKLING PIG

Truly a wonder, so small and so tender, the suckling pig is known as *cochinillo* in Castilian, *tostón* in central Spain and *porcella* in the Balearics.

Old Castile is famous for its ovens, which are used to roast either milk-fed piglets or lamb. The west, Arévolo and Segovia, is piglet country. There they are roasted in a huge domed brick or refractory oven, heated by holm oak – just imagine thirty piglets sizzling on a revolving turntable.

With the pig being killed at 15 to 20 days old, the shoulder blade is only the size of a car key. To roast the pigs, they are split through the belly and opened out flat with their legs and tail out. Each splayed pig is displayed in an earthenware dish, which catches the fat and juices as the pig roasts. The roasted meat is carved using the side of a plate.

Above right: Calf's liver is good cooked with sweet Málaga wine sauce.

Right: Strongly flavoured pig's liver is stewed on the first day of pig killing with sweet, pungent sauces.

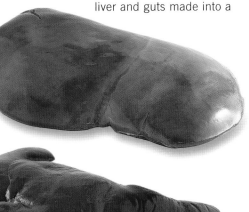

OFFAL

It is said that everything from the pig can be eaten except its squeak. The pig is the principal source of offal (variety meats) in Spain, although other animals are also used.

Pigs' heads and tails can be salted. Pickled ears are breaded and fried, as well as being used to make some wonderful delicatessen salads. Trotters and tails may be found in stews and rice dishes. Ham bones are used to flavour beans; as they grow older they become highly prized, with neighbours lending each other bones for stews. Pig's caul is used to baste faggots, and ham fat (*unto*) sold in great rolls, is used for frying – aged fat is prized in Galicia for its extra flavour.

Lamb and veal kidneys are to be found cooked in wine sauces in tapas bars. Sweetbreads (*mollejas*) are usually fried. Brains are used in two good gypsy dishes: they are minced (ground) to stuff *tortilla Sacromonte*; and are served fried, with lemon, as *sesos a la flamenca*. *Criadillas* (testicles) are called white kidneys; a delicacy for matadors, they are breadcrumbed and fried. Another "man's dish" is blood, solidified in squares with vinegar, which is offered in tapas bars.

The first dish to be eaten at the *matanza* (pig killing) is *asadura*, the liver and guts made into a

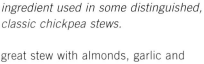

Above: Tripe (callos) is the essential ingredient used in some distinguished, classic chickpea stews.

great stew with almonds, garlic and oregano. The similar *chanfaina*, with lungs (lights) and liver, is cooked, often in vast vats for festivals. A more elegant calf's liver dish from the south contains sweet Málaga wine and aromatic herbs.

Tripe, called *menudo* in Andalusia, is one of the surprises of Spanish cuisine. Resembling a woollen blanket when raw, it has a repertoire of dishes. *Callos a la madrilena* (from veal or pig) is tavern fare in the capital city. It is seasoned with onion, thyme and tomato, and includes *morcilla*, chorizo and ham too. Depending on the region, tripe is usually cooked with chickpeas or beans, along with a ham bone for extra flavour. One Catalan dish combines tripe with potatoes, pine nuts and a glass of old *rancio* wine.

Pork tongues (*lengua*) are commoner than lambs' tongues. The former are cooked in a Majorcan dish, with pomegranate seeds. But larger veal tongues are also served cold, and as a *fiambre* (pressed delicatessen meat).

White *manitas*, lambs' feet, come 16 to a portion and leave pearl-like bones on the plate. *Zarajos* are the lamb's intestines; they are wrapped around two twigs, then grilled (broiled). Lambs' tails are eaten in Aragón, where they are called mountain asparagus, with (bell) peppers and tomatoes. In the markets you will find beef muzzles, too, and cow's heel with the horn off.

SAUSAGES

The pig is virtually a "larder on trotters" and is valued more for what can be made out of it than for fresh meat. It is turned into sausages, frequently home-made, which will last the whole year. The raw pork is minced (ground), or hand-chopped, mixed with back fat and spices, then stuffed into casings. The bigger the pieces of meat, and the lower the fat content, the sweeter the meat is.

Some sausages (chiefly *morcillas*) include extra ingredients such as onion or rice, and additions such as nuts are included in regions where there was once a strong Moorish presence. Garlic is used in the south and west, but too much would turn the sausage rancid. There are also sausages made using pork blends – with beef, vegetables other than onion, and even the occasional cereal sausage such as the *farinata* of Salamanca. There are game sausages too, made from venison.

The mixture is stuffed into casings made from pigs' guts. These natural casings vary in size so some sausages are fatter than others. The sausages are then hung on strings in the cold dry air and will lose as much as 35 per cent of their weight if left for a full year. Smoked sausages are found across Spain, usually coinciding with the old pilgrim routes, as in Bierzo in León. The dry sausages used in the Asturian *fabada* (pork and bean stew) are smoked and swell with cooking.

Sausages tend to be classed by colour, and this provides some guidance as to how they should be cooked and served. Many dried sausages may be eaten raw, although this is not always the rule.

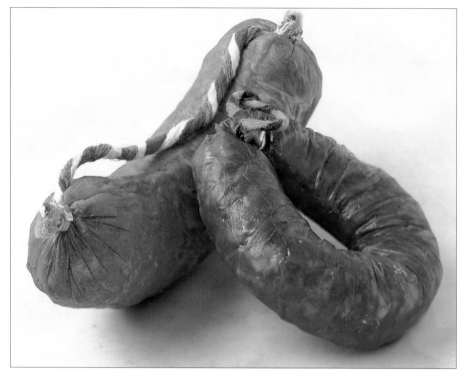

BLACK SAUSAGES

Morcillas are blood puddings, and are the first to be made from the newly killed pig, straight after slaughter. They are made as links, or as rings in Seville and Ronda in the south. Once made, they are boiled in cauldrons, then dried for storage. Occasionally they may also be smoked, and they are almost always cooked again before being eaten.

These wonderful sausages are a speciality of the north, the most famous being those of Extremadura and Asturias, which are flavoured with aniseed and cloves, and plumped with either rice or onions. Rice is typically used in some parts of Aragón, and the Burgos *morcilla* also contains pine nuts. *Morcilla dulce* is eaten raw, and can be found in tapas bars. The spicing, sweetness and rich tongue-clinging fat make it irresistible.

Botifarra is the black sausage from the east of the country. It is made in links, or occasionally in rings. The *bisbe* (meaning

Left: Ring-shaped black and white botifarras *are made in Catalonia.*

Above: The fat chorizo from Cantimpalo, and the ring-shaped one from Jabugo are two famous versions of this classic spicy paprika sausage.

bishop) is an outsize sausage, while the *bull* contains tongue and cheek. There are Valencian *morcillas* too, which are sometimes very spicy, and a Majorcan version, *camiot*, which is flavoured with cumin and cinnamon.

RED SAUSAGES

Paprika is used in sausages right across Spain, apart from in Catalonia, the Levante and the Balearics (except for the *sobrasada* from Majorca). Chorizos are named after the *choricero* chilli that gives them both spiciness and colour. There are at least 50 varieties of chorizo, but two main types.

Red chorizos, made in links, contain minced (ground) meat, which is mottled with fat. They may be fried or boiled. The longer varieties are usually sweeter, while small round ones are *picante* (hot and spicy). The knobbly, garlicky *chorizos de Cantimpalos*, from Segovia, are typical of central Spain and are the first choice for the Madrid *cocido* (the national stew of salt and fresh meats).

Above:
Lomo *is*
not actually
a sausage,
but cured pork
loin flavoured with herbs and spices.

The second type is the tapas or cured chorizo. The meat filling is stuffed into a larger gut casing and so is much longer and fatter. These are sliced thinly and eaten with bread, or they are cut into little batons and added to salads. The meat in these sausages may be marbled or chopped.

There are many varieties of cured chorizo, and each one attracts an enthusiastic and loyal following. *Pamplona* resembles salami, with its thoroughly minced (ground) meat, and the coloured fat that looks like orange rice grains. *Chorizo de Rioja* has big swirls of paprika-red marbled meat around the fat. *Chistorra* is typically Basque and Navarran. This narrow, cigar-shaped sausage includes beef as well as pork. *Morcón* is widely distributed in Andalusia. It is made from marinated loin and shoulder, and seasoned with paprika. It is tied with string to make a round sausage that resembles a hand grenade. There is also a larger Murcian version. However, it is *sobrasada de Mallorca* that probably wears the crown and is the pride of the Balearic islands. The sausage is more or less spherical in shape, although it is sometimes long, and is air-cured for up to a year. It is spreadable and has a smooth pâté-like texture that is achieved by grinding and regrinding the pork several times. The sausage meat is also sold in pots.

Lomo embuchado (or *cinta*) looks like a sausage but is actually the spinal loin muscle (*caña*). It is marinated in garlic and paprika, sometimes with sugar, oregano and nutmeg, then encased and dried for two to six months. A good variety is produced in Teruel. It has a delicate flavour and compact texture, but is expensive so is quite a treat.

Sausages that are named after a place famed for ham also attract a following. *Jabugocitos* are little frying sausages from Jabugo, *guijuelo* is a fat tapas sausage from Extremadura, and *ibéricos* are made from the meat of the prized black pig.

Below: Long, fat cured salchichones *are sliced and served for tapas.*

WHITE SAUSAGES

Sausages that are neither black nor red are classified as white sausage, although they are not necessarily white in appearance. The cured varieties are a dark cerise colour inside and are cased in the smaller gut.

Salchichón comes in rings and strings, and is usually powdered on the outside with ambient bacteria. The meat and fat are easily distinguishable. Some famous examples are made in Vic in Catalonia. These sausages are dry, like salami, and laced with peppercorns. *Fuet* is a Catalonian sausage containing white pepper and sugar. It is long and thin so dries fast, and is consequently very chewy.

Longaniza covers a variety of sausages. A few are dry, while others are fresh and coiled in a bowl, and still more hang in a wonderful hank. Short lengths are used for cooking. If the sausages are thin, they tend to be hard, bland and can be rather fatty.

White *botifarras* (known as *blancas*) are the brothers of the black ones. These fresh sausages are usually grilled (broiled), and are often eaten with beans all along the east coast. And of course there are *embutidos* (fresh sausages) that are made everywhere.

Above: Fuet *is a chewy, dry Catalonian sausage.*

HAMS

Spain produces some of Europe's finest hams, one-third of which are exported. About one-fifth of Spanish pigs are used for hams, so it is not surprising more ham is eaten in Spain than elsewhere in Europe – the Basques alone eat nearly one whole ham each per year.

The mountain-cured *jamón serrano* rules supreme, but lesser hams – *jamón cocido* – are cured for boiling. The front leg of the pig (*paleta*, or *lacón* in Galicia) is also cured. It is a coarser cut but with a very even flavour). In the north-west it is used for *caldo gallego*, while *lacón con grelos* (with turnip tops) is definitely their national dish.

JAMON SERRANO

Serrano is the adjective from *sierra* (mountain). It means mountain ham, and indicates that it is raw and dried in cold air. Typically, these hams are long and thin, and almost triangular at the meaty end. Better ones are marketed with the trotter (foot) still attached.

Big names in ham production in Andalusia are Jabugo in the Aracena (near Huelva) and Trévelez, in the high mountains south of Granada. *Jabugo* is probably the Spanish choice for the best ham, but *Trévelez* is better known abroad. Being so far south, these hams need heavier salting, and so are less sweet and melt-in-the-mouth than hams from cooler climes such as those from Extremadura and Lérida.

Teruel in Aragón and *Guijuelo* in Salamanca have D.O. status for local hams. The former is famous for its white hams; the latter for lighter salting and sweet-flavoured hams. The whole

Below: Serrano *ham from the black* ibérico *pig is highly prized.*

of Extramadura is pig country and *Montanchez* in Cáceres and *Cumbre Mayores* are both popular hams.

As well as the big names, who don't need to advertise, as they sell all the ham that they can produce, there are also many small producers. Many hams are sold packed off the bone, or sliced. Other parts of the pig (including the loin and front shoulder) are also cured.

Thinly sliced *serrano* is eaten for tapas or sandwiched with cheese, but it is also used to wrap fish. Little batons are added to salads and bean dishes.

Breeds and grades

White hams come from crosses of Landrace, Duroc and the Large White pigs. Just 5 per cent of hams now come from the incomparable black native pig called *ibérico*. This ham is sold under this name *ibérico* abroad but, in Spain, it is known as *pata negra*. *Ibérico* meat is leaner and tougher than other pigs', while the surface fat attracts a little blue penicillin mould, which adds flavour.

These expensive "black" hams are graded by the animals' food. *Bellota* (acorn) indicates a pig fed in the wild, and this is terribly expensive. *Recebo* refers to a pig fed on a diet of grain and acorns for its last month. *Pienso* means the pig was entirely grain fed.

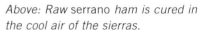

Above: Raw serrano *ham is cured in the cool air of the sierras.*

Curing

It takes 12 months to cure a *serrano* ham. All hams take at least 9 months to cure, and *pata negra* is cured for 18 months. The ham is salted once, for 40 to 60 days, then matured hanging in the dry winter air. When summer temperatures return, it is cellar-rested.

Fat

The fat is distributed between the muscles in fine layers, increasing the flavour of the meat. When black pigs forage on grass and acorns, this fat has a very high oleic oil content, and so liquifies at a lower temperature than other meat fats. It also has a lower cholesterol content than farmed or other free-range (farm-fresh) meat.

Carving

Serrano hams need their own stands to support them, as they are very long. They are carved into paper-thin slices, lengthways with the grain of the meat. The meat is faintly chewy, varying in colour from deep red to scarlet. The fat appears as tiny lengthways threads in the meat. The best cuts come from close to the bone on the *manza* (the rounder side).

Other salazones
Parts of lamb, kid and beef can also be salted, and smoked for more flavour. *Cecina* (*ceniza* in Catalan) is cured beef that is thinly sliced. There are also bull hams and duck breast hams.

THE BARNYARD

Poultry cluck around the many farms of Spain. However, the chickens are mainly kept for their eggs; the birds are not the main family meat.

CHICKEN

More popular now than it used to be, there was a time when chicken was more expensive than beef. The well-known Catalan dish, chicken with lobster, recalls its luxury status.

There are numerous Spanish chicken dishes, reflecting regional tastes and using local produce. Chicken is cooked with sherry in the south; with (bell) peppers in Rioja; *alli-pebre* (with garlic and paprika) in Valencia, and with tomatoes and cumin in Extremadura.

Below: The boiling hen is tastier than a young chicken and has its own repertoire of dishes in Spain.

Below: Huge capons are a favourite at Christmas time.

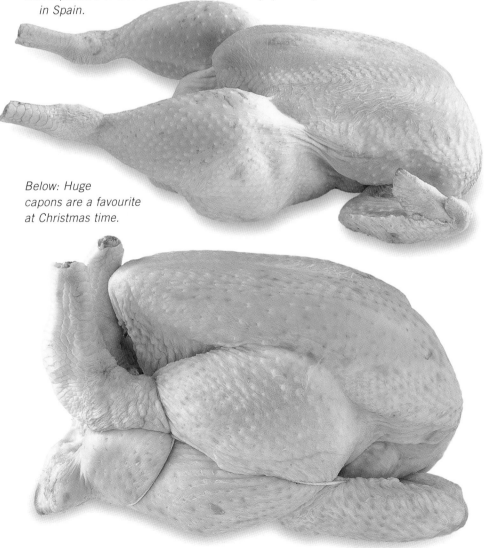

The smell of chickens roasting, basted with pork fat, in chicken shops at the weekend is quite mouthwatering.

Gallina is a boiling hen. In *gallina en pepitoria*, it is simmered slowly, then the sauce is thickened with ground nuts. Capons are sold in the Christmas market in Villalba in Galicia. These large birds weigh about 5kg/11lb. Some are fattened on maize (like foie gras ducks) and they are sold in Madrid dressed and stuffed with Roquefort or chestnuts.

Chicken offal (variety meats) is widely used. The gizzards are added to lentil dishes, and accompany the chicken meats in *arroces* (rice dishes). Chicken livers cooked in sherry is a popular tapas dish.

Above: Guinea fowl are regarded as a substitute for true game birds.

OTHER POULTRY

Goose and duck are cooked in Catalonia, but are not popular in the rest of Spain. Goose with pears (*oca amb peras*) is the famous dish of the region. The Catalans are known for combining birds and fruit, and the reason is not hard to discover – the birds feed on fruit. Duck is combined with figs in another Catalan classic.

Ducks (*pato*) are also reared in Valencia near lake Albufera but they are not widespread elsewhere. Catalonia and Navarra now breed the mallard (a cross between the white duck and the grey barbary), called *anèc* in Catalan. Because of the French influence in these regions, duck hams, foie gras and even duck confit are produced. In Galicia, a popular dish combines duck with turnips. However, Spain's most famous duck recipe comes from Seville. The juice of the Seville orange was added to duck to cut through the fat. Olives do the same job, and there are several dishes that combine duck and olives.

The turkey was introduced to Europe via Spain in the 16th century from America. Called *pavo*, after the peacock (*pavo real*), it was at first cooked like a peacock, stuffed and inserted into a pig's caul. The dark bronze or black turkey are the birds of choice, weighing in at around 3kg/6½–7lb. The best birds come from Aspe, in the Pyrenees.

The guinea fowl (*pintada*) came from Queen Dido's Africa – either directly, or with the Romans. They are now reared in Spain, as are quails (*codornices*).

GAME

Spain is great for wildlife, and out in the country the sign *coto de caza* (shooting reserved) is a constant reminder that hunting is a passion in Spain. *Caza mayor* (game hunting) has always been part of the social/political scene. *Caza menor* (shooting birds) can be pursued by anyone with a gun and a knapsack.

FEATHERED GAME

There are massive migrations of birds across Spain twice a year, on their way to and from Africa. The 27,000 Spanish shooting clubs try to ensure that two-thirds of the birds pass through their land, for breeding. Small birds have always contributed to the poor family's diet: fieldfare, starling, even sparrow, can be added to rice dishes.

Duck

In Spain, duck shooting (*aquatica*) is a specialized sport, with many adherents. There are mallards on all the lakes and salt flats in Spain, and many teal.

Below: The abundant pigeon is meaty and benefits from long, slow cooking.

Above: Tiny quail are one of the most prevalent wild birds found in Spain.

Pigeon

Present all year, pigeons (*palomas*) are netted as they fly over the mountains. They are pot-roasted with vinegar, or with raisins in the Val d'Arran, and stewed with peas or mushrooms in Castile. Murcia has a famous pigeon pie, which mimics the highly spiced Moroccan *b'stilla* (a pie made with filo pastry and a filling of shredded pigeon, ground almonds and spices), revealing its distinct Moorish influences. The pie is then baked until golden and sprinkled with icing (confectioners') sugar and ground cinnamon.

Partridge

The partridge in Spain is the red-legged (French) *perdiz* (which is larger than the grey-legged variety). It is far and away the most popular of game birds. It gorges on the sherry grapes in the south, and from October a million of the birds are eaten each year. La Mancha is the partridge capital of Europe. Once captured, the birds may be

Left: Teal is one of the smallest wild ducks and is highly prized for its fabulous taste and texture.

kept in cages until needed. Celebrated recipes include partridges in chocolate, Pyrenean mushroom stews, and *perdices en escabeche* (a salad of jellied, vinegared birds). They are also stewed with cabbage, in a dish that dates back to the 1400s, and with beans.

Quail

In Spain, it is said to rain quails, rather than cats and dogs because there are so many of these tiny birds (about 10 million), which are trapped in their thousands as they fly south each April. The birds are roasted, barded with bacon and stuffed with their own innards, or casseroled with wine and garlic, or with grapes. A speciality is *codornices con pochas*, quail with freshly shelled haricot (navy) beans, as their seasons coincide.

Woodcock

Chocha (woodcock) are found in Galicia in the winter. The small birds are shot for the pot, and you really need to allow two birds per person.

Pheasant

Because it was recorded by the great French chef, Escoffier, *faisan al modo de Alcántara*, pheasant stuffed with duck liver and truffles, became the most famous bird dish in Europe.

FURRED GAME

Ninety per cent of Spain is mountainous and full of game. The mountain goats are the long-horned ibex (*cabra monte*) and the short-horned chamois (*rebeco* in Catalan). Boars (*jabalí*) are hunted by moonlight. They are numerous in the rugged north and in the southern mountains. Because the wild boar does so much damage to young woodland, it is now culled. Boar is stewed with thyme or wine and nuts.

Venison

The red *ciervo común* is Europe's largest deer, pre-eminent in the Sierra Morena and the mountains of the south, in the coastal Coto Doñana, and reintroduced into the northern

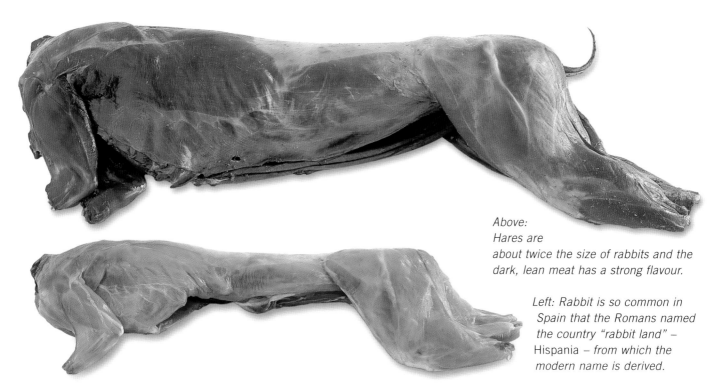

Above:
Hares are
about twice the size of rabbits and the
dark, lean meat has a strong flavour.

Left: Rabbit is so common in
Spain that the Romans named
the country "rabbit land" –
Hispania – *from which the*
modern name is derived.

Cantabrian *cordillera*. Here, you can find all three types of deer: the *ciervo común*, the small *corzo* (roe deer), and the *gamo* (fallow deer). Venison (*venado*) is cooked in wine, roasted or grilled (broiled) and served with a creamy *Cabrales* sauce.

Hare

In Extremadura, hare (*liebre*) is served at engagement parties, the sauce finished with blood, sherry and brandy. It is also often cooked with chocolate. Sometimes it is cooked in the field, in a pot with charcoal on the lid, and accompanied by beans. *Morteruelo*, a pâté of mixed game meats pounded together, is a speciality of Cuenca on the edge of La Mancha.

Rabbit

There are rabbits (*conejos*) all across Spain – so many that the Spanish bred spaniels to chase them. Rabbits are often cooked with snails, which impart the flavour of rosemary, or wild thyme. A Navarran speciality is a pie whose pastry is aromatized by thyme and rosemary. In the south, saffron rice with rabbit is eaten in preference to paella. Rabbit is also cooked with vinegar and garlic (*salmorego*), giving rise to the proverb for a good match – *el salmorejo para el conejo*.

Gathering wild food

Hunters out with a gun and a dog often also collect wild mushrooms, herbs, grubs and snails in their knapsacks – for they are free food. Lizards are caught in Extremadura; the hunters tighten a small noose around the tail of the creature. The lizard's white flesh, which tastes like a cross between a young rabbit and a frog, is eaten in little pots with a tomato sauce. Frogs are a popular food, too, and the hind legs may be battered or fried.

There are many different snails that can be eaten, and they come in all sizes and many flavours. The great black *negros* and *moros* are best grilled (broiled) and eaten with vinegar. The most expensive are the prized Valencia *vaquetas de oliva*; grey and black with a flavour of wild rosemary, upon which they feed. They are commonly added to rice dishes such as paella. In Lérida there is the *caracol de viña* (the same as Burgundy's *petit gris* snail), while in Seville there is the small *caracol* (the generic word for a snail) and the larger *cabrilla*, which means chanterelle, with its pretty whorls of black and white.

Preparing snails

To make an appetizer for four people, you will need about 60 snails. They must be purged before cooking.

1 To purge the snails, put them in a bucket with a weighted lid. After 3 days sprinkle in flour, then leave for another 4 days.

2 The day before cooking, splash the snails with a little fresh water. Discard any that aren't moving. Clean the shells with salt and vinegar, then leave them for 30 minutes before rinsing under cold running water.

3 To cook, put the snails in a pan and cover with warm water, then bring slowly to the boil. Drain, then return to the pan and cover in fresh salted water and bring to the boil again, with a handful of herbs such as wild fennel or bruised parsley stalks. Cook for at least 30 minutes.

4 Drain the snails and add them to a spicy tomato sauce. Simmer for 30 minutes, then serve in individual earthenware dishes. To eat, put a pin into the end, and twist the shell anticlockwise (counterclockwise).

FRUIT AND DESSERTS

More often than not, dessert in Spain is simply a beautifully fragrant piece of fruit. There are only a few true desserts, but they are deeply traditional – and usually incredibly sweet.

FRUIT

Spain is blessed with a huge wealth of fruit. The apricot trees are the first to flower every spring. But it is apples (*manzanas*) that are grown across the country, especially Asturias, with *reinetas* (a Cox type) being a speciality. The orchards of Lérida and Navarra are red with *melocotones* (peaches).

Any Spaniard will boast of the date groves of Elche, of the plums (*ciruelas*) and pears (*peras*), and of the Valle de Jerte that is filled with cherries (*cerezas*). Dark *picota* cherries have no stalks. Quinces are made into a delicious orange paste, *membrillo*, which is often served with cheese.

Golden grapes (*uvas*) drape across houses in the south, and the coast from Alicante to Valencia is famous for fat, juicy muscats. They are dried in Málaga as huge black *pasas*. Red-fleshed figs grow wild in the southern scrub, while Granada gained its name from the pomegranate (*granada*). The orange "tomatoes", growing high on bare trees in December, are persimmons (*cakis*).

Below: Pasas de Málaga *are the huge, fat raisins made from muscat grapes.*

Melons (*melones*) have been grown in Spain since the Roman times. The dark-skinned, white-fleshed honeydew melons (*piel de sapo*) are the most highly prized. Strawberries (*fresas*) are another success story. In times past, a train used to run from Madrid to Aranjuez in the summer, carrying picnickers out to the strawberry farms. Now, in Huelva, the strawberries are ripe by Christmas.

Below: Pomegranates are used to make drinks, sorbets and a sauce for chicken.

Above: Spain is renowned for its honeydew melons.

Left: Strawberries are an important Spanish crop.

Citrus fruit

It was the Moors who first planted citrus trees in Spain. The bitter orange came from India in the 11th century, and the juice was squeezed over fish – and still is – in the way we now use lemons. Sweet oranges (*naranjas*) came from China and were planted across the country in the 1550s.

Valencia is the orange capital of Spain and oranges are picked from September to late spring. The small Valencia orange has now been replaced by the seedless Washington navel, and small clementines now represent a quarter of citrus exports. More lemons (*limones*) are grown in Murcia than in Valencia. The summer lemon is the *verna*, with thick peel and juicy flesh, and in winter it is the thin-skinned *fino*.

Tropical fruit

Microclimates allow passion fruit (*pasionara*), loquat (*níspero*) and the custard apple (*cherimoya*) to grow in the south, while in Galicia kiwi and feijoas are cultivated. The Canary Islands are known for a small, sweet banana and the pineapple (*piña*).

Above: Small Valencia oranges have a sweet, tangy, juicy flesh.

FRUIT DESSERTS

Peaches in syrup (*almibar*) are a favourite dessert in Spain, although peaches (or pears) baked whole in red wine are also very popular. Traditional desserts often feature preserved fruit and nuts and are made in winter. Dried figs go into *pan de alá*. The Galicians make superb *marrons glacées* as well as an excellent chestnut and chocolate mousse. They also like freshly roasted chestnuts in a glass of brandy. The Basque Christmas Eve *intxausalsa* is a creamy purée of walnuts.

In Aragón, the crystallized fruit are coated in chocolate. In Cáceres, they make tiny chocolate-coated figs that are out of this world.

MILK PUDDINGS

Custards reign supreme in Spain, and there is a great trio of desserts: *flan* (baked custard), *crema catalana* (crème brulée) and *tocino de cielo*, which is a baked caramel custard turned out and dark-topped. It looks like an uncut slab of pork, hence its name, which means blissful bacon. Custards (*natilla*) are traditionally made in convents, to sell outside. They may be piled high with *suspiros de mona* (poached meringue); the name means nun's sighs and it is said that the nuns making them sigh regretfully, "Would that I could eat them."

Rice found a sweet niche in the north. The Asturian milk pudding, *arroz con leche*, is flavoured with cinnamon or caramel. Fried custard squares (*leche frita*) are a Basque speciality, and further west pancakes (*filloas*) are popular, served with cream and liqueur. Sugared *flores manchegos* are cooked on special irons and are shaped like flowers. Junket (*cuajada*) and whipped cream (*nata*) are topped with nuts, and *mel y mato* is Catalan cream cheese with honey. Two good cheesecakes are the Santander *quesada*, made with fresh *pasiega*, and the Ibizan *flaó*, which is flavoured with mint.

ICES

The Moors in Granada used to send runners up the mountains to cut ice, even in summer, starting a tradition of *granizados* (grainy iced desserts), made with lemon and sweet fruit syrups (*jarabes*), and later with coffee. The popular frozen dessert today is *tarta helada quemada*, which has a crispy caramel topping.

ALMOND SWEETMEATS

The tradition of serving almond sweet-meats such as *alfajores* (almonds crushed to a paste with honey and wrapped in paper) started in the Moorish harems. *Mazapán* (marzipan) was invented in Toledo when the Moors, besieged by Alfonso VI, ran out of bread and turned to almonds instead. The city now sells little baked half moons of

Honey

Spain specializes in single-flower honey – and there are a great many varieties due to the many mountains, herbs and flowering trees. Valencia is famous for rosemary, *azahar* (citrus blossom) and thyme honeys. Lavender and thyme honeys are produced in the hills behind Cordoba. *Miel de bosque*, from the blossom of Extrameduran oaks, is very dark. Alcarría D.O. is a famous honey centre in Guadalajarra.

Honey is traditionally served with fruit juice, or with almonds or figs, but it is also served with unusual savoury foods such as *bacalao* and *sobrasada* sausage.

marzipan. *Figuritas de mazapán* are sold at Christmas and you will find them in many different shapes, including little fish, animals, bread shapes, and even miniature musical instruments.

Turrón (nougat) used to be seasonal too, but is now available all year round. In Jijona you can buy a soft almond and honey paste, and in Alicante one with whole marcona almonds embedded in it, while *torta imperiale*, sandwiched between layers of rice paper, is the best in Spain. *Almendras garapiñadas* (crunchy nuts tossed in sweet caramel) are sold at street fairs.

Left: Traditional Spanish sweetmeats date back to the Moorish traditions.

BREAD AND CAKES

Bread is a very important part of the Spanish diet, while cakes and sweet buns are eaten less often than in other countries. Bread shops (*panaderias*) sell bread alone. Cakes and other sweet things are bought from a *pastelería*.

BREAD

As in many European countries, *pan* is Spain's basic food and taken very seriously. Not so long ago consumption was 1kg/2¼lb a head per day. In Galicia, if a piece of bread is dropped, it will be picked up and kissed. It plays a ritual part in weddings, anniversaries and death ceremonies.

Bread accompanies all meals in Spain. It is bought twice a day and eaten very fresh. The *barra* (long loaf) is better, some claim, than French bread. But there are a host of rolls with local names such as *bollas* (balls) and *chicas* (little girls).

Traditional breads

The wheat granary of Spain is the Tierra de Campos in León and south towards Zamora. Here they make the *hogaza* (large loaf) of Castile and the round, white *candeal* bread, which is a classic. In Catalonia, where everything tends to be done slightly differently, the bread is shaped like a three-corned hat, with slashes across the corners. (Salvador

Above: Pan de cebada *is a coarse-textured country bread from Galicia, which is exceptional for its barley flour.*

Dalí used them to decorate his house.) *Pan cateto* is sourdough bread with a close crumb and chewy crust (*cateto* means country bumpkin); it is dry but long lasting. Bread is also made with pork crackling in it.

Corn meal is used to make corn bread (*pan de maíz*) in Galicia; it is wrapped in leaves and baked overnight in the dying embers of the fire. *Borona* is made with both rye flour and corn meal. Galicians also use bread dough to make their flat two-crust pies, while *bollas preñadas* (pregnant buns) consist of dough folded round sausage meat.

Cocas

Hot from the bread oven, *cocas* are a speciality of the Balearics and Levante. They resemble an Italian pizza but date back much further than that. Once they were just bread dough topped with sardines or salted meat, but today they are spread with tomato sauce, too, and scattered with onions, black olives and herbs. At festival time, there are sweet ones for sale, topped with glistening candied fruit. *Cocarois* are little pastries, folded over with a filling of meat or vegetables.

Using bread

Bread is used in a variety of ways, both in the kitchen and at the table.

Mojado The bread used to scoop up sauced vegetables and seafood tapas.

Rebanada A slice of bread, which is used as a "polite" plate mop at the end of a course.

Pa amb tomàquet Very lightly toasted bread, topped with olive oil and squashed fresh tomato. It is eaten at the start of every meal in Catalonia.

Torrijas These are bread dipped in milk or wine, then fried and sugared.

Migas Breadcrumbs fried in olive oil and a food for all occasions, for every meal and with almost everything. They can be eaten for breakfast after a night on the town, with bacon and eggs; or with fresh fruit as dessert; even with chocolate and sardines – together.

Sobras Yesterday's stale bread is ideal for frying, before being pounded and used to thicken sauces and soups.

Sopa Stale pieces of bread were once common breakfast fare, dunked in coffee, milk and sugar, and eaten with a spoon.

Jam

The best jam is *cabello de angél* (angel's hair) made from the citron melon (*cidra*) which is large and blotched dark green. Jam is used to fill sweet *empanadillas* and cakes, or spread on bread.

FRITTERS

Dulces de sartén (frying-pan sweets) are the Spanish doughnut, sold on the streets at fairs and in tapas bars. Delicately flavoured with crushed aniseed, and steeped in honey or anis syrup, they betray their Moorish past. *Borrachuelos* are "drunk" on their syrup. Many of them are made in the same way as choux pastry, by beating flour and egg (with wine) in a pan. They may be baked or fried, both of which causes the pastry to puff up.

Plain *empanadillas* (pies) are rolled out with a special rolling pin to stripe the pastry, then sugared; others are filled with angel's hair jam. *Pestiños* (honey-coated fritters) are often hollow – a square folded with opposite corners meeting – to soak up more syrup. *Huesos de santos* (saints' bones) are hollow too, sometimes made of potato dough or almond pastry. *Buñuelos de viento* (*bunyols* in Catalan) are choux puffs, which are eaten on All Saints' Day and at Christmas.

BISCUITS AND COOKIES

Small dry cakes are served with sweet liqueurs, and are often dunked into them. Rings (*rosquillos*) are very common. Many little cookies are made from cinnamon pastry. Others have delightfully descriptive names. S-shaped *mostachones* look like a moustache when two of the cookies are held together; *polverones* (crumble cakes)

Below: Small, dry rosquillos, *made from a wine pastry, are found all over Spain.*

Above: Sobaos pasiegas, from the dairy valley of Pas, are made with butter.

have a powdery texture. *Mantecados*, which are famous in Old Castile, are lardy cookies containing ground almonds. *Macarrones* (macaroons) are made with whisked egg whites and ground almonds, while *almendrados*, made with almonds, and *almori* (honey cakes) reflect the Moorish influence. Moors' sighs (*suspiros de Moros*) are ground almond meringues.

Nuns are traditionally bakers in Old Castile and the south. The nuns of San Leandro in Seville make *yemas* (yolks), whose name describes their colour, shape and content.

LITTLE CAKES AND BUNS

Breakfast is the occasion for some real treats. The melting pastry of Majorcan *ensaimada*, curled like a turban, is also a favourite in Madrid. *Sobaos pasiegas* are rich butter sponges baked in little individual rectangles in papers.

Pan quemado is an all-day Valencian snack. The name means burnt bread, because it is brushed with meringue and sugar before baking, to give it a dark golden crust. For tea time in Madrid, custard-filled puff pastry *bartillos* are eaten. *Medias noches* (midnight buns) are worth sneaking down for at night.

Above: Small, soft bread rolls are good at any time of day.

CAKES

Sponge cakes, made with egg whites only, are light and airy and perfect for soaking up syrups and brandies – as is the tradition in Spain. *Brazo de gitano* (gypsy's arm) is the best-known cake – long and brown and rolled up round *cremadina* (custard). The big traditional cake is *Roscón de Reyes*, an enriched bread-dough ring made for Twelfth Night. It is generously topped with almonds and candied fruit, of which there seems to be more every year.

Below: Simple little magdalenas *(butter cakes) make a delightful treat.*

WINE

There are two great wine styles that are particular to Spain – Rioja and sherry. In Rioja, red wine (but also some white wine) is aged in oak casks, which gives it a light aroma of vanilla. Sherry is a highly sophisticated fortified white wine, and classed with the world's great wines. In Spain, it is drunk as a wine, not just as an aperitif as it is elsewhere.

Spain's viticulture is the largest in the world, and is undergoing a rapid modernization programme. Once behind

---

The language of wine
Drinking wine is part of Spanish culture and has its own terms.
Vino de la mesa This is the house wine, usually in *una jarra* (a jug or pitcher). *Una media* is a 500ml/ 17fl oz/2¼ cup measure.
Vino corriente This is table wine in its first or second year.
Crianza These wines must be stored for two years after harvest (*cosecha*). For the first six months the wine is stored in casks, whose oak gives the wine its distinctive flavour. Better quality wines may be held back before they are sold. However, you should beware of five- to six-year-old wines because they may have developed a very oxidized, stale taste.
Reserva This means that the wine has been matured for three years. For whites and *rosados* (rosé) wines, this means they are in the cask for six months; for reds, this means at least a year, often much more, plus a year in the bottle. Both modest regional wines and good brands carry this label.
Gran reserva This includes much of the best wine, which is only made in fine vintage years or from the best grapes. Cellar-aged for six years, they have at least two years in the cask and three in the bottle – and are splendid value for the quality of wine offered.
Viña This means vineyard, but is a brand not a place. There are few estate-bottled wines.

---

other countries in technology, Spain's expenditure on modern equipment is resulting in better wines all the time.

Spanish wine drinking is not a very complicated matter. There are no rules about matching food and drink and the Spanish enjoy young wines as well as those that have been aged in oak casks in the traditional way.

RED WINE

Much of Spain's wine is red, with top quality wine produced on the northern rivers and hefty reds with a high alcohol content further south.

Wines on the Ebro river

These are the Riojas; they are soft but not delicate, with a fruity taste. They are blended wines, and some wine firms grow no grapes themselves. Good wines are matured partly in casks, partly in the bottle, which gives an opportunity for a "house taste". Popular brands are San Ascensio made by Campo Viejo, the biggest *bodega* (wine firm) in Rioja, CUNE and Banda Azul (Blue Stripe) from top exporter Frederick Paternina.

At the expensive end, two traditional houses, Marqués de Murrieta and Marqués de Riscal make big-bodied, oaky reds. With them a newer house in the same style, Marqués de Muga, makes up "the three mighty Ms" of Rioja. However, many modern *bodegas* favour time maturing in the bottle (not the cask), for example Marqués de Cáceres, Lagunilla and the big exporter Faustino Martínez.

Vintages are important here, as grapes may not always ripen to full potential. There are three regions of Rioja, each with its own distinct style, which will also give clues as to what you are

Right: Campo Viejo is one of the biggest Rioja-producing wine firms in Spain.

---

buying. Rioja Baja is low-lying, producing everyday fruity wines. The high Rioja Alta produces wines with more tannin, making them hard and acidic if young, but maturing to a more complex taste. The Rioja Alavesa makes softer, aromatic wines. Part of this region is in Navarra, on the other side of the river, which has a good line in young reds, not unlike Beaujolais.

Wines on the Duero river

Ribera del Duero produces Vega Sicilia, Spain's masterpiece, which is, unfortunately, almost unobtainable. Based on Cabernet Sauvignon, it is aged in casks for ten years or so, and is often 16 years old when sold. Pesquera del Duero is the affordable alternative.

Central Spain

Valdepeñas produces better-quality reds than La Mancha which surrounds it. Huge *tinajas* (unglazed urns) stand at the roadsides and are used for wine. Here they make *aloques*, strong but light red wines, and *claretes*, not claret but a wine of mixed red and white grapes.

The red grapes

Tempranillo is Spain's principal red grape (*Ull de Llebre* in Catalonia). Used on its own, it makes good, berry-scented young wines, but about 70 per cent of the crop goes into the great Riojas, chiefly supported by the garnacha grape.

Spain's quest for better grapes has been hampered by old D.O. (*Denominación de Origen*) restrictions. However, new grapes and irrigation, which have been introduced increasingly since the 1960s, have helped to improve quality. Landmarks are the Raimat estate in Costers del Segre, while Jean León introduced Cabernet Sauvignon to Penedès. The palm of honour, however, goes to two generations of the Torres family in Penedès, who produce splendid new wines (white, pink and red) with fabulous wines such as Gran Coronas' Black Label, Mas la Plana.

Vast acres of Spain are under vines. La Mancha, with half the vineyards in Spain, produces red wine mainly from the *monastrell* grape. Poor Aragón makes purplish reds, often 15 per cent by volume, because the sun raises alcohol content at the same time as it diminishes quality. Cariñena and Borja in the south-east, and Alicante, Jumilla and Yecla nearer the coast all make hefty reds. Priorato may be Spain's answer to Burgundy. Lighter reds come from Utiel-Requeña and Somontana in the north-east.

PINK WINE

The *rosados* (rosé wines) of Navarra such as Gran Feudo are justly famous, and good ones are made in Aragón, Ribera del Duero, Tarragona and Utiel-Requeña. The cherry-coloured wines, a speciality of Ampurdán, are very good.

WHITE WINE

Good whites are produced on Spain's fringes – north and east – with the masterpiece, sherry, in the south.

Green wine

The *Alberiño* grape produces German-style wines on the slopes of Rías Bajas and Ribera del Duero. Delicately fruity, they give a slight prickle in the mouth and are perfect with shellfish.

Chacoli

The Basques are proud of this wine which they call *txacoli*. It is thin, rather acidic, appley and slightly sparkling.

Rioja whites

White wine is made with the traditional *viura* grape, usually without being aged in the cask. Marqués de Cáceres is a good example of the type. CUNE's Monopole *blanco* is balanced between the two styles, while good oaked examples come from Marqués de Murrieta, Monte Real from Bodegas Riojanas and López de Heredía.

French-style whites

Lighter, fruitier and less alcoholic wines are in demand today, so styles are changing accordingly. New technology is also helping to improve white wines. Typical ones are Antonio Barbadillo in Huelva and Palacio de Bornos, made from the *verdejo* grape, in Rueda.

Whites are a tradition on the north-east coast, with French grapes making French-style wines in the cooler hills. Delicate young whites come from Marqués de Alella just outside Barcelona. Torres makes Viña Sol, which is fresh and slightly lemony (from the Spanish *parellada* grape), Gran Viña Sol (half Chardonnay), or the estate-bottled version, green label, which is matured in oak. Torres' Milmanda is the top Chardonnay in Spain.

South-west Spain

The white wines in the south-west have a strong resemblance to sherry and include *cañamero* and *chiclana*. Most famous, however, is Montilla-Moriles, which has the same nutty scent as sherry, though it is made by conventional methods. Alvear is well-known, especially C.B. (the proprietor's initials), which is the white for cooking.

Sparkling wines

Cavas are wines made by the champagne method in Penedès (although the grapes may come from elsewhere), mainly in San Sadurní de Nova. Codorníu is the largest champagne-style wine producer in the world. Their lovely top-of-the-range wine is the Chardonnay *cava*. Raimat is a good alternative, or Freixenet *cordon negro*, in the black bottle. The Spanish favour sweet *champáns* so do look for "brut" on the label.

Right: Freixenet Cordon Negro is a good quality cava *with a lovely flavour.*

Sherry styles

Fino This is the lightest and driest sherry. It is a pale straw colour.
Manzanilla Meaning camomile, this is similar to *fino*, but has a tang aquired as a result of being stored by the sea.
Amontillado This is matured until it is a soft, dark tawny colour.
Palo cortado This is sweeter still.
Oloroso With more body and a nutty flavour, *olorosos*, as a class, are on the sweet side, sometimes reminiscent of port, but they are also made in dry styles.
Cream sherry This has sweet Pedro Ximénes juice added, which gives it a voluptuous flavour.

Sherry

The name sherry is actually a mispronounciation of the place Jerez de la Frontera. Jerez de la Frontera produces exceptional fortified wines, mainly from the *Palomino* grape, and is one of the few places in Spain with a long tradition of fine wines. Because of its high alcohol content (17 per cent by volume) and the way it is made, it is regarded as an aperitif by the outside world. But in Spain it is a white wine, the natural choice for fish, or a flamenco evening, drunk chilled from the tulip-shaped *copita*, which is never more than two-thirds full. Sherry is made in a *solera* system, a tier of barrels, where the bottom barrels are tapped and the upper barrels are made up with younger wine. The sherry is fortified with brandy, then exposed to air in the cask, where a yeast *flor* grows on the surface to protect it. Darker sherries have oxidized more. Among the great names are Tio Pepe, Barbadillo and Domecq's La Ina.

ALCOHOLIC AND OTHER DRINKS

The Spanish are immensely social, and can match any occasion throughout the day with the perfect drink.

SWEET AND FORTIFIED WINES

The scented muscat grape gives its name to many sweet wines including the *moscatels* of Alicante and Valencia and Málaga *Virgen*. The *Malvasía* grape is used to make a honeyed wine of the same name. Pedro Ximénes is made into luscious dessert wines. *Vino de lágrima* is made from very ripe grapes.

Dry or sweet fortified wine (*generoso*) can be enjoyed before or after dinner, as can the mellowed *rancio*. Tarragona is known for the 20-year-old copper-coloured Fondillón.

BRANDY

Coñac is very popular. (Some people even enjoy it with coffee for breakfast.) The Spanish prefer brandies that are caramelized with added syrup and perfume such as Soberano. Magno and Veterano are big medium-priced sellers, while Carlos III (*te-thero*) is more elegant. Catalonia has always produced brandies that are closer to cognac such as Mascaró and Torres' Black label.

Below: The top quality brandy Lepanto is sold in a decanter-shaped bottle.

Above: The light Valencia moscatel is widely available abroad.

SPIRITS AND LIQUEURS

Aguardiente is any distilled liquor, often colourless. In the north, the dark *orujo* is a rough, strong brandy, made from grape skins. *Anís* is the true taste of Spain, and there are both dry and *dulce* (sweet) varieties. Aniseed-flavoured and colourless, the famous brands are Anís de Mono and Chinchón. *Dulce* is served neat in liqueur glasses or combined in mixtures such as *sol y sombra* (anís with brandy). *Pacharán* (sloe brandy), such as Zoco, is the top generic liqueur and is drunk on the rocks.

Both gin and rum are popular. Gin is made by the huge firm Larios in the south, while a grape gin is made in Menorca by Xoviguer. Bacardi is made under licence, but there is also brown *ron*. They are drunk short over ice, with mixers, or soda and lemon. *Cubalibre* is rum and coke, poured 50:50.

Above: Anís de Mono comes in a very distinctive cut glass bottle.

Herb liqueurs

Hierbas are popular throughout Spain. Those made in Ibiza are really strong – like the dangerous green absinthe – and should be mixed with ice and water. *Izarra*, meaning star, is the Basque green liqueur, made with 48 herb flowers and plants. It is served chilled in short glasses. *Ponche*, meaning punch, is a sweet, herbalized old brandy that comes in a silver bottle; Cabellero and De Soto are well-known varieties. *Ratafias* are liqueurs flavoured with almonds and are particularly popular in Navarra and Aragón.

In this land of liqueurs there are many more to choose from. Chartreuse is made in Tarragona, for it became the home of monks when they were expelled from France. The golden Calisay is quinine-based, while vanilla is included in Liquor 43 (*Cuarenta y tres*).

Right: Liquor 43 is a brandy-based liqueur with an infusion of forty-three different herbs.

CIDER AND BEER

In the north of Spain, cider (*sidra*) replaces wine as the drink of choice. Strongly alcoholic, it is drunk in *sidrerías* with its own rituals. Guests are not permitted to pour their own *sidra*. The bottle is held high in one hand, the tumbler low in the other, and the cider is poured in a great arc, to aerate it.

Spanish-style beer, *cerveza*, is light and refreshing – well suited to the climate. *Un caño* is beer from the pump. Well-known brands include San Miguel, Aguila and Victoria, which are all pilsner types. Cruz Campo is Seville's best beer, and Majou is the best bitter.

Below: San Miguel is one of the most popular summer beers in Spain.

SUMMER DRINKS

Refrescos are cool, non-alcoholic drinks. The big names in bottled water, *con gas* or *sin gas* (sparkling or still) are Solares, Font Vella and Lanjarón. Vichy Catalan is the leading sparkling water. Spanish lemonades (*gaseoso*) are fizzy and very sweet. Freshly squeezed juice (*zumo*) is available in bars, while the brand Rives produces colourful fruit syrups for diluting, including bright red *granadina* (pomegranate).

Tinto de verano is the beach drink, made with half red wine and half lemonade. More elegant, chilled *horchata* is made from tiger nuts (*chufas*), which grow in the Moorish-owned fine black sand round Alboraya in Valencia. The nuts are ground, diluted with water and sweetened with honey. Good shops such as Santa Catalina in Valencia, make it fresh every day.

Finally, *leche merenguada* is made with half milk and half cream. It is flavoured with cinnamon and lemon, and made light with whisked egg whites – rather like an ice cream.

TEA, CHOCOLATE AND COFFEE

Teas are known as *infusiones*, but hot *te con limón* is less popular than the many herb teas that are available. Camomile (*manzanilla*) is the firm favourite. Other popular flavourings are mint (*poleomenta*), lime (linden) flowers (*tila*) and lemon verbena (*hierba luisa*).

Chocolate came from America, but acquired its connection with cinnamon in Spain. Louis XIV's Spanish bride took to it with her to France as a breakfast drink. Today, there are still traditional bars dedicated to serving chocolate in Seville. It is sold as a powder or in tablet form with thickener added.

The national passion is for coffee, which is always made the same way – dark and strong. In former days breakfast coffee was poured over bread in a bowl, then hot milk and sugar were added before it was eaten.

Sangría

There are many variations of this classic, refreshing mixture of iced wine and citrus juice.

MAKES ABOUT 2 LITRES/
4 PINTS

INGREDIENTS
2 pared lemon rind strips
juice of 2 lemons
juice of 4 oranges
30ml/2 tbsp caster
  (superfine) sugar
1 litre/1¾ pints/4 cups red wine,
  chilled
750ml/1¼ pints/3 cups soda
  water, chilled
ice cubes

1 Put the lemon rind, fruit juice and sugar in a large jug and chill.

2 To serve, pour the wine, soda water and ice cubes into the jug. Stir, then pour into tall glasses.

A nice cup of coffee

Coffee in Spain is always freshly made and there are many ways to drink it.

Café con leche A mellow coffee drunk at breakfast. It is made with its own volume of hot milk.

Café solo Black coffee.

Un cortado A *demi-tasse*, with room for a little bit of milk.

Café helado This iced coffee is made by pouring hot coffee into a tumbler of ice cubes.

Un blanco y negro A glass of milky iced coffee, heavily scented with cinnamon, and drunk through a straw.

Batido de café A cold coffee milkshake.

Mazagrán Iced coffee with rum.

El carajillo Coffee with brandy.

Un cremàt Brandy or rum flamed with coffee. (*Cremàt* is the Catalan word for burnt.)

TAPAS

In Spain, the motto is "eat when you drink, drink when you eat"
— and tapas would seem to have been invented for just this.
Tapas are finger food, a choice of delicious morsels to tempt the
drinker to have another glass and with it another tapas dish.
They range from simple dishes of olives and nuts to richly
flavoured shellfish, marinated fish and titbits on skewers.

OLIVE AND ANCHOVY BITES

THESE LITTLE MELT-IN-THE-MOUTH MORSELS ARE MADE FROM TWO INGREDIENTS THAT ARE FOREVER ASSOCIATED WITH TAPAS — OLIVES AND ANCHOVIES. THE REASON FOR THIS IS THAT BOTH CONTAIN SALT, WHICH HELPS TO STIMULATE THIRST AND THEREFORE DRINKING.

3 Preheat the oven to 200°C/400°F/ Gas 6. Roll out the dough thinly on a lightly floured surface.

4 Cut the dough into 5cm/2in wide strips, then cut across each strip in alternate directions, to make triangles. Transfer to baking sheets and bake for 8–10 minutes until golden. Cool on a wire rack. Sprinkle with sea salt.

VARIATIONS

• To add a little extra spice, dust the olive and anchovy bites lightly with cayenne pepper before baking.

• Crisp little nibbles set off most drinks. Serve these bites alongside little bowls of seeds and nuts such as sunflower seeds and pistachios. These come in the shell, the opening of which provides a diversion while gossiping. Toasted chickpeas are another popular tapas snack.

MAKES FORTY TO FORTY-FIVE

INGREDIENTS
   115g/4oz/1 cup plain
      (all-purpose) flour
   115g/4oz/½ cup chilled
      butter, diced
   115g/4oz/1 cup finely grated
      Manchego, mature (sharp) Cheddar
      or Gruyère cheese
   50g/2oz can anchovy fillets
      in oil, drained and roughly
      chopped
   50g/2oz/½ cup pitted black olives,
      roughly chopped
   2.5ml/½ tsp cayenne pepper
   sea salt, to serve

1 Place the flour, butter, cheese, anchovies, olives and cayenne pepper in a food processor and pulse until the mixture forms a firm dough.

2 Wrap the dough loosely in clear film (plastic wrap). Chill for 20 minutes.

SWEET AND SALTY VEGETABLE CRISPS

THE SPANISH LOVE NEW AND COLOURFUL SNACKS. TRY THESE BRIGHTLY COLOURED CRISPS, WHICH MAKE AN APPEALING ALTERNATIVE TO POTATO CRISPS. SERVE THEM WITH A BOWL OF CREAMY, GARLICKY ALLIOLI, AND USE THE CRISPS TO SCOOP IT UP.

SERVES FOUR

INGREDIENTS
   1 small fresh beetroot (beet)
   caster (superfine) sugar and fine salt,
     for sprinkling
   olive oil, for frying
   coarse sea salt, to serve

COOK'S TIP
Beetroot crisps are particularly flavoursome, but other naturally sweet root vegetables, such as carrots and sweet potato, also taste delicious when cooked in this way. You might like to make several different varieties and serve them heaped in separate small bowls.

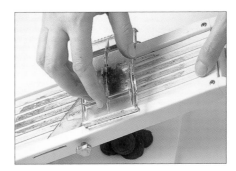

1 Peel the beetroot and, using a mandolin or a vegetable peeler, cut it into very thin slices.

2 Lay the slices on kitchen paper and sprinkle them with sugar and fine salt.

3 Heat 5cm/2in oil in a deep pan until a bread cube turns golden in 1 minute. Cook the slices in batches, until they float to the surface and turn golden at the edge. Drain on kitchen paper and sprinkle with sea salt when cool.

TAPAS OF ALMONDS, OLIVES AND CHEESE

ALMONDS AND OLIVES USED TO BE SERVED FREE IN ALL TAPAS BARS, AND STILL ARE IN SOME. THEY ARE THE PERFECT NIBBLE OR CASUAL STARTER FOR PRE-DINNER DRINKS. MANCHEGO CHEESE IN OIL IS NOW A DELICIOUS SPANISH EXPORT, ALTHOUGH YOU CAN EASILY MARINATE THE CHEESE YOURSELF.

SERVES SIX TO EIGHT

INGREDIENTS
For the marinated olives
   2.5ml/½ tsp coriander seeds
   2.5ml/½ tsp fennel seeds
   2 garlic cloves, crushed
   5ml/1 tsp chopped fresh rosemary
   10ml/2 tsp chopped fresh parsley
   15ml/1 tbsp sherry vinegar
   30ml/2 tbsp olive oil
   115g/4oz/⅔ cup black olives
   115g/4oz/⅔ cup green olives
For the marinated cheese
   150g/5oz Manchego or other
    firm cheese
   90ml/6 tbsp olive oil
   15ml/1 tbsp white wine vinegar
   5ml/1 tsp black peppercorns
   1 garlic clove, sliced
   fresh thyme or tarragon sprigs
   fresh flat leaf parsley or tarragon
    sprigs, to garnish (optional)
For the salted almonds
   1.5ml/¼ tsp cayenne pepper
   30ml/2 tbsp sea salt
   25g/1oz/2 tbsp butter
   60ml/4 tbsp olive oil
   200g/7oz/1¾ cups blanched
    almonds
   extra salt for sprinkling (optional)

1 To make the marinated olives, crush the coriander and fennel seeds in a mortar with a pestle. Work in the garlic, then add the rosemary, parsley, vinegar and olive oil. Put the olives in a small bowl and pour over the marinade. Cover with clear film (plastic wrap) and chill for up to 1 week.

2 To make the marinated cheese, cut the cheese into bitesize pieces, removing any hard rind, and put in a small bowl. Combine the oil, vinegar, peppercorns, garlic, thyme or tarragon and pour over the cheese. Cover with clear film and chill for up to 3 days.

3 To make the salted almonds, combine the cayenne pepper and salt in a bowl. Melt the butter with the oil in a frying pan. Add the almonds and fry them, stirring for 5 minutes, or until golden.

4 Tip the almonds into the salt mixture and toss until the almonds are coated. Leave to cool, then store in an airtight container for up to 1 week.

5 To serve, arrange the almonds, olives and cheese in three separate small, shallow dishes. Garnish the cheese with fresh herbs if you like and scatter the almonds with a little more salt, to taste. Provide cocktail sticks (toothpicks) for guests to pick up the cheese and olives with.

COOK'S TIPS
• Whole olives, sold with the stone, invariably taste better than pitted ones. Don't serve them directly from the brine, but drain and rinse them, then pat dry with kitchen paper. Put the olives in a jar and pour over extra virgin olive oil to cover. Seal and store in the refrigerator for 1–2 months; the flavour of the olives will become enriched. Serve the olives as a tapas dish, or add to salads. When the olives have been eaten, the fruity oil can be used as a dressing for hot food, or made into flavoursome salad dressings.
• A number of exotic stuffed olives are exported from Spain and are widely available in most large supermarkets. Popular varieties include pimiento-stuffed olives, which have been in existence for more than half a century, olives stuffed with salted anchovies, and olives filled with roast garlic.

BUÑUELOS

THE NAME OF THESE CHEESE PUFFS LITERALLY MEANS PUFFBALL. IN SPAIN, THEY ARE USUALLY DEEP-FRIED BUT BAKING IS EASIER AND GIVES WONDERFUL RESULTS. THE DOUGH IS MADE IN THE SAME WAY AS FRENCH CHOUX PASTRY, AND THE BUÑUELOS SHOULD BE EATEN WITHIN A FEW HOURS OF BAKING.

SERVES FOUR

INGREDIENTS
  50g/2oz/¼ cup butter, diced
  1.5ml/¼ tsp salt
  250ml/8fl oz/1 cup water
  115g/4oz/1 cup plain
   (all-purpose) flour
  2 whole eggs, plus 1 yolk
  2.5ml/½ tsp Dijon mustard
  2.5ml/½ tsp cayenne pepper
  50g/2oz/½ cup finely grated
   Manchego or Cheddar cheese

1 Preheat the oven to 220°C/425°F/Gas 7. Place butter and the salt in a pan, then add the water. Bring the liquid to the boil. Meanwhile, sift the flour on to a sheet of baking parchment or greaseproof (waxed) paper.

2 Working quickly, tip the flour into the pan of boiling liquid in one go and stir it in immediately.

3 Beat the mixture vigorously with a wooden spoon until it forms a thick paste that binds together and leaves the sides of the pan clean. Remove the pan from the heat.

4 Gradually beat the eggs and yolk into the mixture, then add the mustard, cayenne pepper and cheese.

5 Place teaspoonfuls of mixture on a non-stick baking sheet and bake for 10 minutes. Reduce the temperature to 180°C/350°F/Gas 4. Cook for 15 minutes until well browned. Serve hot or cold.

CHICHARRONES

THE SPANISH EAT EVERYTHING THAT COMES FROM THE PIG, AND EVEN THE HUMBLE RIND GOES TO MAKE THIS DELICIOUS LITTLE SALTED, PIQUANT SNACK. THIS CRISPY, CRUNCHY PORK CRACKLING IS THE PERFECT ACCOMPANIMENT FOR A GLASS OF WINE OR CHILLED BOTTLE OF SAN MIGUEL.

SERVES FOUR

INGREDIENTS
  115g/4oz pork rind
  vegetable oil, for frying
  paprika and coarse sea salt,
   for sprinkling

COOK'S TIPS
• Make these cracklings spicier, if you wish. Paprika is the pepper of Spain, and any kitchen may well have one sweet variety (our common paprika), as well as one smoked and one hot – hot chilli powder, cayenne and Tabasco sauce can all be substituted.
• Strips of streaky (fatty) belly can be used instead of pork rind. Cut the strips into the same lengths, removing any bones. Cook them until all the fat has run out, and they look like crisp honeycombs. These tasty morsels are known as *torreznos*.

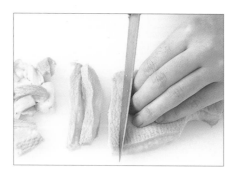

1 Using a sharp knife, cut the pork rind into strips. There is no need to be too precise, but try to make the strips roughly 1cm/½in wide and 2.5cm/1in long.

2 Pour the vegetable oil to a depth of 2.5cm/1in in a deep heavy frying pan. Heat the oil and check that it has reached the correct temperature by immersing a cube of bread, which should brown in 1 minute.

3 Cook the strips of rind in the oil for 1–2 minutes, until they are puffed up and golden brown. Remove with a slotted spoon and drain on kitchen paper.

4 Sprinkle the chicharrones with paprika and salt to taste. Serve them hot or cold. Although they are at their best 1–2 days after cooking, they will keep reasonably well for up to 2 weeks in an airtight container.

PIMIENTO TARTLETS

KNOWN AS TARTALITAS DE PIMIENTO IN SPAIN, THESE PRETTY LITTLE TARTLETS ARE FILLED WITH STRIPS OF ROASTED SWEET PEPPERS AND A DELICIOUSLY CREAMY, CHEESY CUSTARD. THEY MAKE THE PERFECT SNACK TO SERVE WITH DRINKS.

SERVES FOUR

INGREDIENTS
  1 red (bell) pepper
  1 yellow (bell) pepper
  175g/6oz/1½ cups plain
    (all-purpose) flour
  75g/3oz/6 tbsp chilled butter, diced
  30–45ml/2–3 tbsp cold water
  60ml/4 tbsp double (heavy) cream
  1 egg
  15ml/1 tbsp grated fresh
    Parmesan cheese
  salt and ground black pepper

VARIATION
Use strips of grilled aubergine (eggplant) mixed with sun-dried tomatoes in place of the roasted peppers.

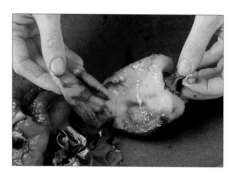

1 Preheat the oven to 200°C/400°F/ Gas 6, and heat the grill (broiler). Place the peppers on a baking sheet and grill for 10 minutes, turning occasionally, until blackened. Cover with a dishtowel and leave for 5 minutes. Peel away the skin, then discard the seeds and cut the flesh into very thin strips.

2 Sift the flour and a pinch of salt into a bowl. Add the butter and rub it in until the mixture resembles fine breadcrumbs. Stir in enough of the water to make a firm, not sticky, dough.

3 Roll the dough out thinly on a lightly floured surface and line 12 individual moulds or a 12-hole tartlet tin (muffin pan). Prick the bases with a fork and fill the pastry cases with crumpled foil. Bake for 10 minutes.

4 Remove the foil from the pastry cases and divide the pepper strips among the pastry cases.

5 Whisk the cream and egg in a bowl. Season well and pour over the peppers. Sprinkle each tartlet with Parmesan cheese and bake for 15–20 minutes until firm. Cool for 2 minutes, then remove from the moulds and transfer to a wire rack. Serve warm or cold.

SPINACH EMPANADILLAS

LITTLE PIES ARE PART OF THE MOORISH TRADITION IN SPAIN. THE ARABS FIRST BROUGHT SPINACH TO EUROPE AND PINE NUTS AND RAISINS ARE TYPICAL ARAB FLAVOURINGS. IN SPAIN THE DOUGH FOR THESE PASTRIES IS SOLD READY-CUT INTO ROUNDS, AND THEY ARE DEEP-FRIED.

MAKES TWENTY

INGREDIENTS
    25g/1oz/¼ cup raisins
    25ml/1½ tbsp olive oil
    450g/1lb fresh spinach
       leaves, washed, drained
       and chopped
    6 canned anchovies, drained
       and chopped
    2 garlic cloves, finely chopped
    25g/1oz/¼ cup pine nuts,
       roughly chopped
    350g/12oz puff pastry
    1 egg, beaten
    salt and ground black pepper

1 To make the filling, soak the raisins in a little warm water for 10 minutes. Drain well, then chop roughly.

2 Heat the olive oil in a large pan, add the spinach, stir, then cover and cook over a low heat for about 2 minutes until the spinach starts to wilt. Remove the lid, turn up the heat and cook until any liquid has evaporated.

3 Add the chopped anchovies, garlic and seasoning to the spinach and cook, stirring, for about 1 minute.

4 Remove the pan from the heat, then stir in the soaked raisins and pine nuts, and set aside to cool.

5 Meanwhile, preheat the oven to 180°C/350°F/Gas 4. Roll out the pastry on a lightly floured surface to a 3mm/⅛in thickness.

6 Using a 7.5cm/3in pastry cutter, cut the pastry into 20 rounds, re-rolling any scraps if necessary. Place about 10ml/2 tsp filling in the middle of each round, then brush the edges with a little water.

7 Bring up the sides of the pastry and seal well. Press the edges together with the back of a fork. Brush with egg.

8 Place the pies, slightly apart, on a lightly greased baking sheet and bake for about 15 minutes, until puffed up and golden brown.

9 Transfer the pies to a wire rack to cool. They are best served while still slightly warm, but not hot.

VARIATIONS
• Little stuffed pies such as these are typical of Catalonia and the Balearic Islands. Elsewhere in Spain these pies are usually plain, deep-fried and then sugared – the one sweet tapas.
• In the Barcelona food markets, pies filled with a canned tuna and vegetable stuffing are a popular hot snack.

COCA <u>WITH</u> ONION <u>AND</u> ANCHOVY TOPPING

NOT UNLIKE ITALIAN PIZZA, COCAS HAVE A VERY LONG TRADITION IN SPAIN. THEY ARE ESSENTIALLY FRESH BREAD DOUGH, BAKED WITH A VARIETY OF SAVOURY TOPPINGS, AND OFTEN INCLUDE SALT FISH. THE FLAVOURINGS OF THIS SNACK GO BACK AT LEAST 1000 YEARS.

SERVES SIX TO EIGHT

INGREDIENTS
  400g/14oz/3½ cups strong white
    bread flour
  2.5ml/½ tsp salt
  15g/½oz easy-blend (rapid-rise)
    dried yeast
  120ml/4fl oz/½ cup olive oil
  150ml/¼ pint/⅔ cup milk and water,
    in equal quantities, mixed together
  3 large onions, thinly sliced
  50g/2oz can anchovies, drained and
    roughly chopped
  30ml/2 tbsp pine nuts
  30ml/2 tbsp Muscatel raisins or
    sultanas (golden raisins), soaked
  5ml/1 tsp dried chilli flakes
    or powder
  salt and ground black pepper

VARIATION
You can eat cocas with a wide range of different toppings. Try spinach sautéed with garlic or sweet red (bell) peppers.

1 Put the flour and salt into a food processor with the yeast. Process, gradually working in 60ml/4 tbsp oil and a little of the milk and water. Gradually add the remaining milk and water, processing until well combined. Turn the dough into a bowl, cover with a dishtowel, then leave in a warm place for about 1 hour to rise.

2 Preheat the oven to 240°C/475°F/Gas 9. Heat the remaining oil in a large frying pan, add the sliced onions, and cook gently until soft.

3 Return the dough to the food processor and use the pulse button to work the dough. On a lightly floured surface roll out the dough to a rectangle about 30 × 38cm/12 × 15in. Place on an oiled baking sheet.

4 Cover the dough with the onions. Scatter with the anchovies, pine nuts, raisins or sultanas and chilli flakes or powder and season. Bake for about 10 minutes, until puffed up and the edges are beginning to brown. Serve hot, cut into wedges.

BANDERILLAS

THESE MINIATURE SKEWERS ARE VERY POPULAR IN THE NORTH OF SPAIN, WHERE THEY ARE CALLED PINCHOS, WHICH LITERALLY MEANS STUCK ON A THORN. TASTE, COLOUR AND SHAPE GUIDE THE CHOICE OF INGREDIENTS, WHICH MAY INCLUDE COLD OR CURED MEAT, PICKLED TUNA, SALTED FISH OR EVEN HARD-BOILED EGGS. IN THE SOUTH, PICKLED VEGETABLES ARE PREFERRED. THERE, THE RESEMBLANCE TO THE BULLFIGHTER'S DART WAS NOTICED AND SO THE SKEWERS WERE RENAMED.

SERVES FOUR

INGREDIENTS
  12 small capers
  12 canned anchovy fillets in
    oil, drained
  12 pitted black olives
  12 cornichons or small gherkins
  12 silverskin pickled onions

VARIATION
You can vary the ingredients if you like, using cold meats, cheeses and vegetables. Choose ingredients with different textures, tastes and colours.

1 Using your fingers, place a caper at the thicker end of each anchovy fillet and carefully roll it up, so that the caper is completely enclosed.

2 Thread one caper-filled anchovy, one olive, one cornichon or gherkin and one pickled onion on to each of 12 cocktail sticks (toothpicks). Chill and serve.

MARINATED ANCHOVIES

THIS IS ONE OF THE SIMPLEST WAYS TO PREPARE THESE TINY FISH BECAUSE IT REQUIRES NO COOKING. MARINATING IS PARTICULARLY ASSOCIATED WITH ANCHOVIES, WHICH TEND TO LOSE THEIR FRESHNESS VERY QUICKLY. THE SPANISH TERM FOR MARINATED ANCHOVIES IS BOQUERONES, *WHILE* ANCHOAS *IS THEIR WORD FOR THE CANNED, SALTED VARIETY.*

2 Using the tip of a small, sharp knife, carefully remove the backbones from the flattened fish, and arrange the anchovies skin side down in a single layer on a large plate.

3 Squeeze two-thirds of the lemon juice over the fish and sprinkle them with the salt. Cover and leave to stand for 1–24 hours, basting occasionally with the juices, until the flesh is white and no longer translucent.

4 Transfer the anchovies to a serving plate and drizzle with the olive oil and the remaining lemon juice. Scatter the fish with the chopped garlic and parsley, then cover with clear film (plastic wrap) and chill until ready to serve.

SERVES FOUR

INGREDIENTS
    225g/8oz fresh anchovies, heads
      and tails removed, and split open
      along the belly
    juice of 3 lemons
    30ml/2 tbsp extra virgin olive oil
    2 garlic cloves, finely chopped
    15ml/1 tbsp chopped fresh parsley
    flaked sea salt

1 Turn the anchovies on to their bellies, and press down with your thumb.

FLASH-FRIED SQUID <u>WITH</u> PAPRIKA <u>AND</u> GARLIC

SQUID ARE PART OF EVERY TAPAS BAR SELECTION, AND ARE USUALLY DEEP-FRIED. HERE IS A MODERN RECIPE, WHICH IS UNUSUAL IN THAT IT USES FRESH CHILLIES. SERVE THE DISH WITH A FINO OR MANZANILLA SHERRY AS A TAPAS DISH. ALTERNATIVELY, SERVE THE CALAMARES ON A BED OF SALAD LEAVES, ACCOMPANIED BY BREAD, FOR A SUBSTANTIAL FIRST COURSE TO SERVE FOUR.

SERVES SIX TO EIGHT

INGREDIENTS
   500g/1¼lb very small squid, cleaned
   90ml/6 tbsp olive oil, plus extra
   1 fresh red chilli, seeded and
     finely chopped
   10ml/2 tsp Spanish mild
     smoked paprika
   30ml/2 tbsp plain (all-purpose) flour
   2 garlic cloves, finely chopped
   15ml/1 tbsp sherry vinegar
   5ml/1 tsp grated lemon rind
   30–45ml/2–3 tbsp finely chopped
     fresh parsley
   salt and ground black pepper

1 Using a sharp knife, cut the squid body sacs into rings and cut the tentacles into bitesize pieces.

2 Place the squid in a bowl and pour over 30ml/2 tbsp of the olive oil, half the chilli and the paprika. Season with a little salt and some pepper, cover with clear film (plastic wrap), place in the refrigerator and leave to marinate for 2–4 hours.

COOK'S TIPS
• Make sure the oil in the pan is very hot before adding the squid. The squid should cook for only 1–2 minutes; any longer and it will begin to toughen.
• Smoked paprika, chiefly from the Valle de Jerte, has a wonderful, subtle flavour. If you cannot find it, you can use mild paprika instead.

3 Toss the squid in the flour and divide it into two batches. Heat the remaining oil in a wok or deep frying pan over a high heat until very hot. Add the first batch of squid and quickly stir-fry for 1–2 minutes, or until it becomes opaque and the tentacles curl.

4 Add half the garlic. Stir, then turn out into a bowl. Repeat with the second batch, adding more oil if needed.

5 Sprinkle with the sherry vinegar, lemon rind, remaining chilli and parsley. Season and serve hot or cool.

KING PRAWNS IN CRISPY BATTER

A HUGE RANGE OF PRAWNS IS ENJOYED IN SPAIN, EACH WITH ITS APPROPRIATE COOKING METHOD. LANGOSTINOS ARE DEEP-WATER PRAWNS, OFTEN WITH TIGER STRIPES, AND CAN BE AMONG THE BIGGEST. THE BEST WAY TO ENJOY THEM IS DIPPED IN A SIMPLE BATTER AND DEEP-FRIED.

SERVES FOUR

INGREDIENTS
  120ml/4fl oz/½ cup water
  1 large egg (US extra large)
  115g/4oz/1 cup plain
    (all-purpose) flour
  5ml/1 tsp cayenne pepper
  12 raw king prawns (jumbo shrimp),
    in the shell
  vegetable oil, for deep frying
  flat leaf parsley, to garnish
  lemon wedges, to serve (optional)

COOK'S TIP
Leaving the tails on the prawns makes them easier to pick up and eat, and also look very pretty once cooked.

1 In a large bowl, whisk together the water and the egg. Whisk in the flour and cayenne pepper until smooth.

2 Peel the prawns, leaving just the tails intact. Make a shallow cut down the back of each prawn.

3 Using the tip of the knife, pull out and discard the dark intestinal tract.

4 Heat the oil in a large pan or deep-fat fryer, until a cube of bread dropped into the oil browns in 1 minute.

5 Holding the prawns by their tails, dip them into the batter, one at a time, shaking off any excess. Carefully drop each prawn into the oil and fry for 2–3 minutes until crisp and golden. Drain on kitchen paper, garnish with parsley and serve with lemon wedges, if you like.

VARIATION
If you have any batter left over, use it to coat thin strips of vegetables such as sweet potato, beetroot (beet), carrot or (bell) pepper, or use small broccoli florets or whole baby spinach leaves. Deep-fry the vegetables until golden.

BUTTERFLIED PRAWNS IN CHOCOLATE SAUCE

THERE IS A LONG TRADITION IN SPAIN, WHICH ORIGINATES IN MEXICO, OF COOKING SAVOURY FOOD – EVEN SHELLFISH – WITH CHOCOLATE. KNOWN AS LANGOSTINOS EN CHOCOLATE *IN SPANISH, THIS IS JUST THE KIND OF CULINARY ADVENTURE THAT BASQUE CHEFS LOVE.*

SERVES FOUR

INGREDIENTS
8 large raw prawns (shrimp), in the shell
15ml/1 tbsp seasoned plain (all-purpose) flour
15ml/1 tbsp pale dry sherry
juice of 1 large orange
15g/½oz dark (bittersweet) chocolate, chopped
30ml/2 tbsp olive oil
2 garlic cloves, finely chopped
2.5cm/1in piece fresh root ginger, finely chopped
1 small dried chilli, seeded and chopped
salt and ground black pepper

1 Peel the prawns, leaving just the tail sections intact. Make a shallow cut down the back of each one and carefully pull out and discard the dark intestinal tract.

2 Turn the prawns over so that the undersides are uppermost, and then carefully slit them open from tail to top, using a small sharp knife, cutting them almost, but not quite, through to the central back line.

3 Press the prawns down firmly to flatten them out. Coat with the seasoned flour and set aside.

4 Gently heat the sherry and orange juice in a small pan. When warm, remove from the heat and stir in the chopped chocolate until melted.

5 Heat the oil in a frying pan. Add the garlic, ginger and chilli and cook for 2 minutes until golden. Remove with a slotted spoon and reserve. Add the prawns, cut side down and cook for 2–3 minutes until golden brown with pink edges. Turn the prawns and cook for a further 2 minutes.

6 Return the garlic mixture to the pan and pour the chocolate sauce over. Cook for 1 minute, turning the prawns to coat them in the glossy sauce. Season to taste and serve hot.

SIZZLING PRAWNS

GARLIC PRAWNS ARE HUGELY POPULAR IN SPAIN, BOTH WITH AND WITHOUT THE ADDITION OF CHILLI. THEY ARE NORMALLY COOKED IN SMALL, INDIVIDUAL EARTHENWARE CASSEROLES, WHICH STAND ON AN IRON BAKING SHEET — LA PLANCHA. A FRYING PAN WILL PRODUCE THE SAME RESULT.

SERVES FOUR

INGREDIENTS
    1–2 dried chillies (to taste)
    60ml/4 tbsp olive oil
    3 garlic cloves, finely chopped
    16 large raw prawns (shrimp),
     in the shell
    salt and ground black pepper
    French bread, to serve

VARIATION

To make classic *gambas al ajillo* – garlic prawns (shrimp) – simply omit the chilli. The word *ajillo* tells you how the garlic is prepared. The diminutive means finely chopped, like the garlic in the final dish. The alternative is *gambas con ajo*, which means with garlic. For this dish, slices of garlic are fried until brown, to flavour the oil, then discarded.

1 Split the chillies lengthways and discard the seeds. It is best to do this with a knife and fork, because the seeds, in particular, contain hot capsicum, which can be very irritating to the eyes, nose and mouth.

2 Heat the oil in a large frying pan and stir-fry the garlic and chilli for 1 minute, until the garlic begins to turn brown.

3 Add the whole prawns and stir-fry for 3–4 minutes, coating them well with the flavoured oil.

4 Remove from the heat and divide the prawns among four dishes. Spoon over the flavoured oil and serve immediately. (Remember to provide a plate for the heads and shells, plus plenty of napkins for messy fingers.)

SPICED CLAMS

Spanish clams, especially in the North, are much larger than clams found elsewhere, and have more succulent bodies. This modern recipe uses Arab spicing to make a hot dip or sauce. Serve with plenty of fresh bread to mop up the delicious juices.

SERVES THREE TO FOUR

INGREDIENTS
  1 small onion, finely chopped
  1 celery stick, sliced
  2 garlic cloves, finely chopped
  2.5cm/1in piece fresh root
    ginger, grated
  30ml/2 tbsp olive oil
  1.5ml/¼ tsp chilli powder
  5ml/1 tsp ground turmeric
  30ml/2 tbsp chopped
    fresh parsley
  500g/1¼lb small clams, in
    the shell
  30ml/2 tbsp dry white wine
  salt and ground black pepper
  celery leaves, to garnish
  fresh bread, to serve

COOK'S TIPS
• There are many different varieties of clam fished off the coast of Spain. One of the best is the *almeja fina* (the carpet shell clam), which is perfect used in this dish. They have grooved brown shells with a yellow lattice pattern.
• Before cooking the clams, check that all the shells are closed. Any clams that do not open after cooking should be discarded.

1 Place the onion, celery, garlic and ginger in a large pan, add the olive oil, spices and chopped parsley and stir-fry for about 5 minutes. Add the clams to the pan and cook for 2 minutes.

2 Add the wine, then cover and cook gently for 2–3 minutes, shaking the pan occasionally. Season. Discard any clams whose shells remain closed, then serve, garnished with the celery leaves.

MUSSELS WITH A PARSLEY CRUST

THE STORMY ATLANTIC COAST OF SPAIN PRODUCES THE BEST MUSSELS IN THE WORLD. KNOWN AS
MEJILLONES IN SPAIN, THEY GROW TO ENORMOUS SIZE IN A VERY SHORT TIME, WITHOUT BECOMING
TOUGH. HERE THEY ARE GRILLED WITH A DELICIOUSLY FRAGRANT TOPPING OF PARMESAN CHEESE,
GARLIC AND PARSLEY, WHICH HELPS TO PREVENT THE MUSSELS FROM BECOMING OVERCOOKED.

SERVES FOUR

INGREDIENTS
    450g/1lb fresh mussels
    45ml/3 tbsp water
    15ml/1 tbsp melted butter
    15ml/1 tbsp olive oil
    45ml/3 tbsp freshly grated
      Parmesan cheese
    30ml/2 tbsp chopped fresh parsley
    2 garlic cloves, finely chopped
    2.5ml/½ tsp coarsely ground
      black pepper
    crusty bread, to serve

COOK'S TIP
Steaming the mussels produces about
250ml/8fl oz/1 cup wonderful shellfish
stock that can be used in other fish and
shellfish recipes. Once the mussels have
been steamed, remove them from the
pan and leave the broth liquor to cool,
then store it in a sealed container in the
refrigerator or freezer.

Combining fish and shellfish stock
is the backbone of many Spanish fish
dishes such as *merluza con salsa verde*
(hake with green sauce). It is said that
the stock from one shellfish makes the
best sauce for another.

1 Scrub the mussels thoroughly,
scraping off any barnacles with a round-
bladed knife and pulling out the gritty
beards. Sharply tap any open mussels
and discard any that fail to close or
whose shells are broken.

2 Place the mussels in a large pan and
add the water. Cover the pan with a lid
and steam for about 5 minutes, or until
the mussel shells have opened.

3 Drain the mussels well and discard
any that remain closed. Carefully snap
off the top shell from each mussel,
leaving the actual flesh still attached
to the bottom shell.

4 Balance the shells in a flameproof
dish, packing them closely together to
make sure that they stay level.

5 Preheat the grill (broiler) to high.
Put the melted butter, olive oil, grated
Parmesan cheese, parsley, garlic and
black pepper in a small bowl and mix
well to combine.

6 Spoon a small amount of the cheese
and garlic mixture on top of each
mussel and gently press down with
the back of the spoon.

7 Grill (broil) the mussels for about
2 minutes, or until they are sizzling
and golden. Serve the mussels in their
shells, with plenty of bread to mop up
the delicious juices.

COOK'S TIP
Give each guest one of the discarded top
shells of the mussels. They can be used
as a little spoon to free the body from
the shell of the next. Scoop up the
mussel in the empty shell and tip the
shellfish and topping into your mouth.

CHICKEN CROQUETTES

CROQUETAS ARE VERY POPULAR TAPAS FARE AND THERE ARE MANY DIFFERENT VARIATIONS. THIS ONE IS BASED ON BECHAMEL SAUCE, WHICH IS PERFECT FOR TAKING ON DIFFERENT FLAVOURS SUCH AS HAM OR CHOPPED PEPPERS. THE CROQUETTES ARE BEST FRIED JUST BEFORE SERVING.

SERVES FOUR

INGREDIENTS
  25g/1oz/2 tbsp butter
  25g/1oz/¼ cup plain
    (all-purpose) flour
  150ml/¼ pint/⅔ cup milk
  15ml/1 tbsp olive oil, plus extra
    for deep-frying
  1 boneless chicken breast
    with skin, diced
  1 garlic clove, finely chopped
  1 small egg, beaten
  50g/2oz/1 cup stale white
    breadcrumbs
salt and ground black pepper
fresh flat leaf parsley, to garnish
lemon wedges, to serve

1 Melt the butter in a pan. Add the flour and cook gently, stirring, for 1 minute. Gradually stir in the milk and cook until smooth and thick. Cover and set aside.

2 Heat the oil in a frying pan and fry the chicken and garlic for 5 minutes.

3 When the chicken is lightly browned and cooked through, tip the contents of the frying pan into a food processor and process until finely chopped. Tip the mixture into the sauce and stir to combine. Season with plenty of salt and pepper to taste, then set aside to cool completely.

4 Once cooled and firm, shape the mixture into eight small sausage shapes. Dip each one in beaten egg, then roll in breadcrumbs to coat.

5 Heat the oil in a large pan, until a cube of bread dropped in the oil browns in 1 minute. Lower the croquettes into the oil and cook for 4 minutes until crisp and golden. Lift out using a slotted spoon and drain on kitchen paper. Serve with lemon wedges and garnish with fresh flat leaf parsley.

PINCHITOS MORUÑOS

THE MOORS INTRODUCED BOTH SKEWERS AND MARINATED MEAT TO SPAIN. THESE LITTLE YELLOW KEBABS ARE A FAVOURITE IN ANDALUSIA, WHERE MANY BUTCHERS SELL THE MEAT READY MARINATED. THE ARAB VERSIONS USED LAMB, BUT PORK IS USED NOW, BECAUSE THE SPICING FITS SO PERFECTLY.

SERVES FOUR

INGREDIENTS

    2.5ml/½ tsp cumin seeds
    2.5ml/½ tsp coriander seeds
    2 garlic cloves, finely chopped
    5ml/1 tsp paprika
    2.5ml/½ tsp dried oregano
    15ml/1 tbsp lemon juice
    45ml/3 tbsp olive oil
    500g/1¼lb lean cubed pork
    salt and ground black pepper

1 Starting a couple of hours in advance, grind the cumin and coriander seeds in a mortar and work in the garlic with a pinch of salt. Add the paprika and oregano and mix in the lemon juice. Stir in the oil.

2 Cut the pork into small cubes, then skewer them, three or four at a time, on to cocktail sticks (toothpicks). Put the skewered meat in a shallow dish, and pour over the marinade. Spoon the marinade back over the meat to ensure it is well coated. Leave to marinate in a cool place for 2 hours.

3 Preheat the grill (broiler) to high, and line the grill pan with foil. Spread the kebabs out in a row and place under the grill, close to the heat. Cook for about 3 minutes on each side, spooning the juices over when you turn them, until cooked through. Sprinkle with salt and pepper, and serve at once.

FRIED BLACK PUDDING

SPANISH MORCILLA — BLACK PUDDING — IS THE FIRST SAUSAGE TO BE MADE FROM THE FRESHLY KILLED PIG AND IS VERY POPULAR THROUGHOUT SPAIN. IT IS FLAVOURED WITH SPICES AND HERBS, USUALLY INCLUDING GARLIC AND OREGANO, AND HAS A WONDERFULLY RICH, SPICY TASTE.

SERVES FOUR

INGREDIENTS

15ml/1 tbsp olive oil
1 onion, thinly sliced
2 garlic cloves, thinly sliced
5ml/1 tsp dried oregano
5ml/1 tsp paprika
225g/8oz black pudding (blood
  sausage), cut into 12 thick slices
1 thin French stick, sliced into 12
30ml/2 tbsp fino sherry
sugar, to taste
salt and ground black pepper
chopped fresh oregano, to garnish

COOK'S TIP

If you can find real *morcilla*, serve it neat: simply fry the slices in olive oil and use to top little rounds of bread. If you cannot find black pudding, you can use red chorizo instead.

1 Heat the olive oil in a large frying pan and fry the sliced onion, garlic, oregano and paprika for 7–8 minutes until the onion is softened and has turned golden brown.

2 Add the slices of black pudding, then increase the heat and cook them for 3 minutes, without stirring. Turn them over carefully with a spatula and cook for a further 3 minutes until crisp.

3 Arrange the rounds of bread on a large serving plate and top each with a slice of black pudding. Stir the sherry into the onions and add a little sugar to taste. Heat, swirling the mixture around the pan until bubbling, then season with salt and black pepper.

4 Spoon a little of the onion mixture on top of each slice of black pudding. Scatter the oregano over and serve.

BARBECUED MINI RIBS

THESE TASTY RIBS ARE KNOWN AS COSTILLAS IN SPAIN. THEY ARE DELICIOUS COOKED ON A BARBECUE AND ALMOST AS GOOD WHEN COOKED UNDER A HOT GRILL. IF YOU PREFER A SWEETER FLAVOUR, USE FRESHLY SQUEEZED ORANGE JUICE INSTEAD OF THE SWEET SHERRY.

SERVES SIX TO EIGHT

INGREDIENTS

    1 sheet of pork ribs, about
      675g/1½lb
    90ml/6 tbsp sweet oloroso sherry
    15ml/1 tbsp tomato purée (paste)
    5ml/1 tsp soy sauce
    2.5ml/½ tsp Tabasco sauce
    15ml/1 tbsp light muscovado
      (brown) sugar
    30ml/2 tbsp seasoned plain
      (all-purpose) flour
    coarse sea salt

COOK'S TIP
Oloroso sherry has a full body and sweet flavour sometimes reminiscent of port.

1 Separate the ribs, then, using a meat cleaver or heavy knife, cut each rib in half widthways to make about 30 pieces.

2 Mix the sherry, tomato purée, soy sauce, Tabasco and sugar in a bowl. Stir in 2.5ml/½ tsp salt.

3 Put the seasoned flour in a strong plastic bag, then add the ribs and toss to coat. Dip each rib in the sauce. Cook on a hot barbecue or under a hot grill (broiler) for 30–40 minutes, turning occasionally until cooked and a little charred. Sprinkle with salt and serve.

EGGS AND SOUP

Tortilla is the classic dish identified with Spain, and eggs hold
a special place in the Spanish heart — for they speak of the
barnyard, and the country, where every Spaniard imagines a
home. Gazpacho is the world-famous soup but there are many
others from shellfish soup to ham-scented broth, and those
that might come before a hearty main course.

GAZPACHO

THIS CLASSIC CHILLED SOUP IS DEEPLY ROOTED IN ANDALUSIA. THE SOOTHING BLEND OF TOMATOES, SWEET PEPPERS AND GARLIC IS SHARPENED WITH SHERRY VINEGAR, AND ENRICHED WITH OLIVE OIL. SERVING IT WITH SAUCERFULS OF GARNISHES HAS VIRTUALLY BECOME A TRADITION.

SERVES FOUR

INGREDIENTS
1.3–1.6kg/3–3½lb ripe tomatoes
1 green (bell) pepper, seeded and roughly chopped
2 garlic cloves, finely chopped
2 slices stale bread, crusts removed
60ml/4 tbsp extra virgin olive oil
60ml/4 tbsp sherry vinegar
150ml/¼ pint/⅔ cup tomato juice
300ml/½ pint/1¼ cups iced water
salt and ground black pepper
ice cubes, to serve (optional)
For the garnishes
30ml/2 tbsp olive oil
2–3 slices stale bread, diced
1 small cucumber, peeled and finely diced
1 small onion, finely chopped
1 red (bell) and 1 green (bell) pepper, seeded and finely diced
2 hard-boiled eggs, chopped

COOK'S TIP
In Spain, ripe tomatoes are used for salads and very ripe ones for sauces and soups. No further flavouring ingredients are needed. If you cannot find really ripe tomatoes, add a pinch of sugar to sweeten the soup slightly.

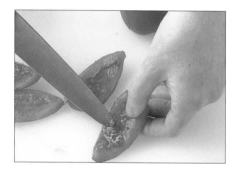

1 Skin the tomatoes, then quarter them and remove the cores and seeds, saving the juices. Put the pepper in a food processor and process for a few seconds. Add the tomatoes, reserved juices, garlic, bread, oil and vinegar and process. Add the tomato juice and blend to combine.

2 Season the soup, then pour into a large bowl, cover with clear film (plastic wrap) and chill for at least 12 hours.

3 Prepare the garnishes. Heat the olive oil in a frying pan and fry the bread cubes for 4–5 minutes until golden brown and crisp. Drain well on kitchen paper, then arrange in a small dish. Place each of the remaining garnishes in separate small dishes.

4 Just before serving, dilute the soup with the ice-cold water. The consistency should be thick but not too stodgy. If you like, stir a few ice cubes into the soup, then spoon into serving bowls and serve with the garnishes.

CHILLED AVOCADO SOUP WITH CUMIN

ANDALUSIA IS HOME TO BOTH AVOCADOS AND GAZPACHO, SO IT IS NOT SURPRISING THAT THIS CHILLED AVOCADO SOUP, WHICH IS ALSO KNOWN AS GREEN GAZPACHO, WAS INVENTED THERE. IN SPAIN, THIS DELICIOUSLY MILD, CREAMY SOUP IS KNOWN AS SOPA DE AGUACATE.

SERVES FOUR

INGREDIENTS

    3 ripe avocados
    1 bunch spring onions (scallions),
      white parts only, trimmed and
      roughly chopped
    2 garlic cloves, chopped
    juice of 1 lemon
    1.5ml/¼ tsp ground cumin
    1.5ml/¼ tsp paprika
    450ml/¾ pint/scant 2 cups fresh
      chicken stock, cooled, and all
      fat skimmed off
    300ml/½ pint/1¼ cups iced water
    salt and ground black pepper
    roughly chopped fresh flat leaf
      parsley, to serve

1 Starting half a day ahead, put the flesh of one avocado in a food processor or blender. Add the spring onions, garlic and lemon juice and purée until smooth. Add the second avocado and purée, then the third, with the spices and seasoning. Purée until smooth.

2 Gradually add the chicken stock. Pour the soup into a metal bowl and chill.

3 To serve, stir in the iced water, then season to taste with plenty of salt and black pepper. Garnish with chopped parsley and serve immediately.

CHILLED ALMOND SOUP <u>WITH</u> GRAPES

Called ajo blanco — white garlic soup — in Spain, this is a chilled Moorish soup of ancient origin. It is a perfect balance of three southern ingredients: crushed almonds, garlic and vinegar, in a smooth purée made luscious with oil.

SERVES SIX

INGREDIENTS
    115g/4oz stale white bread
    115g/4oz/1 cup blanched
      almonds
    2 garlic cloves, sliced
    75ml/5 tbsp olive oil
    25ml/1½ tbsp sherry vinegar
    salt and ground black pepper
For the garnish
    toasted flaked almonds
    green and black grapes, halved
      and seeded
    chopped fresh chives

1 Break the bread into a bowl and pour in 150ml/¼ pint/⅔ cup cold water. Leave to soak for about 5 minutes, then squeeze dry.

2 Put the almonds and garlic in a food processor or blender and process until very finely ground. Add the soaked white bread and process again until thoroughly combined.

3 Continue to process, gradually adding the oil until the mixture forms a smooth paste. Add the sherry vinegar, followed by 600ml/1 pint/ 2½ cups cold water and process until the mixture is smooth.

4 Transfer the soup to a bowl and season with plenty of salt and pepper, adding a little more water if the soup is very thick. Cover with clear film (plastic wrap) and chill for at least 2 hours.

5 Ladle the soup into bowls. Scatter the almonds, halved grapes and chopped chives over to garnish.

COOK'S TIP
To accentuate the flavour of the almonds, dry roast them in a frying pan until they are lightly browned before grinding them. This will produce a slightly darker soup.

SHERRIED ONION SOUP <u>WITH</u> SAFFRON

THE SPANISH COMBINATION OF ONIONS, SHERRY AND SAFFRON GIVES THIS PALE YELLOW SOUP A BEGUILING FLAVOUR THAT IS PERFECT FOR THE OPENING COURSE OF A MEAL. THE ADDITION OF GROUND ALMONDS TO THICKEN THE SOUP GIVES IT A WONDERFUL TEXTURE AND FLAVOUR.

SERVES FOUR

INGREDIENTS
   40g/1½oz/3 tbsp butter
   2 large yellow onions, thinly sliced
   1 small garlic clove, finely chopped
   pinch of saffron threads (0.05g)
   50g/2oz blanched almonds, toasted
      and finely ground
   750ml/1¼ pints/3 cups chicken
      or vegetable stock
   45ml/3 tbsp fino sherry
   2.5ml/½ tsp paprika
   salt and ground black pepper
To garnish
   30ml/2 tbsp flaked or slivered
      almonds, toasted
   chopped fresh parsley

1 Melt the butter in a heavy pan over a low heat. Add the onions and garlic, stirring to ensure that they are thoroughly coated in the melted butter, then cover the pan and cook very gently, stirring frequently, for about 20 minutes, or until the onions are soft and golden yellow.

2 Add the saffron threads to the pan and cook, uncovered, for 3–4 minutes, then add the finely ground almonds and cook, stirring the ingredients constantly, for a further 2–3 minutes.

3 Pour in the chicken or vegetable stock and sherry into the pan and stir in 5ml/1 tsp salt and the paprika. Season with plenty of black pepper. Bring to the boil, then lower the heat and simmer gently for about 10 minutes.

4 Pour the soup into a food processor and process until smooth, then return it to the rinsed pan. Reheat slowly, without allowing the soup to boil, stirring occasionally. Taste for seasoning, adding more salt and pepper if required.

5 Ladle the soup into heated bowls, garnish with the toasted flaked or slivered almonds and a little chopped fresh parsley and serve immediately.

VARIATION
This soup is also delicious served chilled. Use olive oil rather than butter, add a little more chicken or vegetable stock to make a slightly thinner soup, then leave to cool and chill for at least 4 hours. Just before serving, taste for seasoning. (Chilled soups need more seasoning than hot ones.) Float one or two ice cubes in each bowl, then garnish with almonds and parsley and serve immediately.

CATALAN BROAD BEAN AND POTATO SOUP

HABAS ARE FRESH BROAD BEANS, AND ARE A GREAT DEAL NICER THAN THE DRIED VARIETY, KNOWN AS FAVAS. THE WORD HAS VANISHED FROM THE SPANISH DICTIONARY AND THE RATHER INDIGESTIBLE DRIED BEAN HAS ALL BUT DISAPPEARED AS WELL. THIS FRESH SOUP USES A MODERN HERB TOO — CORIANDER IS NOT A COMMON SPANISH INGREDIENT, BUT IT ADDS A DELICIOUS FLAVOUR.

SERVES FOUR

INGREDIENTS

30ml/2 tbsp olive oil
2 onions, chopped
3 large floury potatoes, peeled
    and diced
450g/1lb fresh shelled broad
    (US fava) beans
1.75 litres/3 pints/7½ cups
    vegetable stock
1 bunch fresh coriander (cilantro),
    roughly chopped
150ml/¼ pint/⅔ cup single
    (light) cream, plus a little extra,
    to garnish
salt and ground black pepper

1 Heat the oil in a large pan and fry the onions, stirring, for 5 minutes until soft. Add the potatoes, most of the beans (reserving a few for the garnish) and the stock, and bring to the boil. Simmer for 5 minutes, then add the coriander and simmer for a further 10 minutes.

2 Blend the soup in batches in a food processor or blender, then return to the rinsed pan.

3 Stir in the cream, season, and bring to a simmer. Serve garnished with coriander, beans and cream.

SOPA CASTILIANA

This rich, dark garlic soup, from central Spain, divides people into two groups. You either love it or hate it. The pitiless sun beats down on La Mancha, one of the poorest regions of Spain, and the local soup has harsh, strong tastes to match the climate. Poaching a whole egg in each bowl just before serving transforms the soup into a meal.

SERVES FOUR

INGREDIENTS
    30ml/2 tbsp olive oil
    4 large garlic cloves, peeled
    4 slices stale country bread
    20ml/4 tbsp paprika
    1 litre/1¾ pints/4 cups beef stock
    1.5ml/¼ tsp ground cumin
    4 free-range (farm-fresh) eggs
    salt and ground black pepper
    chopped fresh parsley, to garnish

VARIATION
If you prefer, you can simply whisk the eggs into the hot soup.

1 Preheat the oven to 230°C/450°F/ Gas 8. Heat the olive oil in a large pan. Add the whole peeled garlic cloves and cook until they are golden, then remove and set aside. Fry the slices of bread in the oil until golden, then set these aside.

2 Add 15ml/1 tbsp of the paprika to the pan, and fry for a few seconds. Stir in the beef stock, cumin and remaining paprika, then add the reserved garlic, crushing the cloves with the back of a wooden spoon. Season to taste, then cook for about 5 minutes.

3 Break up the slices of fried bread into bitesize pieces and stir them into the soup. Ladle the soup into four ovenproof bowls. Carefully break an egg into each bowl of soup and place in the oven for about 3 minutes, until the eggs are set. Sprinkle the soup with chopped fresh parsley and serve immediately.

SOPA DE MARISCOS

*THIS HEARTY SEAFOOD SOUP CONTAINS ALL THE COLOURS AND FLAVOURS OF THE MEDITERRANEAN.
IT IS SUBSTANTIAL ENOUGH TO SERVE AS A MAIN COURSE, BUT CAN ALSO BE DILUTED WITH A LITTLE
WHITE WINE AND WATER, TO MAKE AN ELEGANT APPETIZER FOR SIX.*

SERVES FOUR

INGREDIENTS
  675g/1½lb raw prawns (shrimp),
    in the shell
  900ml/1½pints/3¾ cups cold water
  1 onion, chopped
  1 celery stick, chopped
  1 bay leaf
  45ml/3 tbsp olive oil
  2 slices stale bread, crusts removed
  1 small onion, finely chopped
  1 large garlic clove, chopped
  2 large tomatoes, halved
  ½ large green (bell) pepper,
    finely chopped
  500g/1¼lb cockles (small clams)
    or mussels, cleaned
  juice of 1 lemon
  45ml/3 tbsp chopped fresh parsley
  5ml/1 tsp paprika
  salt and ground black pepper

COOK'S TIP
Good fish and shellfish dishes are
normally based on proper fish stock
(including the juices saved from opening
mussels). This is equivalent to the French
court bouillon, and takes 30 minutes'
simmering. The method used here is one
of the quickest, because the prawn heads
come off neatly, and the rest of the shells
are simply added as they are removed.

1 Pull the heads off the prawns and
put them in a pan with the cold water.
Add the onion, celery and bay leaf and
simmer for 20–25 minutes.

2 Peel the prawns, adding the shells to
the stock as you go along.

3 Heat the oil in a wide, deep
flameproof casserole and fry the bread
slices quickly, then reserve them. Fry
the onion until it is soft, adding the
garlic towards the end.

4 Scoop the seeds out of the tomatoes
and discard. Chop the flesh and add
to the casserole with the green pepper.
Fry briefly, stirring occasionally.

5 Strain the stock into the casserole and
bring to the boil. Check over the cockles
or mussels, discarding any that are
open or damaged.

6 Add half the cockles or mussels to
the stock. When open, use a slotted
spoon to transfer some of them out on
to a plate. Remove the mussels or
cockles from the shells and discard
the shells. (You should end up having
discarded about half of the shells.)
Meanwhile, repeat the process to cook
the remaining cockles or mussels.

7 Return the cockles or mussels to the
soup and add the prawns. Add the
bread, torn into little pieces, and the
lemon juice and chopped parsley.

8 Season to taste with paprika, salt and
pepper and stir gently to dissolve the
bread. Serve at once in soup bowls,
providing a plate for the empty shells.

FISH SOUP <u>WITH</u> ORANGE

THE OLD NAME FOR THIS SOUP IS SOPA CACHORREÑA – SEVILLE ORANGE SOUP – AND IT IS GOOD SERVED POST-CHRISTMAS, WHEN BITTER SEVILLE ORANGES ARE IN SEASON. IT HAS A BEAUTIFUL ORANGE COLOUR. THE FISH USED IS NORMALLY SMALL HAKE, BUT ANY WHITE FISH IS SUITABLE.

2 Heat the oil in a large flameproof casserole over a high heat. Smash the garlic cloves with the flat of a knife and fry until they are well-coloured. Discard them and turn down the heat. Fry the onion gently until it is softened, adding the tomato halfway through.

3 Strain in the hot fish stock (adding the orange spiral as well if you wish) and bring back to the boil. Add the potatoes to the pan and cook them for about 5 minutes.

4 Add the fish pieces to the soup, a few at a time, without letting it go off the boil. Cook for about 15 minutes. Add the squeezed orange juice and lemon juice, if using, and the paprika, with salt and pepper to taste. Serve in bowls, garnished with a little parsley.

SERVES SIX

INGREDIENTS
1kg/2¼lb small hake or whiting, whole but cleaned
1.2 litres/2 pints/5 cups water
4 bitter oranges or 4 sweet oranges and 2 lemons
30ml/2 tbsp olive oil
5 garlic cloves, unpeeled
1 large onion, finely chopped
1 tomato, peeled, seeded and chopped
4 small potatoes, cut into rounds
5ml/1 tsp paprika
salt and ground black pepper
15–30ml/1–2 tbsp finely chopped fresh parsley, to garnish

1 Fillet the fish and cut each fillet into three, reserving all the trimmings. Put the fillets on a plate, salt lightly and chill. Put the trimmings in a pan, add the water and a spiral of orange rind. Bring to a simmer, skim, then cover and cook gently for 30 minutes.

CALDO GALLEGO

THIS CLASSIC GALICIAN SOUP FEATURES SALT PORK AND BEANS WITH YOUNG TURNIP TOPS, ALTHOUGH PURPLE SPROUTING BROCCOLI MAKES A PRETTY SUBSTITUTE. MAKE THE SOUP AHEAD OF TIME, THEN LET THE FLAVOURS BLEND. YOU WILL NEED TO START MAKING THE SOUP AT LEAST A DAY IN ADVANCE.

SERVES SIX

INGREDIENTS

   150g/5oz/⅔ cup haricot beans,
     soaked overnight in cold water
     and drained
   1kg/2¼lb smoked gammon (cured
     or smoked ham) hock
   3 potatoes, quartered
   3 small turnips, sliced in rounds
   150g/5oz purple sprouting broccoli
   salt and ground black pepper

1 Put the drained beans and gammon into a casserole and cover with 2 litres/ 3½ pints/8 cups water. Slowly bring to the boil, skim off any scum, then turn down the heat and cook gently, covered, for about 1¼ hours.

2 Drain, reserving the broth. Return the broth to the casserole and add the potatoes, turnips and drained beans.

3 Meanwhile, strip all the gammon off the bone and return the bone to the broth. Discard the rind, fat and gristle and chop half the meat coarsely. Reserve the remaining meat for another recipe.

4 Add the chopped meat to the casserole. Discard the hard stalks from the broccoli and add the leaves and florets to the broth. Simmer for 10 minutes. Season generously with pepper, then remove the bone and leave the soup to stand for at least half a day.

5 To serve, reheat the soup, add a little more seasoning if necessary, and ladle into soup bowls.

COOK'S TIP
The leftover gammon can be chopped into bitesize pieces and added to rice or vegetable dishes, or tortillas.

POTATO TORTILLA

The classic tortilla stands on every tapas bar in Spain. The size of a large cake, it is dense and very satisfying. It can be eaten in wedges with a fork — a meal in itself with salad — or cut up into chunks and speared, to be enjoyed as a snack with drinks.

SERVES SIX

INGREDIENTS

450g/1lb small waxy potatoes, peeled
1 Spanish onion
45ml/3 tbsp vegetable oil
4 large (US extra large) eggs
salt and ground black pepper
fresh flat leaf parsley or tomato
wedges, to garnish

1 Using a sharp knife, cut the potatoes into thin slices and slice the onion into thin rings. Heat 30ml/2 tbsp of the oil in a 20cm/8in heavy frying pan.

2 Add the potatoes and the onions to the pan and cook over a low heat for 20 minutes, or until the potato slices are just tender. Remove from the heat.

3 In a large bowl, beat together the eggs with a little salt and pepper. Stir in the cooked potatoes and onion.

4 Clean the frying pan with kitchen paper then heat the remaining oil and pour in the potato mixture. Cook very gently for 5–8 minutes until set underneath. During cooking, lift the edges of the tortilla with a spatula, and allow any uncooked egg to run underneath. Shake the pan from side to side, to prevent sticking.

5 Place a large heatproof plate upside-down over the pan, invert the tortilla on to the plate and then slide it back into the pan. Cook for 2–3 minutes more, until the underside of the tortilla is golden brown. Cut into wedges and serve, garnished with fresh flat leaf parsley or tomato wedges.

TORTILLA <u>WITH</u> BEANS

THE ADDITION OF CHOPPED HERBS AND A FEW SKINNED BEANS TO THE CLASSIC TORTILLA MAKES THIS A VERY SUMMERY DISH. ENJOY IT AS A LIGHT LUNCH, OR CUT IT INTO SMALL PIECES AND SERVE AS A TAPAS DISH. TORTILLA IS A MUST IN TAPAS SELECTIONS.

SERVES TWO

INGREDIENTS
  45ml/3 tbsp olive oil
  2 Spanish onions, thinly sliced
  300g/11oz waxy potatoes, cut
    into dice
  250g/9oz/1¾ cups shelled broad
    (fava) beans
  5ml/1 tsp chopped fresh thyme or
    summer savory
  6 large (US extra large) eggs
  45ml/3 tbsp mixed chopped fresh
    chives and fresh flat leaf parsley
  salt and ground black pepper

1 Heat 30ml/2 tbsp of the oil in a 23cm/9in deep non-stick frying pan. Add the onions and potatoes and stir to coat. Cover and cook gently, stirring, for 20–25 minutes until the potatoes are cooked and the onions collapsed.

2 Meanwhile, cook the beans in a pan of boiling salted water for 5 minutes. Drain well and set aside to cool.

3 When the beans are cool enough to handle, peel off and discard the grey outer skins. Add the beans to the frying pan, together with the thyme or summer savory and season with salt and pepper to taste. Stir well to mix and cook for a further 2–3 minutes.

4 Beat the eggs with salt and pepper to taste and add the mixed herbs. Pour the egg mixture over the potatoes and onions and increase the heat slightly. Cook gently for about 5 minutes, or until the egg on the bottom sets and browns. During cooking, gently pull the tortilla away from the sides of the pan and tilt to allow the uncooked egg to run underneath.

5 Cover the frying pan with a large, upside-down plate and invert the tortilla on to it. Add the remaining oil to the pan and heat until hot. Slip the tortilla back into the pan, uncooked side down, and cook for 3–5 minutes until the underneath browns.

6 Slide the tortilla out on to a plate. Cut up into wedges or cubes and serve warm rather than piping hot.

SPICY SAUSAGE ᴬᴺᴰ CHEESE TORTILLA

THIS SUBSTANTIAL TORTILLA IS DELICIOUS HOT OR COLD. CUT IT INTO CHUNKY WEDGES AND SERVE FOR SUPPER OR A LIGHT LUNCH WITH A FRESH TOMATO AND BASIL SALAD. THE ADDITION OF SPICY CHORIZO AND TANGY CHEESE GIVES IT A WONDERFUL, RICH FLAVOUR.

2 Add a further 30ml/2 tbsp oil to the pan and fry the potatoes and onions for 2–3 minutes, turning frequently (the pan will be very full). Cover tightly and cook over a gentle heat for about 30 minutes, turning occasionally, until softened and slightly golden.

3 In a large mixing bowl, beat together the eggs, parsley, cheese, sausage and plenty of seasoning. Gently stir in the potatoes and onions until coated, taking care not to break up the potato too much.

4 Wipe out the pan with kitchen paper and heat the remaining 30ml/2 tbsp oil. Add the potato mixture and cook, over a very low heat, until the egg begins to set. Use a metal spatula to prevent the tortilla from sticking and allow the uncooked egg to run underneath.

5 Preheat the grill (broiler) to high. When the base of the tortilla has set, which should take about 5 minutes, protect the pan handle with foil and place the tortilla under the grill until it is set and golden. Cut into wedges and serve garnished with parsley.

SERVES FOUR TO SIX

INGREDIENTS
  75ml/5 tbsp olive oil
  175g/6oz frying chorizo or spicy
    sausage, thinly sliced
  675g/1½lb waxy potatoes,
    thinly sliced
  2 Spanish onions, halved and
    thinly sliced
  4 large (US extra large) eggs
  30ml/2 tbsp chopped fresh parsley,
    plus extra to garnish
  115g/4oz/1 cup grated Cheddar or
    other hard cheese
  salt and ground black pepper

1 Heat 15ml/1 tbsp of the oil in a 20cm/8in non-stick frying pan and fry the sausage until golden brown and cooked through. Lift out with a slotted spoon and drain on kitchen paper.

PIPERADA SANDWICH

The Basque omelette, piperada, is very different from the cake-like tortilla. It oozes butter and tomato juice, and does not hold its shape at all. That is why it makes such a satisfying filling for a bocadilla — the Spanish split-roll sandwich.

SERVES SIX

INGREDIENTS
    120–150ml/8–10 tbsp olive oil
    2 small onions, coarsely chopped
    4 red, orange or yellow (bell)
        peppers, seeded and chopped
    2 large garlic cloves, finely chopped
    pinch of chilli or hot cayenne pepper
    675g/1½lb ripe tomatoes, peeled,
        seeded and chopped
    15ml/1 tbsp chopped fresh oregano
        or 5ml/1 tsp dried
    1 long French loaf
    25g/1oz/2 tbsp butter
    6 large (US extra large)
        eggs, beaten
    salt and ground black pepper
    basil leaves, to garnish (optional)

1 Heat 60ml/4 tbsp of the oil in a large heavy frying pan. Add the onions and cook over a gentle heat, stirring occasionally, for about 5 minutes until they are softened but not coloured.

2 Add the peppers, garlic and chilli powder or cayenne pepper to the pan. Cook for a further 5 minutes, stirring, then add the tomatoes, seasoning and fresh or dried oregano. Cook over a moderate heat for 15–20 minutes until the peppers are soft and most of the liquid has evaporated.

VARIATION
If you prefer, serve the piperada as an open sandwich on toasted bread, rather than in a split French stick.

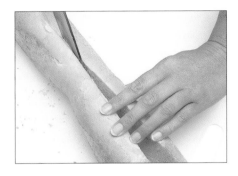

3 Preheat the oven to 200°C/400°F/ Gas 6. Cut the bread in half lengthways, trim off the ends, then cut into six equal pieces and brush with the remaining olive oil. Place the bread on baking trays and bake for 8–10 minutes until crisp and just turning golden.

4 Heat the butter in a pan until it bubbles, add the eggs and cook, stirring, until softly scrambled. Turn off the heat and stir in the pepper mixture. Divide evenly among the pieces of bread and sprinkle with the basil leaves, if using. Serve hot or warm.

SCRAMBLED EGGS WITH SPRING ASPARAGUS

REVUELTO DE ESPÁRRAGOS IS ONE OF THOSE DELICIOUS EGG DISHES THAT SHOW OFF NEW GREEN SPRING VEGETABLES TO PERFECTION. DELIGHTFULLY TENDER FRESH ASPARAGUS AND SWEET PEAS MAKE PERFECT PARTNERS TO LIGHTLY COOKED EGGS.

SERVES FOUR

INGREDIENTS
1 bunch thin asparagus
30–45ml/2–3 tbsp tiny raw
   mangetout (snow peas)
8 large (US extra large) eggs
30ml/2 tbsp milk
50g/2oz/¼ cup butter
salt and ground black pepper
sweet paprika, for dusting

VARIATION
Replace the asparagus with the mangetouts. String 150g/5oz mangetouts, then slice them diagonally into two or three pieces. Cook for 2 minutes.

1 Prepare the asparagus. Using a large sharp knife, cut off and discard any hard stems. Cut the stems into short lengths, keeping the tips separate. Shell some of the fatter mangetout pods, to extract the tiny peas.

2 Tip the stems into a pan of boiling water and simmer for 4 minutes. Add the asparagus tips, and cook for another 6 minutes. If including some pea pod strips, cook them for 2 minutes. Break the eggs into a bowl and beat together with the milk, salt and black pepper.

3 Melt the butter in a large frying pan and pour in the eggs, scrambling them by pulling the cooked outsides to the middle with a wooden spoon. When the eggs are almost cooked, drain the asparagus and pea pod strips, if using, and stir into the eggs. Sprinkle the peas over the top, and dust lightly with paprika. Serve immediately.

SCRAMBLED EGGS <u>WITH</u> PRAWNS

THE SPANISH ARE PARTICULAR ABOUT EGGS, DISTINGUISHING BETWEEN A REVUELTO, *WHICH USES SOFTLY-SET SCRAMBLED EGGS, AND THE MORE SOLID TORTILLA THAT IS COOKED UNTIL SET. THIS* REVUELTO DE GAMBAS *IS AN ECONOMICAL WAY OF USING A FEW SHELLFISH.*

SERVES FOUR

INGREDIENTS

    1 bunch spring onions (scallions)
    25g/1oz/2 tbsp butter
    30ml/2 tbsp oil
    150g/5oz shelled prawns (shrimp)
    8 large (US extra large) eggs
    30ml/2 tbsp milk
    45ml/3 tbsp chopped fresh parsley
    salt and ground black pepper
    crusty bread, to serve

VARIATION

The green shoots from garlic bulbs are another very popular spring ingredient for this type of dish and can be used in place of the spring onions. Called *ajetes* in Spain, they lend a delicate flavour to eggs.

1 Chop the white of the spring onions and reserve, keeping it separate from 30ml/2 tbsp of the green tops.

2 Heat the butter and oil in a large frying pan. Add the spring onion white and cook briefly. Add the prawns and heat through. (If the prawns are raw, cook them for 2 minutes.)

3 Beat the eggs with the milk and then season. Turn the heat to medium-high and pour the egg mixture over the prawns. Cook for about 2 minutes, stirring with a wooden spoon.

4 Sprinkle with parsley and spring onion greens. Divide among four plates and serve immediately with crusty bread.

FLAMENCO EGGS

THIS DISH IS A SWIRL OF RED, GREEN, YELLOW AND WHITE — AS COLOURFUL AS THE MOVING SKIRTS OF FLAMENCO DANCERS. IT IS BASED ON WHATEVER INGREDIENTS ARE AVAILABLE. IN SPRING THAT MIGHT MEAN PEAS, AND LATE IN THE YEAR SQUASH OR PUMPKIN. IT OFTEN CONTAINS A FEW SHRIMPS, TOO. THE MIGAS (FRIED BREADCRUMB) TOPPING IS A POPULAR SPANISH ACCOMPANIMENT TO EGGS.

SERVES FOUR

INGREDIENTS
30ml/2 tbsp olive oil
115g/4oz smoked bacon lardons
  or diced pancetta
2 frying chorizos, cubed
1 onion, chopped
2 garlic cloves, finely chopped
1 red and 1 green (bell) pepper,
  seeded and chopped
500g/1¼lb tomatoes, chopped
15–30ml/1–2 tbsp fino sherry
45ml/3 tbsp chopped parsley
8 large (US extra large) eggs
salt, paprika and cayenne
For the *migas*
4 thick slices stale bread
oil, for frying
2 garlic cloves, bruised

1 Preheat the oven to 180°C/350°F/Gas 4. Warm four individual baking dishes.

2 Heat the oil in a large frying pan and fry the bacon and chorizos, to give off their fat. Add the onion and garlic and cook gently until softened, stirring. Add the peppers and tomatoes and cook and reduce, stirring occasionally. Add some paprika and sherry – the mixture must not be too dry.

3 Divide the vegetable mixture evenly among the baking dishes. Sprinkle with parsley. Swirl the eggs together with a fork (without overmixing) and season well with salt and cayenne. Pour over the vegetable mixture.

4 Bake the eggs and vegetables for 8 minutes, or until the eggs are just set.

5 Meanwhile make the *migas*. Cut the crusts off the bread and reduce to crumbs in a food processor, or use a hand grater.

6 Heat plenty of oil in a large frying pan over a high heat, add the garlic cloves for a few moments to flavour it, then remove and discard them. Throw in the crumbs and brown quickly, scooping them out on to kitchen paper with a slotted spoon. Season with a little salt and paprika, then sprinkle around the edge of the eggs, when ready.

PAN-FRIED HAM <u>AND</u> VEGETABLES <u>WITH</u> EGGS

LITTLE VEGETABLE DISHES, AND ONES THAT CONTAIN HAM OR EGGS, OR BOTH, ARE THE BACKBONE OF THE SPANISH SUPPER SCENE. THIS DELICIOUS DISH IS INCREDIBLY SIMPLE TO MAKE AND IS HEARTY ENOUGH TO SERVE AS A MEAL IN ITSELF. UNLIKE TORTILLA, THE EGGS ARE NOT BEATEN, BUT ARE BROKEN INTO THE VEGETABLE MIXTURE AND COOKED WHOLE.

SERVES FOUR

INGREDIENTS

   30ml/2 tbsp olive oil
   1 onion, roughly chopped
   2 garlic cloves, finely chopped
   175g/6oz cooked ham
   225g/8oz courgettes (zucchini)
   1 red (bell) pepper, seeded and
     thinly sliced
   1 yellow (bell) pepper, seeded
     and thinly sliced
   10ml/2 tsp paprika
   400g/14oz can chopped tomatoes
   15ml/1 tbsp sun-dried tomato
     purée (paste)
   4 large (US extra large) eggs
   115g/4oz/1 cup coarsely grated
     Cheddar cheese
salt and ground black pepper
crusty bread, to serve

1 Heat the olive oil in a deep frying pan. Add the onion and garlic and cook for 4 minutes, stirring frequently.

2 Meanwhile, cut the cooked ham and courgettes into 5cm/2in batons.

3 Add the courgettes and peppers to the pan and cook over a medium heat for 3–4 minutes.

4 Stir in the paprika, tomatoes, tomato purée, ham and seasoning. Bring to a simmer and cook gently for 15 minutes.

5 Reduce the heat to low. Make four wells in the tomato mixture, break an egg into each and season. Cook over a gentle heat until the white begins to set. Preheat the grill (broiler). Sprinkle the cheese over and grill for about 5 minutes until the eggs are set.

SALADS AND VEGETABLES

Salads start the meal in summer, and are typical of Spain's attitude to cooking, using fresh, local seasonal ingredients. Vegetable dishes are inventive too, eaten as a tapas dish, a course on their own, or perhaps as a supper. Simple ingredients are cleverly paired to show off their qualities to perfection.

MARINATED MUSHROOMS

CHAMPIÑONES EN ESCABECHE IS A GOOD WAY TO SERVE MUSHROOMS IN SUMMER, AND MAKES A REFRESHING ALTERNATIVE TO THE EVER-POPULAR MUSHROOMS FRIED IN GARLIC. SERVE WITH PLENTY OF CRUSTY BREAD TO MOP UP THE DELICIOUS JUICES.

SERVES FOUR

INGREDIENTS
    30ml/2 tbsp olive oil
    1 small onion, very finely chopped
    1 garlic clove, finely chopped
    15ml/1 tbsp tomato purée (paste)
    50ml/2fl oz/¼ cup amontillado sherry
    50ml/2fl oz/¼ cup water
    2 cloves
    225g/8oz/3 cups button (white)
      mushrooms, trimmed
    salt and ground black pepper
    chopped fresh parsley, to garnish

VARIATION
In Spain, wild mushrooms, known as *setas*, are served in this way.

1 Heat the oil in a pan. Add the onion and garlic and cook until soft. Stir in the tomato purée, sherry, water and the cloves and season with salt and black pepper. Bring to the boil, cover and simmer gently for 45 minutes, adding more water if it becomes too dry.

2 Add the mushrooms to the pan, then cover and allow to simmer for about 5 minutes. Remove from the heat and allow to cool, still covered. Chill in the refrigerator overnight. Serve the mushrooms cold, sprinkled with the chopped fresh parsley.

ENSALADILLA

KNOWN AS RUSSIAN SALAD ELSEWHERE, THIS "SALAD OF LITTLE THINGS" BECAME EXTREMELY POPULAR DURING THE SPANISH CIVIL WAR IN THE 1930S, WHEN MORE EXPENSIVE INGREDIENTS WERE SCARCE. IT MAY EVEN HAVE BEEN INVENTED IN SPAIN – DESPITE ITS NAME.

SERVES FOUR

INGREDIENTS
  8 new potatoes, scrubbed
    and quartered
  1 large carrot, diced
  115g/4oz fine green beans,
    cut into 2cm/¾in lengths
  75g/3oz/¾ cup peas
  ½ Spanish onion, chopped
  4 cornichons or small
    gherkins, sliced
  1 small red (bell) pepper, seeded
    and diced
  50g/2oz/½ cup pitted black olives
  15ml/1 tbsp drained pickled capers
  15ml/1 tbsp freshly squeezed
    lemon juice
  30ml/2 tbsp chopped fresh fennel
    or parsley
  salt and ground black pepper
For the allioli
  2 garlic cloves, finely chopped
  2.5ml/½ tsp salt
  150ml/¼ pint/⅔ cup mayonnaise

VARIATION
This salad is delicious using any combination of chopped, cooked vegetables. Use whatever is available.

1 Make the allioli. Crush the garlic with the salt in a mortar and whisk or stir into the mayonnaise.

2 Cook the potatoes and diced carrot in a pan of boiling lightly salted water for 5–8 minutes until almost tender. Add the beans and peas to the pan and cook for 2 minutes, or until all the vegetables are tender. Drain well.

3 Tip the vegetables into a large bowl. Add the onion, cornichons or gherkins, red pepper, olives and capers. Stir in the allioli and season to taste with pepper and lemon juice.

4 Toss the vegetables and allioli together until well combined, check the seasoning and chill well. Serve garnished with fennel or parsley.

ORANGE AND RED ONION SALAD WITH CUMIN

DURING WINTER IN THE SOUTH OF SPAIN, WHEN OTHER SALAD INGREDIENTS ARE IN SHORT SUPPLY, ORANGES OFTEN FORM THE BASIS OF SALADS. IN THIS ENSALADA DE NARANJAS *THEY ARE PARTNERED WITH THINLY SLICED RED ONIONS AND BLACK OLIVES, AND FLAVOURED WITH TWO POPULAR MIDDLE EASTERN INGREDIENTS — CUMIN SEEDS AND MINT.*

SERVES SIX

INGREDIENTS
  6 oranges
  2 red onions
  15ml/1 tbsp cumin seeds
  5ml/1 tsp coarsely ground
    black pepper
  15ml/1 tbsp chopped fresh mint
  90ml/6 tbsp olive oil
  salt
  fresh mint sprigs and black olives,
    to garnish

COOK'S TIP
It is important to let the salad stand before serving. This allows the flavours to develop and the pungent taste of the onion to soften slightly.

1 Using a sharp knife, slice the oranges thinly, working over a bowl to catch any juice. Then, holding each orange slice in turn over the bowl, cut round the middle fleshy section with scissors to remove the peel and pith. Reserve the juice. Slice the two red onions thinly and separate the rings.

2 Arrange the orange and onion slices in layers in a shallow dish, sprinkling each layer with cumin seeds, pepper, mint, olive oil and salt. Pour in the reserved orange juice. Leave to marinate in a cool place for about 2 hours. Just before serving, scatter with the mint sprigs and black olives.

MIXED SALAD WITH OLIVES AND CAPERS

COLOURFUL SALADS START MANY SUMMER MEALS IN SPAIN, AND ARE A COMMUNAL AFFAIR. THE BOWL IS PUT IN THE CENTRE OF THE TABLE AND EVERYONE HELPS THEMSELVES, WITH A FORK.

SERVES FOUR

INGREDIENTS
  4 large tomatoes
  ½ cucumber
  1 bunch spring onions (scallions)
  1 bunch watercress or rocket
    (arugula), washed
  8 pimiento-stuffed olives
  30ml/2 tbsp drained pickled capers
For the dressing
  1 garlic clove, finely chopped
  30ml/2 tbsp red wine vinegar
  5ml/1 tsp paprika
  2.5ml/½ tsp ground cumin
  75ml/5 tbsp virgin olive oil
  salt and ground black pepper

COOK'S TIP
In Spain, tomatoes are always used when red and ripe. Firm tomatoes should be used in salads and soft ones in sauces.

1 To peel the tomatoes, place them in a heatproof bowl, pour over boiling water to cover and leave to stand for 1 minute. Lift out with a slotted spoon and plunge into a bowl of cold water. Leave for 1 minute, then drain. Slip off the skins and dice the flesh finely. Put in a salad bowl.

2 Peel the cucumber, dice finely and add to the tomatoes. Trim and chop half the spring onions, and add to the bowl.

3 Toss the vegetables together, then break the watercress or rocket into small sprigs. Add to the tomato mixture, with the olives and capers.

4 Make the dressing. Crush the garlic to a paste with a little salt, using the flat of a knife. Put in a bowl and mix in the vinegar and spices. Whisk in the oil and taste for seasoning. Dress the salad, and serve garnished with the remaining spring onions.

MUSHROOM, BEAN AND CHORIZO SALAD

THIS REALLY SIMPLE SALAD CAN BE SERVED AS AN ACCOMPANIMENT TO PLAIN FISH OR CHICKEN DISHES, OR SERVED WITH CRUSTY BREAD AS A HEARTY LUNCH OR SUPPER DISH. THE COMBINATION OF SPICY SAUSAGE, TENDER, SWEET BEANS AND DELICATE MUSHROOMS IS QUITE DELICIOUS.

SERVES FOUR

INGREDIENTS
    225g/8oz shelled broad (fava) beans
    175g/6oz frying chorizo
    60ml/4 tbsp extra virgin olive oil
    225g/8oz/3 cups brown cap (cremini)
        mushrooms, sliced
    60ml/4 tbsp chopped fresh chives
    salt and ground black pepper

COOK'S TIP
Although peeling the skins from broad beans can be time consuming, it is well worth it. Beans with tough, bitter skins will spoil the delicate taste and texture of this lovely salad.

1 Cook the broad beans in a pan of salted boiling water for 7–8 minutes. Drain and refresh under cold water.

2 Remove the skin from the sausage. If it doesn't peel off easily, score along the length of the sausage with a sharp knife first. Cut the chorizo into small chunks. Heat the oil in a small pan, add the chorizo and cook for 2–3 minutes.

3 Put the sliced mushrooms in a bowl and tip in the chorizo and oil. Toss to combine then leave to cool.

4 If the beans are large, peel away the tough outer skins. Stir the beans and half the chives into the mushroom mixture, and season to taste. Serve at room temperature, garnished with the remaining chives.

AVOCADO, ORANGE AND ALMOND SALAD

IN ANDALUSIA, AVOCADOS HAVE BECOME ONE OF THE BIG CASH CROPS, REPLACING MANY ORANGE ORCHARDS. IN THIS SALAD, ENSALADA DE AGUACATES, THE SMOOTH, CREAMY AVOCADOS COMBINE PERFECTLY WITH LOCALLY GROWN ORANGES AND ALMONDS.

SERVES FOUR

INGREDIENTS
    2–3 oranges
    2 ripe tomatoes
    2 small avocados
    60ml/4 tbsp extra virgin olive oil
    30ml/2 tbsp lemon juice
    15ml/1 tbsp chopped fresh parsley
    small onion rings
    25g/1oz/¼ cup split, toasted
        almonds
    10–12 black olives
    salt and ground black pepper

COOK'S TIP
Spanish onions are sweet and mild, and pleasant to eat raw, but they are very large. Slice them and use just the small central rings for salads, keeping the large outer rings for frying.

1 Peel the oranges and slice them into thick rounds. Plunge the tomatoes into boiling water for 30 seconds, then refresh in cold water. Peel away the skins, cut the tomatoes into quarters, remove the seeds and chop roughly.

2 Cut the avocados in half, remove the stones and carefully peel away the skin. Cut into chunks.

3 Mix together the olive oil, lemon juice and parsley. Season with salt and pepper, then toss the avocados and tomatoes in half of the dressing.

4 Arrange the sliced oranges on a plate and scatter with the onion rings. Drizzle with the remaining dressing. Spoon the avocados, tomatoes, almonds and olives on top and serve immediately.

CHARRED ARTICHOKES WITH LEMON OIL DIP

YOUNG ARTICHOKES, ALCACHOFAS, ARE COOKED OVER THE FIRST BARBECUES OF THE SUMMER. HOWEVER, THEY ARE ALSO VERY GOOD ROASTED IN THE OVEN. A ROAST HEAD OF GARLIC COMBINED WITH OLIVE OIL MAKES A CLASSIC, MILD SAUCE — CON MOJETE — FOR VEGETABLES.

SERVES TWO TO FOUR

INGREDIENTS
  15ml/1 tbsp lemon juice or white
    wine vinegar
  2 globe artichokes
  45ml/3 tbsp olive oil
  sea salt
  sprigs of fresh flat leaf parsley,
    to garnish
For the lemon oil dip
  12 garlic cloves, unpeeled
  1 lemon
  45ml/3 tbsp extra virgin olive oil

COOK'S TIP
Artichokes are usually boiled, but if you can get young, tender artichokes, they are delicious roasted over a barbecue.

1 Preheat the oven to 200°C/400°F/ Gas 6. Stir the lemon juice or vinegar into a bowl of cold water.

2 Cut each artichoke lengthways into wedges. Pull the hairy choke out from the centre of each wedge and drop the wedges into the acidulated water.

3 Drain the artichokes and place in a roasting pan with the garlic cloves. Toss in the oil. Sprinkle with salt and roast for 40 minutes, stirring once or twice, until the artichokes are tender.

4 Meanwhile, make the dip. Pare away two strips of rind from the lemon and scrape away any pith. Place the rind in a pan with water to cover. Simmer for 5 minutes, then drain, refresh in cold water and chop roughly.

5 Arrange the artichokes on a plate and set aside to cool for 5 minutes. Flatten the garlic cloves so that the flesh pops out of the skins. Transfer the garlic flesh to a bowl, mash to a purée then add the lemon rind. Squeeze the juice from the lemon, then, using a fork, whisk in the olive oil and lemon juice.

6 Serve the artichokes warm. Garnish them with parsley and accompany them with the lemon dip.

SPINACH WITH RAISINS AND PINE NUTS

RAISINS AND PINE NUTS ARE FREQUENT PARTNERS IN SPANISH RECIPES, AS THE PINE NUTS ARE ASTRINGENT YET RICH, THE RAISINS SWEET. HERE, TOSSED WITH WILTED SPINACH AND CROÛTONS, THEY MAKE A DELICIOUS SNACK OR MAIN MEAL ACCOMPANIMENT.

SERVES FOUR

INGREDIENTS
50g/2oz/⅓ cup raisins, preferably
   Malaga raisins
1 thick slice crusty white bread
45ml/3 tbsp olive oil
25g/1oz/¼ cup pine nuts
500g/1¼lb young spinach,
   stalks removed
2 garlic cloves, finely chopped
salt and ground black pepper

VARIATION
Swiss chard, also known as spinach beet and leaf beet, may be used instead of the spinach. It has a very similar flavour to spinach, but the leaves require slightly longer cooking.

1 Put the raisins in a small bowl and pour over enough boiling water to cover. Leave the raisins to soak for about 10 minutes, then drain well.

2 Cut off the crusts and cut the bread into cubes. Heat 30ml/2 tbsp of the oil in a frying pan and fry the cubes of bread until golden. Drain.

3 Heat the remaining oil in the pan. Gently fry the pine nuts until just colouring. Add the spinach and garlic and cook quickly, turning the spinach until it has just wilted.

4 Add the raisins and season lightly. Transfer to a warmed dish. Scatter with the croûtons and serve immediately.

AMANIDA

THE WORD AMANIDA IS CATALAN FOR AN ARRANGED SALAD THAT INCLUDES FISH, MEAT AND VEGETABLES IN EQUAL PROPORTIONS. THESE SALADS CAN BE A WONDER TO BEHOLD, BUT ARE ALSO SIMPLE TO MAKE, BECAUSE THEY COMBINE SMALL QUANTITIES OF READY-TO-EAT INGREDIENTS.

SERVES SIX

INGREDIENTS
   1 lolla green lettuce
   50g/2oz cured, sliced chorizo or
     in a piece skinned and diced
   4 thin slices Serrano ham
   130g/4½oz can sardines
     in oil, drained
   130g/4½oz can albacore tuna
     steak in oil, drained
   8 canned white asparagus
     spears, drained
   2–3 canned palm hearts, drained
   115g/4oz/⅔ cup tiny arbequina
     olives
   115g/4oz/⅔ cup big gordas or queen
     olives, preferably purplish ones
   10 medium red tomatoes
   15ml/1 tbsp chopped fresh parsley,
     to garnish
For the vinaigrette
   1 garlic clove, split lengthways
   30ml/2 tbsp sherry vinegar
   30ml/2 tbsp red wine vinegar
   60ml/4 tbsp olive oil
   60ml/4 tbsp extra virgin olive oil
   salt and ground black pepper

COOK'S TIP
The salad selection is largely about what you can get. Fresh asparagus spears (cut to length) can replace canned ones and celery hearts may replace palm heart.

1 Make the vinaigrette. Wipe the cut side of the garlic round a bowl, then discard. Whisk the other ingredients together in the bowl, then tip the vinaigrette into a small jug (pitcher).

2 Choose a large serving plate. Select eight lettuce leaves, to make small bunches round it. Break off the stem ends. Tip the leaves into the vinaigrette bowl and toss to coat in a little dressing. Arrange them around the serving plate.

3 Position the chorizo slices on one side of the plate. Roll the ham and arrange opposite. Drain and blot the canned fish and arrange the sardines and tuna across the plate, in a cross.

4 Arrange the asparagus, spears outwards, and the palm hearts (split lengthways), on opposite sides of the plate. Pile the two types of olive in the remaining spaces.

5 Put the tomatoes in a bowl and pour over boiling water. Leave to stand for 10 minutes, then drain. Peel and quarter two-thirds of the tomatoes and cut out the centres.

6 Arrange the tomatoes, round side up, in the centre of the plate, just touching all the prepared sections. Prepare more tomatoes as they are needed. Arrange them in a flower shape, each new ring just overlapping the previous one. The final ring, in the centre of the pile, should make a flower shape.

7 Brush vinaigrette dressing over the tomatoes, palm hearts and asparagus spears and season lightly with salt and black pepper. Sprinkle parsley very discreetly on the tomatoes and white vegetables. Serve at room temperature. (Refrigerate if you must, while waiting to serve.)

BRAISED CABBAGE WITH CHORIZO

CABBAGES — BERZAS — MARK THE LANDSCAPE IN GALICIA, WHERE THE HUGE VEGETABLES GROW MORE THAN HIP HIGH. THEY ARE POPULARLY COOKED IN STEWS IN THE MANY MOUNTAIN REGIONS OF THE SOUTH, AND ARE FREQUENTLY SERVED WITH CHICKPEAS OR SAUSAGES, AS IN THIS RECIPE.

SERVES FOUR

INGREDIENTS
  50g/2oz/¼ cup butter
  5ml/1 tsp coriander seeds
  225g/8oz green cabbage, shredded
  2 garlic cloves, finely chopped
  50g/2oz cured chorizo sausage,
    roughly chopped
  60ml/4 tbsp dry sherry or white wine
  salt and ground black pepper

VARIATION
Smoked bacon makes a good substitute
for chorizo sausage in this recipe, but it
should only be cooked briefly.

1 Melt the butter in a frying pan, add
the coriander seeds and cook for
1 minute. Add the cabbage to the pan
with the garlic and chorizo. Stir-fry for
5 minutes until the cabbage is tender.

2 Add the sherry or wine and plenty of
salt and pepper to the pan. Cover and
cook for 15–20 minutes until the
cabbage is tender. Check the seasoning,
adding more if necessary, and serve.

LA CALÇOTADA

SPRING ONIONS (CALÇOT) HAVE THEIR OWN FESTIVAL IN THE PROVINCE OF TARRAGONA. IT IS A DAY TO MARK THE RETURN OF BETTER WEATHER, AND IN THE PAST THE ONIONS, WHICH WERE PICKED WHEN RATHER BIGGER THAN OUR STANDARD SPRING ONIONS, WERE BARBECUED IN THE FIELDS.

SERVES SIX

INGREDIENTS
   3 bunches of plump spring onions
      (scallions), or Chinese green onions,
      which are about 2.5cm/1in across
      the bulb
   olive oil, for brushing
For the romesco sauce
   2–3 *ñoras* or other mild dried red
      chillies, such as Mexican
      anchos or *guajillos*
   1 large red (bell) pepper, halved
      and seeded
   2 large tomatoes, halved and seeded
   4–6 large garlic cloves, unpeeled
   75–90ml/5–6 tbsp olive oil
   25g/1oz/¼ cup hazelnuts, blanched
   4 slices French bread, each about
      2cm/¾in thick
   15ml/1 tbsp sherry vinegar
   squeeze of lemon juice (optional)
   chopped fresh parsley, to garnish

1 Prepare the sauce. Soak the dried chillies in hot water for about 30 minutes. Preheat the oven to 220°C/425°F/Gas 7.

2 Place the pepper, tomatoes and garlic on a baking sheet and drizzle with 15ml/1 tbsp olive oil. Roast, uncovered, for 30–40 minutes, until the pepper is blistered and blackened and the garlic is soft. Cool slightly, then peel the pepper, tomatoes and garlic.

COOK'S TIP
This piquant romesco sauce is a variation on the classic, roasting the vegetables rather than frying them.

3 Heat the remaining oil in a small frying pan and fry the hazelnuts until lightly browned, then transfer them to a plate. Fry the bread in the same oil until light brown on both sides, then transfer to the plate with the nuts and leave to cool. Reserve the oil from cooking.

4 Drain the chillies, discard as many of their seeds as you can, then place the chillies in a food processor. Add the red pepper halves, tomatoes, garlic, hazelnuts and bread chunks together with the reserved olive oil. Add the vinegar and process to a paste. Check the seasoning and thin the sauce with a little more oil or lemon juice, if necessary. Set aside.

5 Trim the roots from the spring onions or trim the Chinese onion leaves so that they are about 15–18cm/6–7in long. Brush with oil.

6 Heat an oiled ridged grill pan and cook the onions for about 2 minutes on each side, turning once and brushing with oil. (Alternatively, place under a preheated grill (broiler) 10cm/4in away from the heat and cook for 3 minutes on each side, brushing with more oil when turned; roast in a preheated oven at 200°C/400°F/Gas 6 for 5–6 minutes; or barbecue over grey charcoal for 3–4 minutes on each side, brushing with oil as needed.) Serve immediately with the sauce.

PATATAS BRAVAS

THERE ARE SEVERAL VARIATIONS ON THIS CHILLI AND POTATO DISH, BUT THE MOST IMPORTANT THING IS THE SPICING, WHICH IS MADE HOTTER STILL BY ADDING VINEGAR. THE CLASSIC VERSION IS MADE WITH FRESH TOMATO SAUCE FLAVOURED WITH GARLIC AND CHILLI. THE NAME BRAVAS IMPLIES THAT THE POTATOES ARE SO HOT THAT IT IS MANLY TO EAT THEM.

SERVES FOUR

INGREDIENTS

675g/1½ lb small new potatoes
75ml/5 tbsp olive oil
2 garlic cloves, sliced
3 dried chillies, seeded
  and chopped
2.5ml/½ tsp ground cumin
10ml/2 tsp paprika
30ml/2 tbsp red or white
  wine vinegar
1 red or green (bell) pepper,
  seeded and sliced
coarse sea salt, for sprinkling
  (optional)

1 Scrub the potatoes and put them into a pan of salted water. Bring to the boil and cook for 10 minutes, or until almost tender. Drain and leave to cool slightly. Peel, if you like, then cut into chunks.

2 Heat the oil in a large frying or sauté pan and fry the potatoes, turning them frequently, until golden.

3 Meanwhile, crush together the garlic, chillies and cumin using a mortar and pestle. Mix the paste with the paprika and wine vinegar, then add to the potatoes with the sliced pepper and cook, stirring, for 2 minutes. Scatter with salt, if using, and serve hot as a tapas dish or cold as a side dish.

MOJETE

THE SPANISH LOVE TO SCOOP UP COOKED VEGETABLES WITH BREAD, AND THE NAME OF THIS DISH, WHICH IS DERIVED FROM THE WORD MEANING TO DIP, REFLECTS THAT. PEPPERS, TOMATOES AND ONIONS ARE BAKED TOGETHER TO MAKE A COLOURFUL, SOFT VEGETABLE DISH THAT IS STUDDED WITH OLIVES. IN THE SUMMER THE VEGETABLES CAN BE COOKED ON THE BARBECUE.

SERVES EIGHT

INGREDIENTS

2 red (bell) peppers
2 yellow (bell) peppers
1 red onion, sliced
2 garlic cloves, halved
50g/2oz/¼ cup black olives
6 large ripe tomatoes, quartered
5ml/1 tsp soft light brown sugar
45ml/3 tbsp amontillado sherry
3–4 fresh rosemary sprigs
30ml/2 tbsp olive oil
salt and ground black pepper
fresh bread, to serve

1 Halve the peppers and remove the seeds. Cut each pepper lengthways into 12 strips. Preheat the oven to 200°C/400°F/Gas 6.

2 Place the peppers, onion, garlic, olives and tomatoes in a large roasting pan.

3 Sprinkle the vegetables with the sugar, then pour in the sherry. Season well with salt and pepper, cover with foil and bake for 45 minutes.

4 Remove the foil from the pan and stir the mixture well. Add the rosemary sprigs and drizzle with the olive oil. Return the pan to the oven and cook for a further 30 minutes, uncovered, until the vegetables are very tender. Serve hot or cold with plenty of chunks of fresh crusty bread.

COOK'S TIP
Spain is the world's chief olive producer, with half the crop being exported. Try to use good quality Spanish olives for this recipe. Choose unpitted ones as they have a better flavour.

STUFFED TOMATOES AND PEPPERS

COLOURFUL PEPPERS AND TOMATOES MAKE PERFECT CONTAINERS FOR A SIMPLE RICE, NUT AND HERB STUFFING. THE VEGETABLES BECOME DELICIOUSLY SWEET AND JUICY WHEN BAKED. SERVE TOMATOES Y PIMIENTAS RELLENOS AS A SUBSTANTIAL STARTER OR A SUPPER DISH.

3 Halve the peppers, leaving the cores intact. Scoop out the seeds. Brush the peppers with 15ml/1 tbsp of the oil.

4 Fry the onions and garlic in 30ml/ 2 tbsp oil. Stir in most of the almonds. Add the rice, tomato pulp, drained raisins, mint and 30ml/2 tbsp parsley. Season well, then spoon the mixture into the vegetable cases.

5 Bake uncovered for 20 minutes. Finely chop the remaining almonds and parsley in a food processor and sprinkle over the top. Drizzle with 15–30ml/ 1–2 tbsp olive oil. Return to the oven and bake for a further 20 minutes, or until turning golden. Serve, garnished with more chopped parsley if wished.

VARIATION

Small aubergines (eggplant) or large courgettes (zucchini) are also good stuffed. Scoop out the centres, then oil the vegetable cases and bake for about 15 minutes. Chop the centres, fry to soften and add to the stuffing mixture, then fill and bake as for the peppers and tomatoes.

SERVES FOUR

INGREDIENTS
  2 large tomatoes
  1 green (bell) pepper
  1 yellow or orange (bell) pepper
  75ml/5 tbsp olive oil
  2 onions, finely chopped
  2 garlic cloves, finely chopped
  75g/3 oz/¾ cup almonds, chopped
  175g/6oz/1½ cups cooked rice, or
    75g/3oz/scant ½ cup long grain
    rice, cooked and drained
  30ml/2 tbsp Malaga raisins or
    muscatels, soaked in hot water
  30ml/2 tbsp chopped fresh mint
  45ml/3 tbsp chopped fresh flat
    leaf parsley
  salt and ground pepper

1 Preheat the oven to 190°C/375°F/ Gas 5. Cut the tomatoes in half and scoop out the pulp and seeds.

2 Put the tomato halves on kitchen paper with the cut sides down and leave to drain. Roughly chop the centres and seeds and place in a bowl.

STEWED AUBERGINE

THE ARABS INTRODUCED THIS STRANGE VEGETABLE-FRUIT TO ANDALUSIA, WHERE IT WAS COOKED WITH THE ARAB FLAVOURINGS OF CUMIN AND GARLIC. LATER, DISHES SIMILAR TO FRENCH RATATOUILLE BECAME POPULAR. THIS IS A MODERN VERSION OF BERENJENA GUISADA, WITH RED WINE.

SERVES FOUR

INGREDIENTS
1 large aubergine (eggplant)
60–90ml/4–6 tbsp olive oil
2 shallots, thinly sliced
4 tomatoes, quartered
2 garlic cloves, thinly sliced
60ml/4 tbsp red wine
30ml/2 tbsp chopped fresh parsley, plus extra to garnish
30–45ml/2–3 tbsp virgin olive oil (if serving cold)
salt and ground black pepper

3 Heat 30ml/2 tbsp of the oil in a large frying pan until smoking. Add one layer of aubergine slices and fry, turning once, until golden brown. Remove to a plate covered with kitchen paper. Heat more oil and fry the second batch in the same way.

4 Heat 15ml/1 tbsp of oil in a pan and cook the shallots for 5 minutes until golden. Cut the aubergine into strips. Add, with the tomatoes, garlic and wine. Cover and simmer for 30 minutes.

5 Stir in the parsley, and check the seasonings. Sprinkle with a little more parsley and serve hot. To serve cold, dribble a little virgin olive oil over the dish before it goes on the table.

COOK'S TIP
Be sure to heat the oil before adding the aubergine slices and do not be tempted to add more oil once the aubergines are cooking. They will absorb cold oil, resulting in a greasy dish.

1 Slice the aubergine into 1cm/½in rounds. Place them in a large colander and sprinkle with 5–10ml/1–2 tsp salt. Leave to drain for 30 minutes.

2 Rinse the aubergine slices well, then press between several layers of kitchen paper to remove any excess liquid.

MENESTRA

THIS VEGETABLE DISH, WHICH CONTAINS AN ASSORTMENT OF YOUNG, NEW VEGETABLES, IS EATEN ALL ALONG THE NORTHERN COAST OF SPAIN TO CELEBRATE THE ARRIVAL OF SPRING. CHOOSE BY EYE, KEEPING THE QUANTITIES IN PROPORTION, AND PAYING CAREFUL ATTENTION TO THE COOKING TIME EACH VEGETABLE REQUIRES TO STAY JUST CRISP.

SERVES SIX

INGREDIENTS
   15ml/1 tbsp olive oil
   115g/4oz streaky (fatty) bacon
     lardons or diced pancetta
   1 onion, chopped
   3 garlic cloves, finely chopped
   90ml/6 tbsp chopped fresh parsley
   175ml/6fl oz/¾ cup dry white wine
   150g/5oz green beans
   200g/7oz bunched young carrots
   6 small new best potatoes, scrubbed
   300ml/10fl oz/1¼ cups
     chicken stock
   1 corn cob, kernels removed
     (optional)
   200g/7oz/2 cups peas
   50g/2oz mangetout (snow peas)
   salt and ground black pepper
   2 hard-boiled eggs, chopped,
     to garnish

VARIATION
Change the vegetables at will – the stalk end of asparagus, for example, is excellent. But don't vary the amount of liquid used in the casserole, or the sauce will become watery.

1 Heat the oil in a small flameproof casserole and fry the bacon or pancetta over a gentle heat for about 5 minutes, or until it crisps. Remove with a slotted spoon and reserve. Add the onion to the casserole and cook in the bacon fat until softened, adding the garlic towards the end.

2 Remove the cooked onion to a food processor, add 30ml/2 tbsp of the chopped parsley and purée with a little of the white wine.

3 Meanwhile prepare all the vegetables. Cut the beans into short lengths, and the carrots to the same size.

4 Bring a pan of salted water to the boil and add the potatoes. Cook for about 10 minutes. Add the carrots to the pan of potatoes, and cook for a further 5 minutes.

5 Meanwhile, return the bacon to the casserole and add the stock. Put in the beans, sweetcorn and peas and lay the mangetout over the top. Half cover the casserole and leave to simmer for 5–10 minutes, until the vegetables are just cooked.

6 Drain the potatoes and carrots and add them to the casserole.

7 Add the rest of the wine and the onion purée to the casserole, warming the liquid and turning the vegetables gently with a wooden spoon. Check the seasoning, adding more if necessary, and serve with the juices. Garnish with chopped egg and the remaining parsley.

VARIATION
This dish can also be made with tender meats such as lamb and veal with various combinations of new vegetables. Good combinations include lamb with artichokes and sherry, and veal with carrots and peas. Chop the meat and fry before adding to the casserole with the vegetables for further cooking.

PISTO MANCHEGO

A RICH-FLAVOURED AND SIMPLE SUMMER VEGETABLE DISH, FROM THE POOREST AND HOTTEST PART OF SPAIN, LA MANCHA. IT MAY BE EATEN HOT, ALONE OR WITH SUCH THINGS AS FRIED HAM AND EGGS. IT ALSO MAKES A SUBSTANTIAL SALAD, OFTEN WITH CANNED TUNA, OR HARD-BOILED EGGS.

SERVES FOUR

INGREDIENTS
  45–60ml/3–4 tbsp olive oil
  2 Spanish onions, thinly sliced
  3 garlic cloves, finely chopped
  3 large green (bell) peppers,
    seeded and chopped
  3 large courgettes (zucchini),
    thinly sliced
  5 large ripe tomatoes or 800g/
    1¾ lb canned tomatoes,
    with juice
  60ml/4 tbsp chopped fresh parsley
  2 hard-boiled eggs (optional)
  30–45ml/2–3 tbsp virgin olive oil
    (if serving cold)
  salt and ground black pepper

1 Heat the oil in a large heavy pan or flameproof casserole and cook the onions and garlic gently, until soft.

2 Add the peppers, courgettes and tomatoes. Season and cook gently for 20 minutes until the flavours blend.

3 Stir in 30ml/2 tbsp parsley and serve hot, if wished, topped with chopped hard-boiled egg, if using, and more parsley. To serve cold, check the seasoning, adding more if needed, and sprinkle with a little virgin olive oil before adding the garnish.

ESCALIVADA

THE CATALAN NAME OF THIS CELEBRATED DISH MEANS "BAKED OVER EMBERS" AND, LIKE MANY OTHER BARBECUE DISHES, IT TRANSFERS VERY SUCCESSFULLY TO THE OVEN. COOKING THE VEGETABLES IN THIS WAY BRINGS OUT THEIR FLAVOUR MAGNIFICENTLY.

SERVES FOUR

INGREDIENTS

2–3 courgettes (zucchini)
1 large fennel bulb
1 Spanish onion
2 large red (bell) peppers
450g/1lb butternut squash
6 whole garlic cloves, unpeeled
75ml/5 tbsp olive oil
juice of ½ lemon
pinch of cumin seeds, crushed
4 sprigs fresh thyme
4 medium tomatoes
salt and ground black pepper

1 Preheat the oven to 220°C/425°F/ Gas 7. Cut the courgettes lengthways into four pieces. Cut the fennel into similar-sized wedges. Slice the onion lengthways into chunks. Halve and seed the peppers, and slice thickly lengthways. Cut the squash into thick chunks. Smash the garlic cloves with the flat of a knife, but leave the skins on.

2 Choose a roasting pan into which all the vegetables will fit in one layer. Put in all the vegetables except the tomatoes. Mix together the oil and lemon juice. Pour over the vegetables and toss them. Sprinkle with the cumin seeds, salt and pepper and tuck in the thyme sprigs. Roast for 20 minutes.

3 Gently stir the vegetables in the oil and add the tomatoes. Cook for a further 15 minutes, or until the vegetables are tender and slightly charred around the edges.

VARIATIONS
• This is a very easy, pretty dish and you can vary the choice of vegetables according to what is in the market. Baby vegetables are excellent roasted. Tiny fennel, leeks and squash appear seasonally in supermarkets. Judge the roasting time by their volume.
• Aubergines (eggplant) are frequently included in this mixture, and their flavour is delicious, but they turn a slightly unappetizing grey colour when cooked and served plain.

BROAD BEANS WITH BACON

THIS DISH IS PARTICULARLY ASSOCIATED WITH RONDA, IN SOUTHERN SPAIN, THE HOME OF BULL FIGHTING, WHERE BROAD BEANS ARE FED TO FIGHTING BULLS TO BUILD THEM UP. IT IS ALSO FOUND ELSEWHERE IN SPAIN WHERE IT IS KNOWN AS HABAS ESPAÑOLAS. IF YOU HAVE TIME, REMOVE THE DULL SKINS FROM THE BROAD BEANS TO REVEAL THE BRIGHT GREEN BEANS BENEATH.

SERVES FOUR

INGREDIENTS
    30ml/2 tbsp olive oil
    1 small onion, finely chopped
    1 garlic clove, finely chopped
    50g/2oz rindless smoked streaky
      (fatty) bacon, roughly chopped
    225g/8oz broad (fava) beans, thawed
      if frozen
    5ml/1 tsp paprika
    15ml/1 tbsp sweet sherry
    salt and ground black pepper

VARIATION
For a vegetarian version of this dish use
sun-dried tomatoes in oil instead of bacon.

1 Heat the olive oil in a large frying
pan or sauté pan. Add the chopped
onion, garlic and bacon and fry over a
high heat for about 5 minutes, stirring
frequently, until the onion is softened
and the bacon browned.

2 Add the beans and paprika to the
pan and stir-fry for 1 minute. Add the
sherry, lower the heat, cover and cook
for 5–10 minutes until the beans are
tender. Season with salt and pepper
to taste and serve hot or warm.

LENTILS WITH MUSHROOMS AND ANIS

THE GREAT PLAINS OF CASTILE PRODUCE LENTILS FOR THE WHOLE OF EUROPE. LOCALLY THEY ARE WEEKLY FARE. IN THIS RECIPE, LENTEJAS CON CHAMPIÑONES, THEY ARE FLAVOURED WITH ANOTHER PRODUCT OF THE REGION, ANIS SPIRIT, PLUS A GREAT DEAL OF PARSLEY. SERVE THIS DISH ON ITS OWN, OR PARTNERED WITH GRILLED PORK RIBS OR SLICES OF PORK BELLY.

SERVES FOUR

INGREDIENTS
    30ml/2 tbsp olive oil
    1 large onion, sliced
    2 garlic cloves, finely chopped
    250g/9oz/3 cups brown cap (cremini)
      mushrooms, sliced
    150g/5oz/generous ½ cup brown
      or green lentils, soaked overnight
    4 tomatoes, cut in eighths
    1 bay leaf
    25g/1oz/½ cup chopped fresh parsley
    30ml/2 tbsp anis spirit or anisette
    salt, paprika and black pepper

COOK'S TIP
If you forget to soak the lentils, add at least 30 minutes to the cooking time.

1 Heat the oil in a flameproof casserole. Add the onion and fry gently, with the garlic, until softened but not browned.

2 Add the sliced mushrooms and stir to combine with the onion and garlic. Continue cooking, stirring gently, for a couple of minutes.

3 Add the lentils, tomatoes and bay leaf with 175ml/6fl oz/¾ cup water. Simmer gently, covered, for 30–40 minutes until the lentils are soft, and the liquid has almost disappeared.

4 Stir in the parsley and anis. Season with salt, paprika and black pepper.

RICE AND PASTA

Paella – that glorious combination of saffron rice, with shellfish, chicken or rabbit – is probably the dish most commonly associated with Spain. But there are many more classic festival and family dishes that combine rice with vegetables and even bananas. Pasta is a 500-year-old tradition, and comes in the same versatile combinations as the rice.

RICE TORTITAS

Like miniature tortillas, these little rice pancakes are good served hot, either plain or with tomato sauce for dipping. They make an excellent scoop for any soft vegetable mixture or dip — a very Spanish way of eating.

SERVES FOUR

INGREDIENTS
   30ml/2 tbsp olive oil
   115g/4oz/1 cup cooked long grain
     white rice
   1 potato, grated
   4 spring onions (scallions),
     thinly sliced
   1 garlic clove, finely chopped
   15ml/1 tbsp chopped fresh parsley
   3 large (US extra large)
     eggs, beaten
   2.5ml/½ tsp paprika
   salt and ground black pepper

COOK'S TIP
These *tortitas* can be used as a base, for example for cooked chicken livers, instead of the usual sliced bread.

1 Heat half the olive oil in a large frying pan and stir-fry the rice, with the potato, spring onions and garlic, over a high heat for 3 minutes until golden.

2 Tip the rice and vegetable mixture into a bowl and stir in the parsley and eggs, with the paprika and plenty of salt and pepper. Mix well.

3 Heat the remaining oil in the frying pan and drop in large spoonfuls of the rice mixture, leaving room for spreading. Cook the *tortitas* for 1–2 minutes on each side.

4 Drain the *tortitas* on kitchen paper and keep hot while cooking the remaining mixture. Serve hot.

ARTICHOKE RICE CAKES WITH MANCHEGO

THESE UNUSUAL LITTLE CROQUETAS CONTAIN ARTICHOKE IN THE RICE MIXTURE, AND THEY BREAK OPEN TO REVEAL A MELTING CHEESE CENTRE. MANCHEGO IS MADE FROM SHEEP'S MILK AND HAS A TART FLAVOUR THAT GOES WONDERFULLY WITH THE DELICATE TASTE OF THE RICE CAKES.

SERVES SIX

INGREDIENTS
   1 large globe artichoke
   50g/2oz/¼ cup butter
   1 small onion, finely chopped
   1 garlic clove, finely chopped
   115g/4oz/⅔ cup paella rice
   450ml/¾ pint/scant 2 cups hot
     chicken stock
   50g/2oz/⅔ cup grated fresh
     Parmesan cheese
   150g/5oz Manchego cheese, very
     finely diced
   45–60ml/3–4 tbsp fine corn meal
   olive oil, for frying
   salt and ground black pepper
   fresh flat leaf parsley, to garnish

1 Remove the stalks, leaves and choke to leave just the heart of the artichoke; chop the heart finely.

2 Melt the butter in a pan and gently fry the chopped artichoke heart, onion and garlic for 5 minutes until softened. Stir in the rice and cook for about 1 minute.

3 Keeping the heat fairly high, gradually add the stock, stirring occasionally until all the liquid has been absorbed and the rice is cooked – this should take about 20 minutes. Season well, then stir in the Parmesan cheese. Transfer the mixture to a bowl. Leave to cool, then cover and chill for at least 2 hours.

4 Spoon about 15ml/1 tbsp of the mixture into the palm of one hand, flatten slightly, and place a few pieces of diced cheese in the centre. Shape the rice around the cheese to make a small ball. Flatten slightly, then roll in the corn meal, shaking off any excess. Repeat with the remaining mixture to make about 12 cakes.

5 Shallow fry the rice cakes in hot olive oil for 4–5 minutes until they are crisp and golden brown. Drain on kitchen paper and serve hot, garnished with flat leaf parsley.

COOK'S TIP
Manchego is a hard cheese very similar to Italian Parmesan.

SIMPLE RICE SALAD

IN THIS QUICK AND EASY SIDE DISH, RICE AND A SELECTION OF CHOPPED SALAD VEGETABLES ARE
SERVED IN A WELL-FLAVOURED DRESSING TO MAKE A PRETTY SALAD.

SERVES SIX

INGREDIENTS
   275g/10oz/1½ cups long grain rice
   1 bunch spring onions (scallions),
     finely sliced
   1 green (bell) pepper, seeded and
     finely diced
   1 yellow (bell) pepper, seeded and
     finely diced
   225g/8oz tomatoes, peeled, seeded
     and chopped
   30ml/2 tbsp chopped fresh flat leaf
     parsley or coriander (cilantro)
For the dressing
   75ml/5 tbsp mixed olive oil and extra
     virgin olive oil
   15ml/1 tbsp sherry vinegar
   5ml/1 tsp strong Dijon mustard
   salt and ground black pepper

1 Cook the rice in a large pan of lightly salted boiling water for 10–12 minutes, until tender but still *al dente*. Be careful not to overcook it.

2 Drain the rice well in a sieve (strainer), rinse thoroughly under cold running water and drain again. Leave the rice to cool completely.

3 Place the rice in a large serving bowl. Add the spring onions, peppers, tomatoes and parsley or coriander.

4 Make the dressing. Place all the ingredients in a screw-top jar, put the lid on and shake vigorously until well mixed. Stir the dressing into the rice and check the seasoning.

MOORS AND CHRISTIANS

THIS TRADITIONAL DISH IS MADE EVERY YEAR AT THE MOROS Y CRISTIANOS *FESTIVAL IN* VALENCIA, *WHICH COMMEMORATES AN ANCIENT VICTORY OF THE* CHRISTIANS *OVER THE* MOORS. *THIS IS AN ELEGANT MODERN VERSION OF THE RECIPE.*

SERVES SIX

INGREDIENTS
    400g/14oz/2 cups black beans,
        soaked overnight
    1 onion, quartered
    1 carrot, sliced
    1 celery stick, sliced
    1 garlic clove, finely chopped
    1 bay leaf
    5ml/1 tsp paprika
    45ml/3 tbsp olive oil
    juice of 1 orange
    300g/11oz/1½ cups long grain rice
    salt and cayenne pepper
For the garnish
    chopped fresh parsley
    thin wedges of orange
    sliced red onion

1 Put the beans in a large pan with the onion, carrot, celery, garlic and bay leaf and 1.75 litres/3 pints/7½ cups water. Bring to the boil and cook rapidly for 10 minutes, then reduce the heat and simmer for 1 hour, topping up the water if necessary. When the beans are almost tender, drain, discarding the vegetables. Return the beans to a clean pan.

2 Blend the paprika and oil with cayenne pepper to taste and stir into the beans with the orange juice. Top up with a little water, if necessary. Heat gently until barely simmering, then cover and cook for 10–15 minutes until the beans are completely tender. Remove from the heat and allow to stand in the liquid for 15 minutes. Season with salt to taste.

3 Meanwhile, cook the rice in boiling water until tender. Drain, then pack into a buttered bowl or individual moulds and allow to stand for 10 minutes.

4 Unmould the rice on to a serving plate and arrange the black beans around the edge. Garnish with parsley, orange wedges and red onion slices.

CUBAN-STYLE RICE

ARROZ A LA CUBANA, GARNISHED WITH FRIED EGGS AND BANANAS, IS POPULAR IN THE CANARY ISLANDS AND CATALONIA. IT MAKES AN EASY AND SUBSTANTIAL SUPPER DISH. BACON IS SOMETIMES ADDED TO THE TOMATO SAUCE, OR IS FRIED AND SERVED WITH THE EGGS.

SERVES FOUR

INGREDIENTS
    3 garlic cloves
    120ml/4fl oz/½ cup olive oil
    300g/11oz/1½ cups long
      grain rice
    15g/½oz/1 tbsp butter
    4 small bananas or 2 large bananas
    4 large (US extra large) eggs
    salt and paprika
For the tomato sauce
    30ml/2 tbsp olive oil
    1 onion, chopped
    2 garlic cloves, finely chopped
    800g/1lb 12oz can tomatoes
    4 thyme or oregano sprigs
    ground black pepper

1 Make the tomato sauce. Heat the oil in a pan, add the onion and garlic and fry gently, stirring, until soft. Stir in the tomatoes and thyme or oregano sprigs and simmer gently for 5 minutes. Add seasoning to taste. Remove the herb sprigs and keep the sauce warm.

2 Put 850ml/1 pint 8fl oz/3½ cups water in a pan with two whole garlic cloves and 15ml/1 tbsp oil. Bring to the boil, add the rice and cook for 18 minutes until it is done, and the liquid has been absorbed.

3 Heat a pan with 30ml/2 tbsp oil and gently fry one chopped garlic clove. Tip in the rice, stir, season well, then turn off the heat and cover the pan.

4 Heat the butter in a frying pan with 15ml/1 tbsp oil. Halve the bananas lengthways and fry briefly on both sides. Keep them warm.

5 Add 60ml/4 tbsp oil to the pan and fry the eggs over a medium-high heat, so that the edges turn golden. Season with salt and paprika. Serve the rice surrounded by tomato sauce and garnish with bananas and fried eggs.

ALICANTE CRUSTED RICE

PAELLA CON COSTRA IS AN UNUSUAL PAELLA WITH AN EGG CRUST THAT IS FINISHED IN THE OVEN. THE CRUST SEALS IN ALL THE AROMAS UNTIL IT IS BROKEN OPEN AT THE TABLE.

SERVES SIX

INGREDIENTS

  45ml/3 tbsp olive oil
  200g/7oz *butifarra*, fresh sausages
    or frying chorizo, sliced
  2 tomatoes, peeled, seeded
    and chopped
  175g/6oz lean cubed pork
  175g/6oz skinless, boneless chicken
    breast or rabbit, cut into chunks
  350g/12oz/1¾ cups paella rice
  900ml–1 litre/1½–1¾ pints/
    3¾–4 cups hot chicken stock
  pinch of saffron threads (0.2g)
  150g/5oz/⅔ cup cooked chickpeas
  6 large (US extra large) eggs
  salt and ground black pepper

1 Preheat the oven to 190°C/375°F/ Gas 5. Heat the oil in a flameproof casserole and fry the sausage until browned. Add the tomatoes and fry until reduced. Stir in the pork and chicken or rabbit pieces and cook for 2–3 minutes until the meat has browned lightly, stirring.

2 Add the rice to the pan, stir over the heat for about 1 minute, then pour in the hot stock. Add the saffron, season to taste, and stir well.

3 Bring to the boil, then lower the heat and add the chickpeas. Cover the casserole tightly with the lid and cook over a low heat for about 20 minutes or until the rice is tender.

4 Beat the eggs with a little water and a pinch of salt and pour over the rice. Place the casserole, uncovered, in the oven and cook for about 10 minutes, until the eggs have set and browned slightly on top. Serve the paella straight from the casserole.

PAELLA VALENCIANA

A WORLD FAMOUS MIXTURE OF THE FINEST SPANISH INGREDIENTS, VALENCIA'S PAELLA CONTAINS CHICKEN, SHELLFISH AND VEGETABLES IN SUCCULENT SAFFRON RICE. IT HAS BECOME A CELEBRATION DISH THROUGHOUT SPAIN, AND SPAIN'S BEST-KNOWN DISH ABROAD. TO DRINK, CHOOSE A RED VALDEPEÑAS, WHICH WILL GO WELL WITH THE ROBUST FLAVOURS OF THE PAELLA.

SERVES SIX TO EIGHT

INGREDIENTS

   90ml/6 tbsp white wine
   450g/1lb fresh mussels, scrubbed
   115g/4oz/scant 1 cup small
     shelled broad (fava) beans
   150g/5oz green beans, cut into
     short lengths
   90ml/6 tbsp olive oil
   6 small skinless, boneless
     chicken breast portions, cut
     into large pieces
   150g/5oz pork fillet, cubed
   6–8 large raw prawn (shrimp) tails,
     deveined, or 12 smaller raw prawns
   2 onions, chopped
   2–3 garlic cloves, finely chopped
   1 red (bell) pepper, seeded
     and sliced
   2 ripe tomatoes, peeled, seeded
     and chopped
   60ml/4 tbsp chopped fresh parsley
   900ml/1½ pints/3¾ cups
     chicken stock
   pinch of saffron threads (0.25g),
     soaked in 30ml/2 tbsp hot water
   350g/12oz/1¾ cups paella rice,
     washed and drained
   225g/8oz frying chorizo, sliced
   115g/4oz/1 cup peas
   6–8 stuffed green olives, sliced
   salt, paprika and black pepper

COOK'S TIP

Paella is a very easy dish to make with the right pan and, more importantly, the right heat. Traditionally it is cooked outdoors on a wide bed of hot charcoal. Indoors a big heat source such as a large hot plate is needed.

   Without this steady heat, the pan needs to be moved constantly, or the rice cooks in the centre, but not round the outside. Overcome this problem by cooking it in a hot oven.

1 Heat the wine and add the mussels, discarding any that do not close when tapped. Cover and steam until opened. Reserve the liquid and mussels separately, discarding any that do not open.

2 Briefly cook the broad beans and green beans in boiling water, then drain. Pop the broad beans out of their skins.

3 Heat 45ml/3 tbsp oil in a large paella pan or wide flameproof casserole. Season the chicken with salt and paprika, and put in, skin downwards. Fry, turning until browned on all sides. Reserve on a plate. Season the pork with salt and paprika. Add 15ml/1 tbsp oil and fry the seasoned pork until browned evenly. Reserve with the chicken. Fry the prawns briefly in the same pan, but reserve them separately.

4 Heat the remaining oil and fry the onions and garlic for 3–4 minutes until golden brown. Add the red pepper, cook for 2–3 minutes, then stir in the chopped tomatoes and parsley and cook until thick.

5 If cooking in the oven (see Cook's Tip) preheat to 190°C/375°F/Gas 5. Stir the chicken stock, the reserved mussel liquid and the saffron liquid into the vegetables. Season well with salt and pepper and bring the mixture to the boil. When the liquid is bubbling, throw in all the rice. Stir once, then add the chicken pieces, pork, shellfish, beans, chorizo and peas.

6 Transfer the pan to the oven and cook for 15–18 minutes until the rice is done. Alternatively, cook over medium-high heat for about 10 minutes. Then lower the heat and start to move the pan. A big pan needs to shift every 2–3 minutes, moving the edge of the pan round over the heat, then back to the centre. Cook until the rice is done – another 10–12 minutes.

7 Arrange the mussels and olives on top. Cover with a lid (or damp dishtowel) and leave to stand for 10 minutes, until all the liquid is absorbed. Serve straight from the pan.

COOK'S TIP

Spain exports saffron in little boxes labelled with the weight. A 0.3g packet contains 50–60 threads, enough to flavour three small dishes. A dish such as paella needs two-thirds – measured by eye. The amount of rice used in this recipe could take the whole 0.3g – and in Spain it probably would – so enjoy.

SEAFOOD PAELLA

THIS IS A GREAT DISH TO SERVE TO GUESTS ON A SPECIAL OCCASION. A SEAFOOD PAELLA ALWAYS LOOKS SPECTACULAR AND A BED OF SCENTED RICE IS THE PERFECT WAY TO DISPLAY A SELECTION OF MARISCOS (SEAFOOD). THIS PARTICULAR PAELLA CONTAINS A MAGNIFICENT COMBINATION OF SQUID, PRAWNS, MUSSELS AND CLAMS AS WELL AS SPICY CHORIZO AND SUCCULENT VEGETABLES.

SERVES FOUR

INGREDIENTS
  45ml/3 tbsp olive oil
  1 Spanish onion, chopped
  2 large garlic cloves, chopped
  150g/5oz frying chorizo, sliced
  300g/11oz small squid, cleaned
  1 red (bell) pepper, cut into strips
  4 tomatoes, peeled, seeded and
    diced or 200g/7oz can tomatoes
  500ml/17fl oz/2¼ cups chicken
    stock, plus a little extra
  105ml/7 tbsp dry white wine
  200g/7oz/1 cup paella rice
  pinch of saffron threads (0.2g),
    crumbled
  150g/5oz/generous 1 cup peas
  12 large cooked prawns (shrimp),
    in the shell or 8 peeled scampi
    (extra large shrimp)
  450g/1lb fresh mussels, scrubbed
  450g/1lb clams, scrubbed
  4 cooked king prawns (jumbo shrimp)
    or scampi, in the shells
  salt and ground black pepper
  chopped fresh parsley and lemon
    wedges, to garnish

1 Heat the olive oil in a paella pan or large frying pan, add the onion and garlic and fry until translucent. Add the chorizo and fry until lightly golden.

2 If the squid are very small, leave them whole, otherwise cut the bodies into rings and the tentacles into pieces. Add the squid to the pan and sauté over a high heat for 2 minutes.

3 Stir in the pepper and tomatoes and simmer gently for 5 minutes, until the pepper is tender. Pour in the stock and wine, stir well and bring to the boil. Stir in the rice and saffron and season well. Spread the contents evenly over the base of the pan. Bring the liquid back to the boil, then lower the heat and simmer for about 10 minutes.

4 Gently stir the peas, prawns or scampi, mussels and clams into the rice, then cook for a further 15–20 minutes, until the rice is tender and all the mussels and clams have opened. (Discard any that remain closed.) If the paella seems dry, stir in a little more hot stock.

5 Remove the pan from the heat and arrange the king prawns or scampi on top. Cover and leave to stand for 5 minutes. Sprinkle the paella with chopped parsley and serve from the pan, accompanied by lemon wedges.

VEGETABLE RICE POT

IN THIS ARROZ DE VERDURAS, FRESH SEASONAL VEGETABLES ARE COOKED IN SLIGHTLY SPICED RICE. ALWAYS TASTE STOCK BEFORE ADDING IT TO RICE: THIS IS YOUR CHANCE TO REDUCE AND CONCENTRATE IT, OR TO ADD WINE, A BIT OF A STOCK CUBE, OR EVEN SOY SAUCE FOR EXTRA FLAVOUR. IF THE STOCK LACKS TASTE, SO WILL THE FINAL DISH.

SERVES FOUR

INGREDIENTS

1 large aubergine (eggplant)
45ml/3 tbsp olive oil
2 onions, quartered and sliced
2 garlic cloves, finely chopped
1 red (bell) pepper, halved, seeded and sliced
1 yellow (bell) pepper, halved, seeded and sliced
200g/7oz fine green beans, halved
115g/4oz/1½ cups brown cap (cremini) mushrooms, halved
300g/11oz/1½ cups paella rice, washed and drained
1 dried chilli, seeded and crumbled
1 litre/1¾ pints/4 cups chicken stock
115g/4oz/1 cup peas
60ml/4 tbsp chopped fresh parsley
salt and ground black pepper
fresh parsley or coriander (cilantro) leaves, to garnish

1 Halve the aubergine lengthways, then cut it into slices. Spread them out in a large colander or on a draining board, sprinkle with salt and leave for about 30 minutes to drain, then rinse under cold running water and pat dry with kitchen paper.

2 Heat 30ml/2 tbsp olive oil in a wide flameproof casserole or sauté pan over a high heat. Add the aubergine slices and sauté until slightly golden, stirring occasionally, then transfer to kitchen paper to drain.

3 Add the remaining oil to the pan and cook the onion and garlic until soft. Add the peppers, green beans and mushrooms and cook briefly.

4 Add the drained rice and stir for 1–2 minutes, then add the aubergine and stir. Add the chilli and seasoning. Taste the stock and pour in. Add the peas and parsley and mix together.

5 Bring to boiling point, cover and cook over a low heat, for 20–25 minutes, checking the liquid level towards the end (the rice should absorb the liquid, but not burn). When the rice is tender, turn off the heat, cover the pan and leave to stand for 10 minutes for the remaining liquid to be absorbed. Garnish with parsley or coriander and serve.

VARIATIONS

• Almost any roughly chopped or sliced vegetables can be used in this dish. Broccoli, carrots, cauliflower, courgettes (zucchini) and okra are all suitable – or try using frozen corn in place of all or some of the peas.
• To make a tomato-flavoured rice, use a 400g/14oz can chopped tomatoes in place of 350ml/12fl oz/1½ cups of the chicken stock.

CALDERETE OF RICE WITH ALLIOLI

COOKING RICE IN FISH STOCK GIVES IT SUCH A SPLENDID FLAVOUR THAT IT IS OFTEN EATEN ON ITS OWN — ARROZ ABANDA — SERVED IN A LITTLE CAULDRON AND ACCOMPANIED BY ALLIOLI. THE FISH THEN FOLLOWS AS A SEPARATE COURSE. IF YOU PREFER, THE FISH CAN BE RETURNED TO THE CASSEROLE WHILE THE DISH IS STILL LIQUID, AND THE FISH AND RICE EATEN WITH THE SAUCE.

SERVES SIX

INGREDIENTS
1.6kg/3½lb mixed fish on the
  bone, such as snapper, bream,
  grey or red mullet, or bass
45ml/3 tbsp olive oil
6 garlic cloves, smashed
1 *ñora* chilli or 1 hot dried chilli,
  seeded and chopped
250g/9oz ripe tomatoes, peeled,
  seeded and chopped
pinch of saffron threads (0.25g)
30ml/2 tbsp dry Martini or
  white wine
1 tomato, finely diced
30ml/2 tbsp chopped
  fresh parsley
400g/14oz/2 cups paella
  rice, washed
115g/4oz tiny unshelled shrimps
salt and ground black pepper
For the stock
  1 onion, chopped
  2 garlic cloves, chopped
  1 celery stick, chopped
  1 carrot, chopped
  1 litre/1¾ pints/4 cups water
For the allioli
  4 garlic cloves, finely chopped
  2.5ml/½ tsp salt
  5ml/1 tsp lemon juice
  2 egg yolks
  250ml/8fl oz/1 cup olive oil

1 Remove the heads from the fish. Working from the head end, cut the skin along the top of the back and work the fillets off the bone. Trim as needed, put the fillets on a plate, salt them lightly, cover and place in the refrigerator until required.

2 Make the fish stock. Put the bones, heads, tails and any other remaining bits into a large pan with the onion, garlic, celery, carrot and water. Bring to the boil, then reduce the heat, cover with a lid and simmer gently for about 30 minutes.

3 Make the allioli. Put the chopped garlic in a large mortar (or small blender) with the salt and lemon juice and reduce to a purée. Add the egg yolks and mix thoroughly. Gradually work in the oil (drop by drop at first if using a mortar) to make a thick, mayonnaise-like sauce.

4 Put 15ml/1 tbsp of the olive oil in a small pan and add the whole smashed garlic cloves and dried chilli pieces. Fry for a few minutes until the garlic looks roasted. Add the chopped tomato halfway through, crumble in the saffron and cook to form a sauce. Pour the sauce into a small blender and purée until smooth.

5 Heat the remaining 30ml/2 tbsp oil in a large pan or a wide flameproof casserole and fry the fish pieces until they begin to stiffen. Strain the fish stock into a jug (pitcher), then add 900ml/1½ pints/3¾ cups stock and the tomato sauce to the fish. Cook the fish gently for a further 3–4 minutes, until slightly underdone.

6 Remove the fish pieces from the pan with a slotted spoon to a serving dish. Season lightly, sprinkle with the Martini or wine, diced tomato and parsley. Cover with foil and keep warm.

7 Add the rice to the stock, stir, season and bring to a simmer. Cook for 18–20 minutes. Before all the liquid is absorbed, stir in the shrimps. When the rice is tender, cover and turn off the heat. Stand until all the liquid is absorbed: about 5 minutes. Serve from the pan, accompanied by the allioli.

8 When the rice course is almost finished, uncover the fish. Stir the fish juices into the remains of the allioli, then pour over the fish. Eat on the same plates as the rice.

FIDEOS CON ALMEJAS

PASTA THE EAST COAST WAY, FIDEOS ARE LENGTHS OF SPAGHETTI, SHORTER THAN A FINGER. THIS SENSATIONAL DISH IS RATHER LIKE PAELLA MADE WITH PASTA — JUST AS NICE, AND A GREAT DEAL EASIER. IT IS POPULAR ALONG THE MEDITERRANEAN COAST — THE LEVANTE AND THE SOUTH AROUND MALAGA. THE MILKY FLESH OF CLAMS CONTRASTS WONDERFULLY WITH THE FIRMER PASTA AND FENNEL.

SERVES FOUR TO SIX

INGREDIENTS
  30ml/2 tbsp olive oil
  1 large Spanish onion, chopped
  1 garlic clove, finely chopped
  2 large ripe tomatoes
  750ml/1¼ pint/3 cups fish stock
  1kg/2¼lb clams, cleaned
  120ml/4fl oz/½ cup anis spirit, such
    as Ricard or Pernod
  120ml/4fl oz/½ cup dry white wine,
    such as Torres Viña Sol
  juice of ¼ lemon
  300g/11oz spaghetti, broken into
    5cm/2in lengths
  1 fennel bulb, sliced in thin strips
  30ml/2 tbsp chopped fresh parsley
  salt and ground pepper
  fennel fronds or fresh dill, to garnish

1 Heat the oil in a casserole big enough to contain all the ingredients. Fry the onion gently until soft. Add the garlic.

2 Put the tomatoes in a bowl, pour over boiling water and leave for 10 minutes. Peel the tomatoes on a plate and discard the seeds. Chop the flesh, add to the casserole and strain in the tomato juices into the pan. Cook until reduced to a pulp, then add 250ml/8fl oz/1 cup of the stock.

3 Discard any open or cracked clams. Add the rest to the pan in three batches. As they open, remove most from the shells and transfer to a plate. Discard any clams that remain shut.

4 Add the anis spirit and white wine to the sauce, plus the remaining fish stock and lemon juice, to taste. Add the pasta and sliced fennel. Season and simmer, partially covered, for 10 minutes. Stir every now and then to separate the strands, and to make sure the pasta is not sticking.

5 When the pasta is cooked, stir in the parsley and check the seasoning. Tip the clams across the top and cover tightly. Leave to stand for 10 minutes, so the clams warm through and all the liquid is absorbed. Serve in bowls, sprinkled with the fennel fronds or dill.

SAN ESTEBAN CANELONES

CATALANS ARE FOND OF PASTA, AND CANELONES ARE TRADITIONAL ON SAN ESTEBAN, THE DAY AFTER CHRISTMAS DAY, AND ARE OFTEN MADE IN LARGE QUANTITIES. TRY TO KEEP ALL THE CHOPPED STUFFING INGREDIENTS THE SAME SIZE — SMALL DICE. SPANISH STORES SELL SQUARES OF PASTA FOR COOKING THEN ROLLING, BUT READY PREPARED CANNELLONI TUBES HAVE BEEN USED HERE.

SERVES FOUR TO EIGHT

INGREDIENTS
   60ml/4 tbsp olive oil
   1 onion, finely chopped
   1 carrot, finely chopped
   2 garlic cloves, finely chopped
   2 ripe tomatoes, peeled and
     finely chopped
   2.5ml/½ tsp dried thyme
   150g/5oz raw chicken livers
     or cooked stuffing
   150g/5oz raw pork or cooked ham,
     gammon or sausage
   250g/9oz raw or cooked chicken
   25g/1oz/2 tbsp butter
   5ml/1 tsp fresh thyme
   30ml/2 tbsp brandy
   90ml/6 tbsp crème fraîche or
     double (heavy) cream
   16 no pre-cook cannelloni tubes
   75g/3oz/1 cup grated fresh
     Parmesan cheese
   salt and ground black pepper
   green salad, to serve
For the white sauce
   50g/2oz/¼ cup butter
   50g/2oz/½ cup plain
     (all-purpose) flour
   900ml/1½ pints/3¾ cups milk
   fresh nutmeg, to taste

1 Heat the oil in a large frying pan, add the onion, carrot, garlic and tomatoes and cook over a low heat, stirring, for about 10 minutes or until very soft. Meanwhile, chop all the meats to the same size, keeping the fresh and cooked meat apart.

2 Add the butter, then the raw meat, to the centre of the frying pan and cook until coloured. Then add the remaining meats and sprinkle first with thyme, then with the brandy. Stir, then warm through and reduce the liquid.

3 Pour in the crème fraîche or cream, season to taste and leave to simmer for about 10 minutes. Allow to cool briefly.

4 Preheat the oven to 190°C/375°F/ Gas 5. Make the white sauce. Melt the butter in a small pan, add the flour and cook, stirring, for 1–2 minutes. Gradually stir in the milk, a little at a time. Bring to simmering point, stirring until the sauce is smooth. Grate in nutmeg to taste, then season with plenty of salt and black pepper.

5 Spoon a little of the white sauce into a baking dish. Fill the cannelloni tubes with the meat mixture and arrange in a single layer in the dish. Pour the remaining white sauce over them, then sprinkle with the Parmesan cheese. Bake for 35–40 minutes, or until the pasta is tender. Leave for 10 minutes before serving with green salad.

ANDRAJOS

This is a rich dish of hare, wine and mushrooms, flavoured with herbs and pine nuts. The name means "rags and tatters"; it was a shepherds' dish and the shepherd would have made his own simple flour and water pasta, cut into squares. Dried pasta squares are still sold in Spain to make cannelloni. This recipe uses bought lasagne, which needs to be broken up. The sauce permeates the pasta and transforms the chicken.

SERVES SIX

INGREDIENTS

800g/1¾lb hare meat and bone
(the front legs and rib end)
200ml/7fl oz/scant 1 cup red wine
120–150ml/4–5fl oz/½–⅔ cup
olive oil
150g/5oz smoked bacon lardons,
or diced pancetta
2 onions, chopped
2 fat garlic cloves, finely chopped
8 baby onions, peeled
4 carrots, diced
4 chicken thighs, halved along the
bone and seasoned
seasoned plain (all-purpose) flour,
for dusting
350g/12oz small open cap
mushrooms
600ml/1 pint/2½ cups stock
5ml/1 tsp dried thyme
1 bay leaf
250g/9oz dried lasagne sheets
90ml/6 tbsp chopped parsley
30ml/2 tbsp pine nuts
salt and ground black pepper

1 Starting at least two days ahead, cut the hare into portions and put in a bowl. Pour over the red wine and 15ml/ 1 tbsp of the oil and leave to marinate in the refrigerator for at least 24 hours.

COOK'S TIP
This dish uses the front part of the hare, while the back legs and saddle are best kept for a grander dish.

2 Heat 30ml/2 tbsp olive oil in a flameproof casserole, add the bacon or pancetta, chopped onion and garlic and fry until the onion is translucent. Halfway through add the whole baby onions and diced carrots, and continue cooking, stirring occasionally.

3 Heat 45ml/3 tbsp oil in a large frying pan and fry the seasoned chicken pieces on both sides until golden brown. Transfer to the casserole.

4 Remove the hare from the red wine marinade, reserving the liquid. Blot the meat well on kitchen paper and dredge with the seasoned flour until well coated. Add more oil to the frying pan, if necessary, and fry the meat on all sides until browned.

5 Meanwhile, reserve eight of the smallest open cap mushrooms. Quarter the remaining mushrooms and add to the casserole. Continue cooking the hare in the frying pan, stirring every now and then, until browned.

6 When the hare is ready, arrange the pieces in the casserole. Pour the reserved marinade into the frying pan to deglaze it, then pour the juices into the casserole. Add the stock, dried thyme and bay leaf and season with salt and pepper. Cook over a low heat for 1½ hours, until the meat is tender. Leave to cool completely.

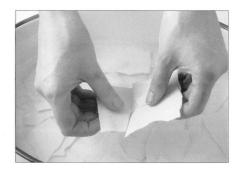

7 When ready to serve, bring plenty of water to the boil in a large roasting pan with 5ml/1 tsp salt and 15ml/1 tbsp oil. Break up the lasagne sheets and spread out the pieces in the pan. Cook for 7–8 minutes until soft, moving the pieces around to prevent them from sticking.

8 Remove all the meat from the bones and return to the casserole with 60ml/ 4 tbsp of the parsley. Bring to a simmer. Stir the drained pasta into the sauce. Heat 15ml/1 tbsp oil in a small pan and fry the reserved mushrooms, then arrange them on top. Sprinkle with the remaining parsley and the pine nuts, and serve.

FISH AND SHELLFISH

Spain is bordered by two different oceans and has the best
fishing in the world. Seafood is, undoubtedly, one of the glories
of Spanish cooking. There is an array of colourful salads and
delightful appetizers, while simple combinations, with lemon or
tomato or potatoes, and hearty stews such as
Zarzuela make delicious main courses.

SEAFOOD SALAD

ENSALADA DE MARISCOS IS A VERY PRETTY ARRANGEMENT OF FRESH MUSSELS, PRAWNS AND SQUID RINGS SERVED ON A COLOURFUL BED OF SALAD VEGETABLES. IN SPAIN, CANNED ALBACORE TUNA IS ALSO OFTEN INCLUDED IN THIS TYPE OF SIMPLE SALAD.

2 Discard any open mussels that do not close when tapped. Cover the base of a large pan with water, add the mussels, then cover and steam for a few minutes until they open. Discard any that remain shut.

3 Using a swivel-style vegetable peeler, cut the carrot into wafer-thin ribbons. Tear the lettuce into pieces and arrange on a serving plate. Scatter the carrot ribbons on top, then sprinkle over the diced cucumber.

4 Arrange the mussels, prawns and squid rings over the salad and scatter the capers over the top.

5 Make the dressing. Put all the ingredients in a small bowl and whisk well to combine. Drizzle over the salad. Serve at room temperature.

SERVES SIX

INGREDIENTS
    115g/4oz prepared squid rings
    12 fresh mussels, scrubbed and
      beards removed
    1 large carrot
    6 crisp lettuce leaves
    10cm/4in piece cucumber,
      finely diced
    115g/4oz cooked, peeled
      prawns (shrimp)
    15ml/1 tbsp drained pickled capers
For the dressing
    30ml/2 tbsp freshly squeezed
      lemon juice
    45ml/3 tbsp virgin olive oil
    15ml/1 tbsp chopped fresh parsley
    salt and ground black pepper

1 Put the squid rings into a metal sieve or vegetable steamer. Place the sieve or steamer over a pan of simmering water, cover with a lid and steam the squid for 2–3 minutes until it just turns white. Cool under cold running water to prevent further cooking and drain thoroughly on kitchen paper.

POTATO, MUSSEL AND WATERCRESS SALAD

THE MUSSELS FOUND ON THE GALICIAN COAST ARE THE BEST IN THE WORLD. THE GALICIANS ARE ALSO VERY PROUD OF THEIR POTATOES AND THEIR WATERCRESS. IN ENSALADA DE MEJILLONES, PATATAS Y BERROS A CREAMY, WELL-FLAVOURED DRESSING ENHANCES ALL THESE INGREDIENTS.

SERVES FOUR

INGREDIENTS
675g/1½lb salad potatoes
1kg/2¼lb mussels, scrubbed
 and beards removed
200ml/7fl oz/scant 1 cup dry
 white wine
15g/½oz fresh flat leaf
 parsley, chopped
1 bunch of watercress
 or rocket (arugula)
salt and ground black pepper
chopped fresh chives or
 spring onion (scallion) tops,
 to garnish
For the dressing
105ml/7 tbsp olive oil
15–30ml/1–2 tbsp white wine vinegar
5ml/1 tsp strong Dijon mustard
1 large shallot, very finely chopped
15ml/1 tbsp chopped fresh chives
45ml/3 tbsp double (heavy) cream
pinch of caster (superfine)
 sugar (optional)

1 Cook the potatoes in salted boiling water for 15–20 minutes, or until tender. Drain, cool, then peel. Slice the potatoes into a bowl and toss with 30ml/2 tbsp of the oil for the dressing.

2 Discard any open mussels. Bring the white wine to the boil in a large, heavy pan. Add the mussels, cover and boil vigorously, shaking the pan occasionally, for 3–4 minutes, until the mussels have opened. Discard any that do not open. Drain and shell the mussels, reserving the cooking liquid.

3 Boil the reserved mussel cooking liquid until reduced to about 45ml/ 3 tbsp. Strain this through a fine sieve over the potatoes and toss to mix.

4 Make the dressing. Whisk together the remaining oil, 15ml/1 tbsp of the vinegar, the mustard, shallot and chives.

5 Add the cream and whisk again to form a thick dressing. Adjust the seasoning, adding more vinegar and/ or a pinch of sugar to taste.

6 Toss the mussels with the potatoes, then gently mix in the dressing and chopped parsley. Arrange the watercress or rocket on a serving platter and top with the salad. Serve sprinkled with extra chives or a little spring onion.

COOK'S TIP
Potato salads such as this one should not be chilled if at all possible because chilling alters the texture of the potatoes. For the best flavour and texture, serve this salad just cool or at room temperature.

SKATE WITH BITTER SALAD LEAVES

THIS DISH IS POPULAR IN GALICIA, WHICH IS FAMOUS FOR BOTH ITS SKATE AND ITS WATERCRESS. SKATE HAS A DELICIOUS SWEET FLAVOUR, ENHANCED HERE BY ORANGE. IT CONTRASTS WELL WITH ANY BITTER LEAVES – BUY A BAG OF MIXED SALAD LEAVES FOR CONTRASTING TEXTURES AND FLAVOURS.

SERVES FOUR

INGREDIENTS
  800g/1¾lb skate wings
  15ml/1 tbsp white wine vinegar
  4 black peppercorns
  1 fresh thyme sprig
  175g/6oz bitter salad leaves,
    such as frisée, rocket (arugula),
    radicchio, escarole, lamb's lettuce
    (mâche) and watercress
  1 orange
  2 tomatoes, peeled, seeded
    and diced
For the dressing
  15ml/1 tbsp white wine vinegar
  45ml/3 tbsp extra virgin olive oil
  1 bunch spring onions (scallions),
    whites finely chopped
  salt, paprika and black pepper
  crusty bread, to serve

1 Put the skate wings into a large shallow pan, cover with cold water and add the vinegar, peppercorns and thyme. Bring to the boil, then poach gently for 8–10 minutes, until the flesh comes away easily from the bones.

2 Make the dressing. Whisk together the vinegar, oil and spring onions and season with salt, paprika and pepper.

3 Put the salad leaves in a large bowl, pour over the dressing and toss well. Remove the rind from the orange using a zester, then peel it, removing all the pith. Slice into thin rounds.

4 Flake the fish, discarding the bones, and add to the salad. Add a pinch of zest, the orange slices and tomatoes, toss gently and serve with bread.

SURTIDO DE PESCADO

THE SPANISH ENJOY AND MAKE THE MOST OF PRESERVED FISH. THIS IS A VERY PRETTY DISH, WHICH USES WHATEVER IS EASILY AVAILABLE, AND IT MAKES AN IDEAL LAST-MINUTE PARTY STARTER. IT IS ALSO EASY TO DOUBLE UP FOR A BUFFET. FOR THE BEST RESULTS TRY TO USE SPANISH CANNED FISH.

SERVES FOUR

INGREDIENTS

  6 eggs
  cos or romaine lettuce leaves
  75–90ml/5–6 tbsp mayonnaise
  90g/3½oz jar Avruga herring roe,
    Eurocaviar grey mullet roe or
    undyed (or black) lumpfish roe
  2 × 115g/4oz cans sardines
    in oil
  2 × 115g/4oz cans mackerel
    fillets in oil
  2 × 150g/5oz jars cockles (small
    clams) in brine, drained
  2 × 115g/4oz cans mussels
    or scallops in tomato sauce
  fresh flat leaf parsley or dill sprigs,
    to garnish

COOK'S TIP
Smoked salmon, kippers (smoked herrings) and rollmops (pickled herring fillets) can also be included on the platter. Try to maintain a balance between fish or shellfish pickled in brine or vinegar, with those in oil or sauce. Huge Spanish mussels *en escabeche* (spicy sauce) are now available in large supermarkets. Also look out for Spanish fish roes to top the eggs.

1 Put the eggs in a pan with enough water to cover and bring to the boil. Turn down the heat and simmer for 10 minutes. Drain immediately, then cover with cold water and set aside until completely cool. Peel the eggs and slice in half.

2 Arrange the lettuce leaves on a large serving platter, with the tips pointing outwards. (You may need to break off the bottom end of each leaf if the leaves are large).

3 Place a teaspoonful or so of mayonnaise on the flat side of each halved egg and top with a spoonful of fish caviar. Carefully arrange in the centre of the dish.

4 Arrange the sardines and mackerel fillets at four points on the plate. Spoon the pickled cockles into two of the gaps, opposite each other, and the mussels in sauce in the remaining gaps. Garnish with parsley sprigs or dill. Place in the refrigerator until needed.

SARDINES EN ESCABECHE

THE ARABS INVENTED MARINADES AS A MEANS OF PRESERVING POULTRY, MEAT AND GAME, AND ESCABECHE MEANS "ACID" IN ARABIC. IN SPAIN THIS METHOD WAS ENTHUSIASTICALLY ADOPTED AS A MEANS OF KEEPING FISH FRESH. THE FISH ARE ALWAYS FRIED FIRST AND THEN STORED IN VINEGAR.

3 Heat the olive oil in a frying pan and fry the sardines for 2–3 minutes on each side. With a metal spatula, remove the fish from the pan to a plate and allow to cool, then pack them in a single layer in a large shallow dish.

4 To make the marinade, add the olive oil to the oil remaining in the frying pan. Fry the onion and garlic gently for 5–10 minutes until soft and translucent, stirring occasionally. Add the bay leaves, cloves, chilli and paprika, with pepper to taste. Fry, stirring frequently, for another 1–2 minutes.

SERVES TWO TO FOUR

INGREDIENTS
 12–16 sardines, cleaned
 seasoned plain (all-purpose) flour,
  for dusting
 30ml/2 tbsp olive oil
 roasted red onion, green (bell) pepper
  and tomatoes, to garnish
For the marinade
 90ml/6 tbsp olive oil
 1 onion, sliced
 1 garlic clove, crushed
 3–4 bay leaves
 2 cloves
 1 dried red chilli, seeded
  and chopped
 5ml/1 tsp paprika
 120ml/4fl oz/½ cup wine
  or sherry vinegar
 120ml/4fl oz/½ cup white wine
 salt and ground black pepper

1 Using a sharp knife, cut the heads off the sardines and split each of them along the belly. Turn the fish over so that the backbone is uppermost. Press down along the backbone to loosen it, then carefully lift out the backbone and as many of the remaining little bones as possible.

2 Close the sardines up again and dust them with seasoned flour.

5 Stir in the vinegar, wine and a little salt. Allow to bubble up, then pour over the sardines. The marinade should cover the fish completely. When the fish is cool, cover and chill overnight or for up to three days. Serve the sardines and their marinade, garnished with the onion, pepper and tomatoes.

VARIATION
Other oily fish such as herrings or sprats (small whitebait) are very good prepared in this way. White fish can also be used.

FRIED WHITEBAIT <u>WITH</u> SHERRY SALSA

SMALL FRESHLY FRIED FISH ARE OFFERED IN EVERY TAPAS BAR IN SPAIN. BLACK-BACKED ANCHOVIES ARE THE BEST, BUT NEED TO BE COOKED WITHIN A DAY OF CATCHING. TINY CHANQUETES ARE ALSO GOOD, BUT ANY SMALL FISH, SUCH AS WHITEBAIT, ARE SUITABLE. SERVE THEM WITH LEMON WEDGES.

SERVES FOUR

INGREDIENTS
   225g/8oz whitebait
   30ml/2 tbsp seasoned plain
    (all-purpose) flour
   60ml/4 tbsp olive oil
   60ml/4 tbsp sunflower oil
For the salsa
   1 shallot, finely chopped
   2 garlic cloves, finely chopped
   4 ripe tomatoes, roughly chopped
   1 small red chilli, seeded and
    finely chopped
   30ml/2 tbsp olive oil
   60ml/4 tbsp sweet oloroso sherry
   30–45ml/2–3 tbsp chopped mixed
    fresh herbs, such as parsley or basil
   25g/1oz/½ cup stale white
    breadcrumbs
   salt and ground black pepper

1 To make the salsa, place the chopped shallot, garlic, tomatoes, chilli and olive oil in a pan. Cover with a lid and cook gently for about 10 minutes.

2 Pour the sherry into the pan and season with salt and pepper to taste. Stir in the herbs and breadcrumbs, then cover and keep the salsa hot until the whitebait are ready.

3 Preheat the oven to 150°C/300°F/ Gas 2. Wash the whitebait thoroughly, drain well and dry on kitchen paper, then dust in the seasoned flour.

4 Heat the oils together in a heavy frying pan and cook the fish in batches until crisp and golden. Drain on kitchen paper and keep warm until all the fish are cooked. Serve at once with the salsa.

SALT COD FRITTERS WITH ALLIOLI

BACALAO — SALT COD — IS ONE OF THE GREAT SPANISH DELIGHTS, ADDING FLAVOUR TO BLAND INGREDIENTS SUCH AS POTATOES. IF YOU ARE UNFAMILIAR WITH IT, THEN THIS IS A DELIGHTFUL WAY TO TRY IT OUT. BITESIZE FISH CAKES, DIPPED INTO RICH, CREAMY, GARLICKY ALLIOLI, ARE IRRESISTIBLE AS A TAPAS DISH OR APPETIZER.

SERVES SIX

INGREDIENTS
  450g/1lb salt cod
  500g/1¼lb floury potatoes
  300ml/½ pint/1¼ cups milk
  6 spring onions (scallions),
    finely chopped
  30ml/2 tbsp extra virgin olive oil
  30ml/2 tbsp chopped fresh parsley
  juice of ½ lemon
  2 eggs, beaten
  plain (all-purpose) flour, for dusting
  90g/3½oz/1¼ cups dried white
    breadcrumbs
  olive oil, for shallow frying
  lemon wedges and salad leaves,
    to serve
  salt and ground black pepper
For the allioli
  2 large garlic cloves, finely chopped
  2 egg yolks
  300ml/½ pint/1¼ cups olive oil
  juice of ½ lemon, to taste

1 Soak the salt cod in cold water for at least 24 hours, changing the water two or three times. The cod should swell as it rehydrates. Sample a tiny piece. It should not taste unpleasantly salty when fully rehydrated. Drain well and pat dry with kitchen paper.

2 Cook the potatoes, unpeeled, in a pan of lightly salted boiling water for about 20 minutes, until tender. Drain. As soon as they are cool enough to handle, peel the potatoes, then mash with a fork or use a potato masher.

3 Pour the milk into a pan, add half the spring onions and bring to a simmer. Add the soaked cod and poach very gently for 10–15 minutes, or until it flakes easily. Remove the cod and flake it with a fork into a bowl, discarding bones and skin.

4 Add 60ml/4 tbsp mashed potato to the cod and beat them together with a wooden spoon. Work in the olive oil, then gradually add the remaining mashed potato. Beat in the remaining spring onions and the parsley.

5 Season with lemon juice and pepper to taste – the mixture may also need a little salt but taste it before adding any. Add one egg to the mixture and beat in until thoroughly combined, then chill until firm.

6 Shape the chilled fish mixture into 12–18 balls, then gently flatten into small round cakes. Coat each one in flour, then dip in the remaining beaten egg and coat with dried breadcrumbs. Chill until ready to fry.

7 Meanwhile, make the allioli. Place the garlic and a good pinch of salt in a mortar and pound to a paste with a pestle. Using a small whisk or a wooden spoon, gradually work in the egg yolks.

8 Beat in about half the olive oil, a drop at a time. When the sauce is as thick as soft butter, beat in 5–10ml/1–2 tsp lemon juice. Continue adding oil until the allioli is very thick. Season to taste, adding more lemon juice if you wish.

9 Heat about 2cm/¾in oil in a large, heavy frying pan. Add the fritters and cook over a medium-high heat for about 4 minutes. Turn them over and cook for a further 4 minutes on the other side, until crisp and golden. Drain on kitchen paper, then serve with the allioli, lemon wedges and salad leaves.

COOK'S TIP
Try to find a thick, creamy white piece of salt cod, preferably cut from the middle of the fish rather than the tail and fin ends. Avoid thin, yellowish salt cod, as it will be too dry and salty.

BAKED TROUT <u>WITH</u> RICE, TOMATOES <u>AND</u> NUTS

TROUT IS VERY POPULAR IN SPAIN, PARTICULARLY IN THE NORTH, WHERE IT IS FISHED IN MANY RIVERS. HERE IS A MODERN RECIPE FOR TRUCHA RELLENA, BAKED IN FOIL WITH A RICE STUFFING IN WHICH SUN-DRIED TOMATOES HAVE BEEN USED IN PLACE OF THE MORE TRADITIONAL CHILLIES.

SERVES FOUR

INGREDIENTS

   2 fresh trout, about 500g/1¼lb each
   75g/3oz/¾ cup mixed unsalted
     almonds, pine nuts or hazelnuts
   25ml/1½ tbsp olive oil, plus extra
     for drizzling
   1 small onion, finely chopped
   10ml/2 tsp grated fresh root ginger
   175g/6oz/1½ cups cooked white
     long grain rice
   4 tomatoes, peeled and very
     finely chopped
   4 sun-dried tomatoes in oil, drained
     and chopped
   30ml/2 tbsp chopped fresh tarragon
   2 fresh tarragon sprigs
   salt and ground black pepper
   dressed green salad leaves,
     to serve

1 Preheat the oven to 190°C/375°F/ Gas 5. If the trout is unfilleted, use a sharp knife to fillet it. Remove any tiny bones remaining in the cavity using a pair of tweezers.

2 Spread out the nuts in a shallow tin (pan) and bake for 3–4 minutes until golden brown, shaking the tin occasionally. Chop the nuts roughly.

3 Heat the olive oil in a small frying pan and fry the onion for 3–4 minutes until soft and translucent. Stir in the grated ginger, cook for a further 1 minute, then spoon into a mixing bowl.

4 Stir the rice, chopped tomatoes, sun-dried tomatoes, toasted nuts and tarragon into the onion mixture. Season the stuffing well.

5 Place the trout on individual large pieces of oiled foil and spoon the stuffing into the cavities. Add a sprig of tarragon and a drizzle of olive oil or oil from the sun-dried tomatoes.

6 Fold the foil over to enclose each trout completely, and put the parcels in a large roasting pan. Bake for about 20 minutes or until the fish is just tender. Cut the fish into thick slices. Serve with the salad leaves.

COOK'S TIP
You will need about 75g/3oz/³⁄4 cup of uncooked rice to produce 175g/6oz/ 1¹⁄2 cups cooked rice.

TRUCHAS A LA NAVARRA

TRADITIONALLY, THE TROUT WOULD HAVE COME FROM MOUNTAIN STREAMS AND BEEN STUFFED AND WRAPPED IN LOCALLY CURED HAM. ONE OF THE BEAUTIES OF THIS METHOD IS THAT THE SKINS COME OFF IN ONE PIECE, LEAVING THE SUCCULENT, MOIST FLESH TO BE EATEN WITH THE CRISPED, SALT HAM.

SERVES FOUR

INGREDIENTS

 4 brown or rainbow trout, about
  250g/9oz each, cleaned
 16 thin slices Serrano ham, about
  200g/7oz
 50g/2oz/¼ cup melted butter, plus
  extra for greasing
 salt and ground black pepper
 buttered potatoes, to
  serve (optional)

1 Extend the belly cavity of each trout, cutting up one side of the backbone. Slip a knife behind the rib bones to loosen them (sometimes just flexing the fish makes them pop up). Snip these off from both sides with scissors, and season the fish well inside.

2 Preheat the grill (broiler) to high, with a shelf in the top position. Line a baking tray with foil and butter it.

3 Working with the fish on the foil, fold a piece of ham into each belly. Use smaller or broken bits of ham for this, and reserve the eight best slices.

4 Brush each trout with a little butter, seasoning the outside lightly with salt and pepper. Wrap two ham slices round each one, crossways, tucking the ends into the belly. Grill (broil) the trout for 4 minutes, then carefully turn them over with a metal spatula, rolling them across on the belly, so the ham doesn't come loose, and grill for a further 4 minutes.

5 Serve the trout very hot, with any spare butter spooned over the top. Diners should open the trout on their plates, and eat them from the inside, pushing the flesh off the skin.

GRILLED RED MULLET WITH BAY LEAVES

RED MULLET ARE CALLED SALMONETES — *LITTLE SALMON* — *IN* SPAIN *BECAUSE OF THEIR DELICATE, PALE PINK COLOUR. THEY ARE SIMPLE TO COOK ON A BARBECUE, WITH BAY LEAVES FOR FLAVOUR AND A DRIBBLE OF TANGY DRESSING INSTEAD OF A MARINADE.*

3 To make the dressing, heat the olive oil in a small pan and fry the chopped garlic with the dried chilli. Add the lemon juice and strain the dressing into a small jug (pitcher). Add the chopped parsley and stir to combine.

4 Serve the mullet on warmed plates, drizzled with the dressing.

COOK'S TIPS
• Nicknamed the woodcock of the sea, red mullet are one of the fish that are classically cooked uncleaned to give them extra flavour. In this recipe however, the fish are cleaned and herbs are used to add extra flavour to the fish.
• If cooking on a barbecue, light the barbecue well in advance. Before cooking, the charcoal or wood should be grey, with no flames.

SERVES FOUR

INGREDIENTS
    4 red mullet, about 225–275g/
        8–10oz each, cleaned and descaled
        if cooking under a grill (broiler)
    olive oil, for brushing
    fresh herb sprigs, such as fennel,
        dill, parsley, or thyme
    2–3 dozen fresh or dried bay leaves
For the dressing
    90ml/6 tbsp olive oil
    6 garlic cloves, finely chopped
    ½ dried chilli, seeded and chopped
    juice of ½ lemon
    15ml/1 tbsp parsley

COOK'S TIP
If you are cooking on the barbecue, the fish do not need to be scaled.

1 Prepare the barbecue or preheat the grill (broiler) with the shelf 15cm/6in from the heat source.

2 Brush each fish with oil and stuff the cavities with the herb sprigs. Brush the grill pan with oil and lay bay leaves across the cooking rack. Place the fish on top and cook for 15–20 minutes until cooked through, turning once.

PAN-FRIED SOLE <u>WITH</u> LEMON <u>AND</u> CAPERS

FLAT FISH OF DIFFERENT SORTS ABOUND IN THE MEDITERRANEAN AND ARE USUALLY FRIED SIMPLY AND SERVED WITH LEMON WEDGES TO SQUEEZE OVER THE TOP. INTENSELY FLAVOURED CAPERS, WHICH GROW EXTENSIVELY IN THE BALEARIC ISLANDS, MAKE A PLEASANT TANGY ADDITION.

SERVES TWO

INGREDIENTS

    30–45ml/2–3 tbsp plain
      (all-purpose) flour
    4 sole, plaice or flounder fillets,
      or 2 whole small flat fish
    45ml/3 tbsp olive oil
    25g/1oz/2 tbsp butter
    60ml/4 tbsp lemon juice
    30ml/2 tbsp pickled capers, drained
    salt and ground black pepper
    fresh flat leaf parsley, to garnish
    lemon wedges, to serve

COOK'S TIP

This is a flavourful, and quick, way to serve the fillets of any white fish. The delicate flavour is enhanced by the tangy lemon juice and capers.

1 Sift the flour on to a plate and season well with salt and ground black pepper. Dip the fish fillets into the flour, to coat evenly on both sides.

2 Heat the oil and butter in a large shallow pan until foaming. Add the fish fillets and fry over a medium heat for 2–3 minutes on each side.

3 Lift out the fillets carefully with a metal spatula and place them on a warmed serving platter. Season with salt and ground black pepper.

4 Add the lemon juice and capers to the pan, heat through and pour over the fish. Garnish with parsley and serve at once with lemon wedges.

SEA BASS ^{IN A} SALT CRUST

BAKING FISH IN A CRUST OF SEA SALT ENHANCES THE FLAVOUR AND BRINGS OUT THE TASTE OF THE SEA. IT IS ALSO THE EASIEST WAY THERE IS TO COOK A WHOLE FISH. IN SPAIN THE GILT-HEAD BREAM IS THE FISH MOST OFTEN USED, BUT ANY FIRM FISH, SUCH AS GREY MULLET, STRIPED BASS AND PORGY, CAN BE COOKED THIS WAY. BREAK OPEN THE CRUST AT THE TABLE TO RELEASE THE GLORIOUS AROMA.

SERVES FOUR TO SIX

INGREDIENTS

    1 sea bass, about 1kg/2¼ lb,
      gutted and scaled
    1 sprig each of fresh fennel,
      rosemary and thyme
    mixed peppercorns
    2kg/4½ lb coarse sea salt
    seaweed or samphire, to garnish
      (optional)
    lemon slices, to serve

COOK'S TIP

In the Mediterranean, fish in salt are often baked whole and ungutted. But supermarkets elsewhere always sell them gutted, so use the opportunity to add flavourings inside.

1 Preheat the oven to 240ºC/475ºF/ Gas 9. Fill the cavity of the sea bass with the fennel, rosemary and thyme sprigs and grind over some of the mixed peppercorns.

2 Spread half the salt in a shallow baking tray and lay the sea bass on it.

3 Cover the fish all over with a 1cm/½ in layer of salt, pressing it down firmly. Bake for 30 minutes, until the salt coagulates and is beginning to colour.

4 To serve, leave the fish on the baking tray and garnish with seaweed or samphire, if using. Bring the fish to the table in its salt crust. Use a sharp knife to break open the crust.

COOK'S TIP

Once baked, the salt sticks to the fish skin, and brings it off. Scrape back the layer of salt and lift out the top fillet in sections. Snip the backbone with scissors and lift out. Discard the herbs and remove the bottom fillet pieces. Add a lemon slice to each plate.

BACALAO IN SPICY TOMATO WITH POTATOES

Salt cod is a popular ingredient in Spain, not just a Lenten necessity. It is the salt that makes the fish so characterful, so don't oversoak it for this traditional Basque recipe. Look out for a loin piece, which has very little waste; if you can't find one, buy a larger piece to ensure you have enough once any very dry bits have been removed.

SERVES FOUR

INGREDIENTS

 400g/14oz salt cod loin, soaked
  in cold water for 24 hours
 30ml/2 tbsp olive oil
 1 large onion, chopped
 2 garlic cloves, finely chopped
 1½ green (bell) peppers, seeded
  and chopped
 500g/1¼lb ripe tomatoes, peeled
  and chopped, or a 400g/14oz
  can tomatoes
 15ml/1 tbsp tomato purée (paste)
 15ml/1 tbsp clear honey
 1.5ml/¼ tsp dried thyme
 2.5ml/½ tsp cayenne pepper
 juice of ½ lemon (optional)
 2 potatoes
 45ml/3 tbsp stale breadcrumbs
 30ml/2 tbsp finely chopped
  fresh parsley
 salt and ground black pepper

1 Drain the salt cod and place in a pan. Pour over water to cover generously and bring to the boil. Remove the pan from the heat as soon as the water boils, then set aside until cold.

2 Heat the oil in a medium pan. Fry the onion, and add the garlic after 5 minutes. Add the chopped peppers and tomatoes, and cook gently to form a sauce. Stir in the tomato purée, honey, dried thyme, cayenne, black pepper and a little salt. Taste for seasoning: a little lemon juice will make it tangier.

3 Halve the potatoes lengthways and cut them into slices just thicker than a coin. Drain the fish, reserving the cooking water.

4 Preheat the grill (broiler) to medium with a shelf 15cm/6in below it. Bring the reserved fish cooking water to the boil and cook the potatoes for about 8 minutes. Do not add extra salt.

5 Remove the skin and bones from the cod, and pull it into small natural flakes. Spoon one-third of the tomato sauce into a flameproof casserole, top with the potatoes, fish and remaining sauce. Combine the breadcrumbs and parsley and sprinkle over. Heat the dish through under a grill for 10 minutes.

MACKEREL IN LEMON SAMFAINA

SAMFAINA IS A SAUCE FROM THE EAST COAST OF SPAIN AND THE COSTA BRAVA. IT SHARES THE SAME INGREDIENTS AS RATATOUILLE AND IS RATHER LIKE A CHUNKY VEGETABLE STEW. THIS VERSION IS PARTICULARLY LEMONY, TO OFFSET THE RICHNESS OF THE MACKEREL.

SERVES FOUR

INGREDIENTS

   2 large mackerel, filleted, or 4 fillets
   plain (all-purpose) flour, for dusting
   30ml/2 tbsp olive oil
   lemon wedges, if serving cold
For the samfaina sauce
   1 large aubergine (eggplant)
   60ml/4 tbsp olive oil
   1 large onion, chopped
   2 garlic cloves, finely chopped
   1 large courgette (zucchini), sliced
   1 red and 1 green (bell) pepper,
    seeded and cut into squares
   800g/1¾lb ripe tomatoes,
    roughly chopped
   1 bay leaf
   salt and ground black pepper

1 Make the sauce. Peel the aubergine, then cut the flesh into cubes, sprinkle with salt and leave to stand in a colander for 30 minutes.

2 Heat half the oil in a flameproof casserole large enough to fit the fish. Fry the onion over a medium heat until it colours. Add the garlic, then the courgette and peppers and stir-fry.

3 Add the tomatoes and bay leaf, partially cover and simmer over the lowest heat, letting the tomatoes just soften without losing their shape.

4 Rinse off the salt from the aubergine. Using three layers of kitchen paper, squeeze the cubes dry.

5 Heat the remaining oil in a frying pan until smoking. Put in one handful of aubergine cubes, then the next, stirring with a wooden spoon and cooking over a high heat until the cubes are brown on all sides. Stir into the tomato sauce.

6 Cut each mackerel fillet into three, and dust the filleted side with flour. Heat the oil in a frying pan over a high heat and put the fish in, floured side down. Fry for 3 minutes until golden. Turn and cook for another 1 minute, then slip the fish into the sauce and simmer, covered, for 5 minutes. Adjust the seasonings before serving.

COOK'S TIP
The fish can be served hot or cold. If serving cold, present the mackerel skin-side up, surrounded by vegetables, and garnished with lemon wedges.

MONKFISH WITH PIMIENTO AND CREAM SAUCE

THIS RECIPE COMES FROM RIOJA COUNTRY, WHERE A SPECIAL HORNED RED PEPPER GROWS AND IS USED TO MAKE A SPICY SAUCE. HERE, RED PEPPERS ARE USED WITH A LITTLE CHILLI WHILE CREAM MAKES A MELLOW PINK SAUCE. TO DRINK, CHOOSE A MARQUES DE CÁCERES WHITE RIOJA.

SERVES FOUR

INGREDIENTS

  2 large red (bell) peppers
  1kg/2¼lb monkfish tail
    or 900g/2lb halibut
  plain (all-purpose) flour,
    for dusting
  30ml/2 tbsp olive oil
  25g/1oz/2 tbsp butter
  120ml/4fl oz/½ cup white Rioja
    or dry vermouth
  ½ dried chilli, seeded and chopped
  8 raw prawns (shrimp), in the shell
  150ml/¼ pint/⅔ cup double
    (heavy) cream
  salt and ground black pepper
  fresh flat leaf parsley, to garnish

1 Preheat the grill (broiler) to high and cook the peppers for 8–12 minutes, turning occasionally, until they are soft, and the skins blackened. Leave, covered, until cool enough to handle. Skin and discard the stalks and seeds. Put the flesh into a blender, strain in the juices and purée.

2 Cut the monkfish or halibut into eight steaks (freeze the bones for stock). Season well and dust with flour.

3 Heat the oil and butter in a large frying pan and fry the fish for 3 minutes on each side. Remove to a warm dish.

4 Add the wine or vermouth and chilli to the pan and stir to deglaze the pan. Add the prawns and cook them briefly, then lift out and reserve.

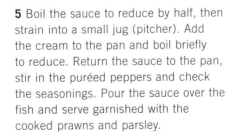

5 Boil the sauce to reduce by half, then strain into a small jug (pitcher). Add the cream to the pan and boil briefly to reduce. Return the sauce to the pan, stir in the puréed peppers and check the seasonings. Pour the sauce over the fish and serve garnished with the cooked prawns and parsley.

HAKE AND CLAMS WITH SALSA VERDE

MERLUZA EN SALSA VERDE IS A FAVOURITE BASQUE WAY OF COOKING HAKE, WHICH IS ONE OF THE MOST POPULAR AND PLENTIFUL FISH IN SPAIN. AS THEY BAKE, THE CLAMS OPEN UP AND ADD THEIR DELICIOUS SEA JUICES TO THE GREEN WINE AND PARSLEY SAUCE.

SERVES FOUR

INGREDIENTS
  4 hake steaks, about 2cm/¾in thick
  50g/2oz/½ cup plain (all-purpose)
   flour, for dusting, plus 30ml/2 tbsp
  60ml/4 tbsp olive oil
  15ml/1 tbsp lemon juice
  1 small onion, finely chopped
  4 garlic cloves, finely chopped
  150ml/¼ pint/⅔ cup fish stock
  150ml/¼ pint/⅔ cup white wine
  90ml/6 tbsp chopped fresh parsley
  75g/3oz/¾ cup frozen petits pois
  16 fresh clams, cleaned
  salt and ground black pepper

COOK'S TIP
To make fish stock, put 450g/1lb fish bones, head and skin in a large pan with 1 sliced onion, 1 sliced carrot, ½ sliced celery stalk, 3–4 thick parsley stalks, snapped in places, 1 bay leaf, 10ml/ 2 tsp lemon juice or wine vinegar and 175ml/6fl oz/¾ cup dry white wine or vermouth. Bring to the boil, then reduce the heat and simmer for 30 minutes. Strain. If you can't buy fish bits, collect fish leftovers in the freezer: prawn (shrimp) heads, the spines from cooked fish, poaching water from a salmon, and mussel or clam stock from opening the shellfish. It is also worth buying a small whole fish to add to the stock.

1 Preheat the oven to 180°C/350°F/ Gas 4. Season the fish, then dust with flour. Heat half the oil in a large pan, add the fish and fry for 1 minute on each side. Transfer to an ovenproof dish and sprinkle with the lemon juice.

2 Heat the remaining oil in a clean pan and fry the onion and garlic, stirring, until soft. Stir in the 30ml/2 tbsp flour and cook for about 1 minute.

3 Slowly add the stock and wine to the pan, stirring until thickened. Add 75ml/5 tbsp of the parsley and the petits pois to the sauce and season with plenty of salt and pepper.

4 Pour the sauce over the fish, and bake for 15–20 minutes, adding the clams 3–4 minutes before the end of the cooking time.

5 Discard any clams that do not open once cooked, then sprinkle the fish with with the remaining parsley and serve.

VARIATION
In Rioja country, on the banks of the River Ebro, this dish often includes fresh young asparagus tips as well as peas. Simply replace half the peas with asparagus tips.

VIEIRAS DE SANTIAGO

SCALLOPS ARE THE SYMBOL OF ST JAMES (SANTIAGO), AND THIS DISH IS ASSOCIATED WITH HIS SHRINE AT SANTIAGO DE COMPOSTELLA IN GALICIA. THE FLAMED SCALLOPS ARE COVERED IN TOMATO SAUCE AND ARE SERVED HOT IN THE CURVED SHELL, WITH CRISP BREADCRUMBS ON TOP.

SERVES FOUR

INGREDIENTS
    30ml/2 tbsp olive oil
    1 onion, finely chopped
    2 garlic cloves, finely chopped
    200g/7oz can tomatoes
    pinch of cayenne pepper
    45ml/3 tbsp finely chopped
      fresh parsley
    50ml/2fl oz/¼ cup orange juice
    50g/2oz/4 tbsp butter
    450g/1lb large shelled scallops,
      or 8–12 large ones on the shell,
      detached and cleaned
    30ml/2 tbsp anis spirit, such as
      Ricard or Pernod
    90ml/6 tbsp stale breadcrumbs
    salt and ground black pepper

1 Heat the oil in a pan and fry the onion and garlic over a gentle heat. Add the tomatoes and cook for 10–15 minutes, stirring occasionally. Season with a little salt and cayenne pepper.

2 Transfer the tomato mixture to a small food processor or blender, add 30ml/ 2 tbsp of the parsley and the orange juice and blend to form a smooth purée.

3 Preheat the grill (broiler) with the shelf at its highest. Arrange four curved scallop shells, or flameproof ramekin dishes, on a baking tray.

4 Heat 25g/1oz/2 tbsp of the butter in a small frying pan and fry the scallops gently, for about 2 minutes, or until sealed but not totally cooked through.

5 Pour the anis spirit into a ladle and set light to it. Pour over the scallops and shake the pan gently until the flames die down. Divide the scallops among the prepared shells (or dishes) and salt them lightly. Add the pan juices to the tomato sauce.

6 Pour the tomato sauce over the scallops. Mix together the breadcrumbs and the remaining parsley, season very lightly and sprinkle over the top.

7 Melt the remaining butter in a small pan and drizzle over the breadcrumbs. Grill (broil) the scallops for about 1 minute to colour the tops and heat through. Serve immediately.

COOK'S TIP
If you can lay your hands on the curved shells of scallops, wash and keep them after use. Fresh scallops are usually sold on the flat shell so the second shell, which can be used as a little dish, is now quite a rarity.

CHAR-GRILLED SQUID

CALAMARES A LA PLANCHA *ARE TRADITIONALLY COOKED ON THE HOT GRIDDLE THAT IS AN ESSENTIAL PART OF EVERY SPANISH KITCHEN. THE METHOD IS FAST AND SIMPLE AND REALLY BRINGS OUT THE FLAVOUR OF THE SQUID. THIS DISH IS AN IDEAL FIRST COURSE FOR FOUR PEOPLE, OR CAN BE SERVED ON A BED OF RICE AS A MAIN DISH FOR TWO.*

3 Heat a ridged griddle pan until hot. Add the body of one of the squid and cook over a medium heat for 2–3 minutes, pressing the squid with a metal spatula to keep it flat. Repeat on the other side. Cook the other squid body in the same way.

4 Cut the squid bodies into diagonal strips. If serving with rice, arrange the squid strips criss-cross on top. Keep hot.

SERVES TWO TO FOUR

INGREDIENTS
  2 whole cleaned squid, with
    tentacles, about 275g/10oz each
  75ml/5 tbsp olive oil
  30ml/2 tbsp sherry vinegar
  2 fresh red chillies, finely
    chopped
  60ml/4 tbsp dry white wine
  salt and ground black pepper
  hot cooked rice, to serve (optional)
  15–30ml/1–2 tbsp chopped parsley,
    to garnish

1 Make a lengthways cut down the side of the body of each squid, then open it out flat. Score the flesh on both sides of the bodies in a criss-cross pattern with the tip of a sharp knife. Chop the tentacles into short lengths. Place all the squid pieces in a non-metallic dish.

2 Whisk together the oil and vinegar in a small bowl. Add salt and pepper to taste, pour over the squid and toss to mix. Cover and leave to marinate for about 1 hour.

5 Add the chopped tentacles and chillies to the pan and toss over a medium heat for 2 minutes. Stir in the wine, then drizzle over the squid. Garnish with chopped parsley.

CALAMARES RELLENOS

Squid are often just stuffed with their own tentacles but, in this recipe, ham and raisins, which contrast wonderfully with the subtle flavour of the squid, are also included. The stuffed squid are cooked in a richly flavoured tomato sauce and make a perfect appetizer. To serve as a main course, simply accompany with plain boiled rice.

SERVES FOUR

INGREDIENTS
 2 squid, about 275g/10oz each
 60ml/4 tbsp olive oil
 1 small onion, finely chopped
 2 garlic cloves, finely chopped
 50g/2oz Serrano ham or gammon
  steak, diced small
 75g/3oz/scant ½ cup long grain rice
 30ml/2 tbsp raisins, chopped
 30ml/2 tbsp finely chopped
  fresh parsley
 ½ small (US medium) egg, beaten
 plain (all-purpose) flour, for dusting
 250ml/8fl oz/1 cup white wine
 1 bay leaf
 30ml/2 tbsp chopped fresh parsley
 salt, paprika and black pepper
For the tomato sauce
 30ml/2 tbsp olive oil
 1 onion, finely chopped
 2 garlic cloves, finely chopped
 200g/7oz can tomatoes
 salt and cayenne pepper

1 Make the tomato sauce. Heat the oil in a flameproof casserole large enough to hold the squid. Cook the onion and garlic over a gentle heat. Add the tomatoes and cook for 10–15 minutes. Season with salt and cayenne pepper.

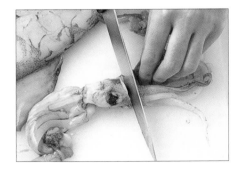

2 To prepare the squid, use the tentacles to pull out the body. Cut off the tentacles, discarding the eyes and everything below. Flex the bodies to pop out the spinal structure. Chop the fin flaps and rinse the bodies well.

3 Heat half the oil in a pan and gently fry the onion and garlic together. Add the ham and squid tentacles and stir-fry. Off the heat stir in the rice, chopped raisins and parsley. Season well and add the egg to bind the ingredients.

4 Spoon the mixture into the squid bodies, then stitch each of them shut using a small poultry skewer. Blot the bodies with kitchen paper, then flour them very lightly. Heat the remaining oil in a frying pan and fry the squid, turning until coloured on all sides.

5 Move the squid with two spoons and arrange them in the tomato sauce. Add the wine and bay leaf. Cover the casserole tightly and simmer for about 30 minutes, turning the squid over halfway through cooking if the sauce does not cover them completely. Serve sliced into rings, surrounded by the sauce and garnished with parsley.

OCTOPUS STEW

In Galicia, octopus stews are particularly popular and a common tapas dish is a simple stew with paprika, served on little wooden plates. Here the octopus is stewed with tomatoes and potatoes, to make a substantial main course. It is an ideal make-in-advance dish, because octopus can be tough, and benefits from long cooking to tenderize it.

SERVES FOUR TO SIX

INGREDIENTS

1kg/2¼lb octopus, cleaned
45ml/3 tbsp olive oil
1 large red onion, chopped
3 garlic cloves, finely chopped
30ml/2 tbsp brandy
300ml/½ pint/1¼ cups dry
  white wine
800g/1¾lb ripe plum tomatoes,
  peeled and chopped or 2 × 400g/
  14oz cans chopped tomatoes
1 dried red chilli, seeded
  and chopped
1.5ml/¼ tsp paprika
450g/1lb small new potatoes
15ml/1 tbsp chopped fresh rosemary
15ml/1 tbsp fresh thyme leaves
1.2 litres/2 pints/5 cups fish stock
30ml/2 tbsp chopped fresh flat leaf
  parsley leaves
salt and ground black pepper
rosemary sprigs, to garnish
salad leaves and French bread,
  to serve

1 Cut the octopus into large pieces, put in a pan and pour over enough cold water to cover. Season with salt, bring to the boil, then lower the heat and simmer for 30 minutes to tenderize it. Drain and cut into bitesize pieces.

2 Heat the oil in a large shallow pan. Fry the onion until lightly coloured, then add the garlic and fry for 1 minute. Add the octopus and fry for 2–3 minutes, stirring, until coloured.

3 Pour the brandy over the octopus and ignite it. When the flames have died down, add the wine, bring to the boil and bubble gently for about 5 minutes. Stir in the chopped tomatoes, with the chilli and paprika, then add the potatoes, rosemary and thyme. Simmer gently for 5 minutes.

4 Pour in the fish stock and season. Cover and simmer for 20–30 minutes, stirring occasionally, until the octopus and potatoes are tender and the sauce has thickened slightly.

5 To serve, check the seasoning and stir in the parsley. Garnish with rosemary and accompany with salad and bread.

COOK'S TIPS

• Octopus skin can be removed with salted fingers. Large octopus often have scaly rings inside the suckers. Run your fingers down the tentacles to pop out.
• You can make this dish the day before. Simply leave to cool, then chill. To serve, reheat gently, then check the seasoning and stir in the parsley.

MARMITAKO

This is a traditional fisherman's stew, often made at sea, with meaty tuna steaks. The substantial fish is wonderfully balanced by sweet peppers and cider, all topped by potatoes. It takes its name from the cooking pot, known in France as a "marmite". Traditionally a one-pot dish, it speeds things along to fry the fish separately.

SERVES FOUR

INGREDIENTS

   60ml/4 tbsp olive oil
   1 onion, chopped
   2 garlic cloves, finely chopped
   3 green (bell) peppers, seeded
     and chopped
   ½ dried hot chilli, seeded
     and chopped
   4 light tuna or bonito steaks,
     about 150g/5oz each
   400g/14oz can tomatoes with juice
   10ml/2 tsp paprika
   3 potatoes, diced
   350ml/12fl oz/1½ cups dry
     (hard) cider
   salt and ground black pepper
   30ml/2 tbsp chopped fresh parsley,
     to garnish

1 Heat half the oil in a shallow flameproof casserole big enough to take the fish. Fry the onion gently until softened, then add the garlic. Add the peppers and chilli and stir-fry gently.

2 Season the fish steaks. Heat the remaining oil in a frying pan and fry the fish steaks for 2 minutes on each side over a high heat. Add the tomatoes to the casserole and stir-fry briefly. Add the paprika, then salt and pepper to taste.

VARIATION

Veal steaks or chops can be cooked in the same way. Fry for 5 minutes on each side in step 2, then continue as with fish.

3 Slip the fish steaks into the sauce, moving the peppers into the spaces between them. Cover with the potatoes, pushing them as flat as possible. Add the cider and bring to a simmer. Cover and cook very gently for about 45 minutes, or until the potatoes are done. Check the seasoning, sprinkle with the chopped parsley and serve immediately, straight from the casserole.

ZARZUELA

THE NAME OF THIS DISH TRANSLATES AS "LIGHT MUSICAL COMEDY", REFLECTING THE COLOUR AND VARIETY OF THE STEW, WHICH IS FULL OF ALL SORTS OF FISH AND SHELLFISH. IT IS DISTINGUISHED FROM OTHER FISH STEWS BY CONTAINING TOMATO AS WELL AS SAFFRON. IT'S A SPLENDID FEAST AND NOT DIFFICULT TO MAKE. IF YOUR PAN IS LARGE ENOUGH, INVITE MORE GUESTS AND SIMPLY ADD A LOBSTER, A GOOD PIECE OF HAKE, ANOTHER BASS AND MORE PRAWNS, COCKLES AND OTHER SHELLFISH. TO DRINK, CHOOSE A BOTTLE OF TORRES GRAN VIÑA SOL.

SERVES SIX

INGREDIENTS

250g/9oz monkfish on the bone
1 gurnard, snapper or other whole
  white fish, about 350g/12oz
1 sole, plaice or flounder or
  other whole flat fish, about
  500g/1¼lb, cleaned
60ml/4 tbsp olive oil
8 small squid, with tentacles
plain (all-purpose) flour, for dusting
30ml/2 tbsp anis spirit, such as
  Ricard or Pernod
450g/1lb mussels, cleaned
250ml/8fl oz/1 cup white wine
4 large scampi (extra large shrimp),
  with heads, uncooked
12 raw king prawns (jumbo shrimp),
  with heads
115g/4oz prawns (shrimp)
salt and ground black pepper
45ml/3 tbsp chopped fresh parsley,
  to garnish
For the stock
1 onion, chopped
1 celery stick, chopped
1 bay leaf
For the fish broth
30ml/2 tbsp oil
1 large onion, finely chopped
2 garlic cloves, finely chopped
500g/1¼lb ripe tomatoes, peeled,
  seeded and chopped
2 bay leaves
1 dried chilli, seeded
  and chopped
5ml/1 tsp paprika
pinch of saffron threads (0.2g)
salt and ground black pepper

1 Prepare the fish. Remove the flesh from the bones and cut into portions. You should have about 500g/1¼lb white fish, both firm and soft. Salt the fish and reserve on a plate in the refrigerator. (Reserve the bones and heads for making the stock.)

2 Make the stock. Put the onion, celery, bay leaf and the fish bones and heads in a pan, pour in 600ml/1 pint/2½ cups water, and bring to the boil, then simmer for about 30 minutes.

3 Make the broth in a large flameproof casserole. Heat the oil and fry the onion and garlic gently until soft. Add the chopped tomatoes, bay leaves, dried chilli, paprika and crumbled saffron and cook gently to make a sauce.

4 To cook the fish and shellfish, heat the oil in a large frying pan. Put in the squid tentacles, face down, and cook for 45 seconds, to make "flowers". Reserve on a plate.

5 Flour and fry the monkfish and white fish for 3 minutes on each side, then the flat fish for 2 minutes on each side. Cut the squid bodies into rings and fry. Pour the anis spirit into a ladle, flame it and pour over the fish remaining in the pan. Remove the fish and reserve.

6 Strain the fish stock into the casserole and add the wine. Bring to a simmer. Add the mussels in two batches. Cover for a couple of minutes, then remove to a plate, discard any closed mussels, and remove the upper shells.

7 Add the scampi and cook for about 8 minutes, then lift out using a slotted spoon. Cut with scissors along the under side from the head to the tail. Add the raw prawns for 3–4 minutes, then lift out and reserve.

8 About 20 minutes before serving, assemble the casserole. Add the seafood to the hot broth in the following order, bringing the liquid back to simmering each time: firm white fish, soft white fish (with squid rings and pan juices), large shellfish in the shell, cooked shellfish in the shell, then any small shelled prawns. If the liquid level falls below the seafood, make it up with more wine. Check the seasonings.

9 Rearrange the soup with the best-looking shellfish and squid flowers on top. Scatter over the mussels, cover and leave to steam for 2 minutes. Garnish with parsley. Take the casserole to the table with a plate for shells.

COOK'S TIP
Don't leave anything stewing in the broth. Keep the broth warm on a low heat, with the fish at room temperature.

POULTRY AND GAME BIRDS

Chicken was once considered a luxury in Spain and there are many traditional recipes. Try serving chicken with spicy red pepper sauce, in saffron rice, with spiced figs, or with ham and peppers. Other poultry, such as duck and turkey, are also on many menus, while game birds are immensely popular. They may be stuffed with grapes, marinaded in wine, cooked with mushrooms or served in delicious sauces.

CHICKEN LIVERS IN SHERRY

HIGADILLAS CON JEREZ IS VERY POPULAR, MADE WITH TRADITIONAL SPANISH INGREDIENTS. IT MAKES A DELICIOUS LITTLE TAPAS DISH AND IS PARTICULARLY GOOD EATEN WITH BREAD OR ON TOAST. FOR A MORE ELEGANT PRESENTATION, SERVE PILED ON TOP OF LITTLE RICE TORTITAS.

SERVES FOUR

INGREDIENTS

225g/8oz chicken livers, thawed
  if frozen, trimmed
15ml/1 tbsp olive oil
1 small onion, finely chopped
2 small garlic cloves, finely chopped
5ml/1 tsp fresh thyme leaves
30ml/2 tbsp sweet oloroso sherry
30ml/2 tbsp crème fraîche or double
  (heavy) cream
2.5ml/½ tsp paprika
salt and ground black pepper
fresh thyme, to garnish

1 Trim any green spots and sinews from the chicken livers. Heat the oil in a frying pan and fry the onion, garlic, chicken livers and thyme for 3 minutes.

2 Stir the sherry into the livers, then add the cream and cook briefly. Season with salt, pepper and paprika, garnish with thyme and serve immediately.

ORANGE CHICKEN SALAD

WITH THEIR TANGY FLAVOUR, ORANGE SEGMENTS ARE THE PERFECT PARTNER FOR TENDER CHICKEN IN THIS TASTY RICE SALAD. TO APPRECIATE ALL THE FLAVOURS FULLY, SERVE THE SALAD AT ROOM TEMPERATURE. IT MAKES THE PERFECT DISH FOR A HOT SUMMER DAY.

SERVES FOUR

INGREDIENTS

   3 large seedless oranges
   175g/6oz/scant 1 cup long grain rice
   10ml/2 tsp strong Dijon mustard
   2.5ml/½ tsp caster (superfine) sugar
   175ml/6fl oz/¾ cup vinaigrette
   450g/1lb cooked chicken, diced
   45ml/3 tbsp chopped fresh chives
   75g/3oz/¾ cup almonds or cashew
     nuts, toasted
   salt and ground black pepper
   mixed salad leaves, to serve

COOK'S TIP

To make a simple vinaigrette, whisk 45ml/3 tbsp wine vinegar with 90ml/ 6 tbsp olive oil. Add 60ml/4 tbsp extra virgin olive oil and season well.

1 Pare one of the oranges thinly, removing only the rind, not the white pith. Put the pieces of orange rind in a pan and add the rice. Pour in 475ml/ 16fl oz/2 cups water, add a pinch of salt and bring to the boil. Cover and cook over a very low heat for about 15 minutes, or until the rice is tender and all the water has been absorbed.

2 Meanwhile, peel the oranges, removing all the white pith. Working over a plate to catch the juices, separate them into segments. Tip in the orange juice from the plate and add to the vinaigrette with the mustard and sugar, whisking to combine. Check the seasoning.

3 When the rice is cooked, remove it from the heat and discard the pieces of orange rind. Spoon the rice into a bowl, let it cool slightly, then add half the dressing. Toss well, then set aside to cool completely.

4 Add the chicken, chives, toasted nuts and orange segments to the cooled rice. Pour over the remaining dressing and toss gently to combine. Serve on a bed of mixed salad leaves.

CHICKEN WITH LEMON AND GARLIC

POLLO CON LIMÓN Y AJILLO IS ONE OF THE SIMPLEST AND MOST DELICIOUS WAYS TO SERVE CHICKEN. IT MAKES A GOOD TAPAS DISH, SERVED WITH COCKTAIL STICKS TO PICK UP THE LITTLE STRIPS OF RICHLY FLAVOURED CHICKEN, OR A SUPPER FOR TWO, WITH FRIED POTATOES.

SERVES TWO TO FOUR

INGREDIENTS

  2 skinless chicken breast fillets
  30ml/2 tbsp olive oil
  1 shallot, finely chopped
  4 garlic cloves, finely chopped
  5ml/1 tsp paprika
  juice of 1 lemon
  30ml/2 tbsp chopped fresh parsley
  salt and ground black pepper
  fresh flat leaf parsley, to garnish
  lemon wedges, to serve

VARIATION

For a variation on this dish, try using strips of turkey breast or pork fillet. They need slightly longer cooking. The whites of spring onions (scallions) can replace shallots, and the chopped green tops replace the parsley.

1 Remove the little fillet from the back of each breast. If the breast still looks fatter than a finger, bat it with a rolling pin to make it thinner. Slice all the chicken meat into strips.

2 Heat the oil in a large frying pan. Stir-fry the chicken strips with the shallot, garlic and paprika over a high heat for about 3 minutes until cooked through.

3 Add the lemon juice and parsley and season with salt and pepper to taste. Serve hot with lemon wedges, garnished with flat leaf parsley.

COOK'S TIP

Chicken breasts have a little fillet strip that easily becomes detached. Collect these, in a bag or container in the freezer, for this dish.

CRUMBED CHICKEN WITH GREEN MAYONNAISE

PECHUGAS DE POLLO REBOZADAS ARE SOLD READY-PREPARED IN EVERY BUTCHER'S IN THE SOUTH. IDENTICAL TO SCHNITZEL, THESE CRISPY, GOLDEN CHICKEN BREAST PORTIONS SHOW THE JEWISH INFLUENCE ON COOKING IN THE REGION. LEMON WEDGES ARE A POPULAR ACCOMPANIMENT.

SERVES FOUR

INGREDIENTS

    4 boneless chicken breasts fillets,
      each weighing about 200g/7oz
    juice of 1 lemon
    5ml/1 tsp paprika
    plain (all-purpose) flour,
      for dusting
    1–2 eggs
    dried breadcrumbs, for coating
    about 60ml/4 tbsp olive oil
    salt and ground black pepper
    lemon wedges (optional), to serve
For the mayonnaise
    120ml/4fl oz/½ cup mayonnaise
    30ml/2 tbsp pickled capers, drained
      and chopped
    30ml/2 tbsp chopped fresh parsley

1 Start a couple of hours ahead, if you can. Skin the chicken breasts. Lay them outside down and, with a sharp knife, cut horizontally, almost through, from the rounded side. Open them up like a book. Press gently, to make a roundish shape, the size of a side plate. Sprinkle with lemon juice and paprika.

2 Set out three plates. Sprinkle flour over one, seasoning it well. Beat the egg with a little salt and pour into the second. Sprinkle the third with dried breadcrumbs. Dip the breasts first into the flour on both sides, then into the egg, then into the breadcrumbs. Chill the crumbed chicken, if you have time.

3 Put the mayonnaise ingredients in a bowl and mix well to combine.

4 Heat the oil in a heavy frying pan over a high heat. Fry the breast portions, two at a time, turning after 3 minutes, until golden on both sides. Add more oil for the second batch if needed. Serve at once, with the mayonnaise and lemon wedges, if using.

POLLO A LA ESPAÑOLA

THIS COLOURFUL CHICKEN DISH IS MADE THROUGHOUT SPAIN IN AN INFINITE NUMBER OF VARIATIONS. CUBED SERRANO HAM CAN REPLACE THE BACON, BUT THE FAT THE LATTER GIVES OFF IS A CONSTANT THEME IN THE SPANISH KITCHEN, SO HELPS TO ADD TO ITS CHARACTER.

SERVES FOUR

INGREDIENTS
    5ml/1 tsp paprika
    4 free-range or corn-fed
      chicken portions
    45ml/3 tbsp olive oil
    150g/5oz smoked bacon lardons,
      or diced pancetta
    1 large onion, chopped
    2 garlic cloves, finely chopped
    1 green (bell) pepper
    1 red (bell) pepper
    450g/1lb tomatoes or 400g/14oz
      canned tomatoes
    30ml/2 tbsp chopped fresh parsley
    salt and ground black pepper
    boiled rice, to serve (optional)

1 Rub paprika and salt into the chicken portions. Heat 30ml/2 tbsp oil in a large frying pan. Put in the chicken portions, skin side down, and fry gently.

2 Heat 15ml/1 tbsp oil in a flameproof casserole and add the bacon or pancetta.

3 When the bacon or pancetta starts to give off fat, add the chopped onion and garlic, frying very gently until soft.

4 Remove and discard the stalks and seeds from the peppers and roughly chop the flesh. Spoon off a little fat from the chicken pan, then add the peppers, fitting them into the spaces between the chicken portions, and cook gently.

5 When the onions are soft, stir in the tomatoes and season. Arrange the chicken pieces in the sauce, and stir in the cooked peppers.

6 Cover the casserole tightly and simmer over a low heat for 15 minutes. Check the seasoning, stir in the chopped parsley and serve with rice, if you like.

ARROZ CON POLLO

Many Spanish families eat rice once a week, referring to it as arroz unless it is paella. Rice with chicken is a casserole, with more liquid than a paella. Seasonal vegetables are included and even peas and sweetcorn can be used.

SERVES FOUR

INGREDIENTS

60ml/4 tbsp olive oil

6 chicken thighs, free-range if possible, halved along the bone

5ml/1 tsp paprika

1 large Spanish onion, roughly chopped

2 garlic cloves, finely chopped

1 chorizo sausage, sliced

115g/4oz Serrano or cooked ham or gammon, diced

1 red (bell) pepper, seeded and roughly chopped

1 yellow (bell) pepper, seeded and roughly chopped

225g/8oz/1 generous cup paella rice, washed and drained

2 large tomatoes, chopped or 200g/7oz can chopped tomatoes

120ml/4fl oz/½ cup amontillado sherry

750ml/1¼ pints/3 cups chicken stock

5ml/1 tsp dried oregano or thyme

1 bay leaf

salt and ground black pepper

15 green olives and chopped fresh flat leaf parsley, to garnish

1 Heat the oil in a wide flameproof casserole. Season the chicken pieces with salt and paprika. Fry until nicely brown all over, then reserve on a plate.

2 Add the onion and garlic to the pan and fry gently until beginning to soften. Add the chorizo and ham or gammon and stir-fry. Add the chopped peppers. Cook until they begin to soften.

3 Sprinkle in the drained rice and cook, stirring, for 1–2 minutes. Add the tomatoes, sherry, chicken stock and dried herbs and season well. Arrange the chicken pieces deep in the mixture, and tuck in the bay leaf.

4 Cover and cook over a very low heat for 30–40 minutes, until the chicken and rice are done. Stir, then garnish and serve.

POLLO CON LANGOSTINOS

Chicken with prawns is another gorgeous Catalan dish. The sauce is thickened with a picada of ground toasted almonds, which is more convenient than making a roux with butter and flour at the last moment. This special picada traditionally includes crumbled butter biscuits, which were considered more sophisticated than the bread that normally goes into picada. The sauce is finished with cream and cayenne, as a modern touch — a splendid dinner-party dish. Serve with a glass of Torres Gran Viña Sol.

SERVES FOUR

INGREDIENTS
1.3kg/3lb free-range chicken
75–90ml/5–6 tbsp olive oil
1 large onion, chopped
2 garlic cloves, finely chopped
400g/14oz tomatoes, peeled and
    seeded then chopped or 400g/14oz
    can tomatoes, drained
1 bay leaf
150ml/¼ pint/⅔ cup dry white wine
450g/1lb large raw prawns (shrimp),
    or 16 large shelled prawn tails
15g/½oz/1 tbsp butter
30ml/2 tbsp anis spirit, such as
    Ricard or Pernod
75ml/2½fl oz/⅓ cup double
    (heavy) cream
1.5ml/¼ tsp cayenne pepper
salt, paprika and ground
    black pepper
fresh flat leaf parsley, to garnish
boiled rice or raw spinach salad,
    to serve
For the *picada*
25g/1oz/¼ cup blanched almonds
15g/½oz/1 tbsp butter
1 garlic clove, finely chopped
3 Marie, Rich Tea or plain all-butter
    biscuits (cookies), broken
90ml/6 tbsp chopped fresh parsley

1 Cut the chicken into eight serving portions, then separate the small fillet from the back of each breast portion. Rub salt and paprika into the chicken.

2 Heat 30ml/2 tbsp oil in a wide flameproof casserole and fry the onion and garlic until soft. Put in the chicken pieces, skin downwards, and fry over a medium heat, turning until they are golden on all sides.

3 Meanwhile, make the *picada*. Dry-fry the almonds in a small frying pan, shaking it regularly, until they are just coloured. Transfer them to a blender.

4 Add 15g/½oz/1 tbsp butter to the pan and gently fry the garlic, then add it to the blender, with the broken biscuits. Reduce the biscuits to crumbs then add the chopped parsley and blend to a purée, adding a little of the wine intended for the casserole.

5 Add the tomatoes to the casserole, tuck in the bay leaf and cook down to a sauce, stirring occasionally. Pour in the remaining wine, season to taste with salt and ground black pepper, and leave to simmer gently.

6 Check the shelled prawn tails, if using: if they have a black thread along the back, nick it out with a knife. Heat 15ml/1 tbsp oil and the 15g/½oz/1 tbsp butter in the frying pan and add the prawns. Cook over a medium heat for 2 minutes on each side.

7 Pour the anis spirit into a ladle and set light to it. Off the heat pour this over the prawns and let it burn off. Stir in the juices from the casserole, then add the pan contents to the casserole.

8 Remove the bay leaf from the pan and stir in the *picada*, then the cream. Add cayenne to taste and check the seasonings, adding a little more if necessary. Heat through gently and serve garnished with more parsley.

VARIATIONS
The classic version of this dish is beef fillet with lobster. Also try veal with scampi, or partridge with large prawns, for equally delicious results.

CHICKEN CHILINDRÓN

THIS FAMOUS CHICKEN DISH FROM NAVARRE HAS A SPICY RED PEPPER SAUCE. IN THE PAST, THE DRIED CHORICERO PEPPER – THE ONE THAT GIVES CHORIZOS THEIR COLOUR AND SPICE – WAS USED ALONE, BUT NOWADAYS THE DISH IS OFTEN MADE WITH FRESH RED PEPPERS, SPICED WITH CHILLI. THE NAME CHILINDRÓN REFERS TO A GAME OF CARDS. SERVE WITH A TEMPRANILLO WINE.

SERVES FOUR

INGREDIENTS

675g/1½lb red (bell) peppers
4 free-range chicken portions
10ml/2 tsp paprika
30ml/2 tbsp olive oil
1 large onion, chopped
2 garlic cloves, finely chopped
200g/7oz Serrano or other ham, in
  one piece, or a gammon chop
200g/7oz can chopped tomatoes
1 dried *guindilla* or other hot
  dried chilli, chopped, or 2.5ml/
  ½ tsp chilli powder, to taste
salt and ground black pepper
chopped fresh parsley, to garnish
small new potatoes, to serve

1 Preheat the grill (broiler) to high. Put the peppers on a baking sheet and grill (broil) for 8–12 minutes, turning occasionally, until the skins have blistered and blackened. Place the blackened peppers in a bowl, cover with clear film (plastic wrap) and leave to cool.

2 Rub salt and paprika into the chicken portions. Heat the oil in a large frying pan and add the chicken portions, skin-side down. Fry over a medium-low heat, turning until golden on all sides.

3 Meanwhile, select a casserole into which the chicken will fit comfortably. Spoon in 45ml/3 tbsp fat from the other pan. Fry the onion and garlic until soft. Dice the ham or gammon and add, stirring occasionally, for a few minutes.

4 Add the chopped tomatoes to the casserole, with the chopped dried chilli or chilli powder. Cook for 4–5 minutes, letting the sauce reduce.

5 Peel the skins off the peppers and discard these and the stalks. Put the peppers into a blender and strain in the juices, discarding the seeds. Process, then add the purée to the casserole and stir in. Heat through.

6 Add the chicken pieces to the casserole, bedding them down in the sauce. Cook, covered, for 15 minutes and check the seasonings, adding more if necessary. Garnish with a little parsley and serve with small new potatoes.

CHICKEN CASSEROLE WITH SPICED FIGS

THE CATALANS HAVE A REPUTATION FOR SERVING FRUIT WITH POULTRY AND MEAT. FIGS GROW WILD AROUND MANY COUNTRY FARMS AND THE POULTRY FEED ON THE FALLEN FRUIT, SO A DISH COMBINING CHICKEN AND FIGS SEEMS LIKE A NATURAL COMBINATION. HERE POLLO CON HIGOS IS COOKED WITH A BEAUTIFULLY SPICED SAUCE, WHICH GOES PERFECTLY WITH A CATALAN CABERNET SAUVIGNON.

SERVES FOUR

INGREDIENTS
   50g/2oz bacon lardons or
     pancetta, diced
   15ml/1 tbsp olive oil
   1.3–1.6kg/3–3½lb free-range
     or corn-fed chicken, jointed
     into eight pieces
   120ml/4fl oz/½ cup white wine
   finely pared rind of ½ lemon
   50ml/2fl oz/¼ cup chicken stock
   salt and ground black pepper
   green salad, to serve
For the figs
   150g/5oz/¾ cup granulated sugar
   120ml/4fl oz/½ cup white
     wine vinegar
   1 lemon slice
   1 cinnamon stick
   120ml/4fl oz/½ cup water
   450g/1lb fresh figs

1 Prepare the figs. Simmer the sugar, vinegar, lemon and cinnamon with the water for 5 minutes. Add the figs and cook for 10 minutes. Remove from the heat and leave to stand for 3 hours.

2 Fry the bacon or pancetta until golden. Transfer to an ovenproof dish. Add the oil to the pan. Season the chicken, brown on both sides, then transfer to the ovenproof dish.

3 Preheat the oven to 180°C/350°F/ Gas 4. Drain the figs. Add the wine and lemon rind to the pan and boil until the wine has reduced and is syrupy. Pour over the chicken.

4 Cook the chicken in the oven, uncovered, for about 20 minutes, then add the figs and chicken stock. Cover and return to the oven for a further 10 minutes. Serve with a green salad.

ROAST TURKEY WITH BLACK FRUIT STUFFING

COLUMBUS INTRODUCED TURKEYS FROM AMERICA TO SPAIN, AND AT FIRST THEY WERE COOKED LIKE PEACOCKS — STUFFED, THEN ROASTED INSIDE A PIG'S CAUL. THE SAUSAGEMEAT INSIDE THIS BIRD IS BLACK MORCILLA, AND PRUNES AND RAISINS MAKE IT EVEN MORE SWEET AND FRUITY. THE SAUCE IS FLAVOURED WITH SWEET GRAPE JUICE AND AN INTRIGUING SPLASH OF ANIS.

SERVES EIGHT

INGREDIENTS
  3kg/6½lb bronze or black turkey,
    weighed without the giblets
  60ml/4 tbsp oil
  200g/7oz rashers (strips) streaky
    (fatty) bacon
For the stuffing
  45ml/3 tbsp olive oil
  1 onion, chopped
  2 garlic cloves, finely chopped
  115g/4oz fatty bacon lardons
  150g/5oz *morcilla* or black pudding
    (blood sausage), diced
  1 turkey liver, diced
  50g/2oz/½ cup Muscatel raisins,
    soaked in 45ml/3 tbsp anis spirit,
    such as Ricard, and chopped
  115g/4oz ready-to-eat pitted
    prunes, chopped
  50g/2oz/½ cup almonds, chopped
  1.5ml/¼ tsp dried thyme
  finely grated rind of 1 lemon
  freshly grated nutmeg
  60ml/4 tbsp chopped fresh parsley
  1 large (US extra large) egg, beaten
  60ml/4 tbsp cooked rice or stale
    breadcrumbs
  salt and ground black pepper
For the sauce
  45ml/3 tbsp plain (all-purpose) flour
  350ml/12fl oz/1½ cups turkey giblet
    stock, warmed
  350ml/12fl oz/1½ cups red
    grape juice
  30ml/2 tbsp anis spirit, such
    as Ricard
  salt and ground black pepper

1 Make the stuffing. Heat 30ml/2 tbsp oil in a pan and fry the onion, garlic and bacon. Remove to a large bowl. Fry the *morcilla* or black pudding for 3–4 minutes and the liver for 2–3 minutes.

COOK'S TIP
Allow 30 minutes to prepare and stuff the bird, and put the turkey in the oven 2¾ hours before carving.

2 Add the soaked raisins, prunes, almonds, thyme, lemon rind, nutmeg, seasoning and parsley. Stir in the egg and rice or breadcrumbs.

3 About 3 hours before carving, preheat the oven, with a low shelf, to 200°C/400°F/Gas 6. Remove the turkey's wishbone, running fingernails up the two sides of the neck to find it. Just nick it out. Season the turkey inside, stuff and retruss it. Season outside. Keep at room temperature.

4 Heat a roasting pan in the oven with 60ml/4 tbsp oil. Put in the turkey and baste the outside. Lay the bacon over the breast and legs. Reduce the oven temperature to 180°C/350°F/Gas 4 and roast for 2¼–2½ hours, basting once. To test, insert a skewer into the thickest part of the inside leg. The juices should run clear. Remove the trussing thread and transfer the turkey to a heated serving plate. Keep warm.

5 Make the sauce. Skim as much fat as possible from the roasting pan. Sprinkle in the flour and cook gently for a few minutes, stirring. Stir in the warm turkey stock and bring to simmering point. Add the grape juice and anis, and bring back to simmering. Taste for seasoning. Pour into a jug (pitcher). Carve the turkey and serve with the sauce.

VARIATION
To make a red stuffing, use frying chorizo instead of *morcilla* or black pudding. Flavour the stuffing with half a chopped dried chilli, and replace the prunes with chopped green or black olives.

SPICED DUCK WITH PEARS

THIS CATALAN SPECIALITY, KNOWN AS ÀNEC AMB PERES IN THE LOCAL LANGUAGE, IS A FABULOUS COMBINATION OF POULTRY AND FRUIT. DUCKS ARE NOT COMMON IN OTHER REGIONS OF SPAIN. TRY TO BUY A BARBARY DUCK IF YOU CAN. THIS DISH FEATURES THE PICADA, A GREAT CATALAN INVENTION MADE OF POUNDED NUTS, WHICH BOTH FLAVOURS AND THICKENS THE FINAL SAUCE. SERVE WITH A BOTTLE OF GRAN SANGRE DE TORO, WHICH WILL STAND UP WELL TO THIS ROBUSTLY FLAVOURED DISH.

SERVES SIX

INGREDIENTS

6 duck portions, preferably Barbary,
   either breast or leg pieces
15ml/1 tbsp olive oil
1 large onion, thinly sliced
1 cinnamon stick, halved
4 thyme sprigs
475ml/16fl oz/2 cups duck
   or chicken stock
3 firm, ripe pears
30ml/2 tbsp olive oil
25g/1oz/¼ cup raisins
salt and ground black pepper
young thyme sprigs or fresh parsley,
   to garnish
mashed potatoes and green
   vegetables, to serve (optional)
For the *picada*
   30ml/2 tbsp olive oil
   ½ slice stale bread, without crusts
   2 garlic cloves, sliced
   15g/½oz/12 almonds, toasted
   15g/½oz/12 hazelnuts, toasted
   15ml/1 tbsp chopped fresh parsley
   salt and ground black pepper

1 Preheat the oven to 180°C/350°F/
Gas 4. Season the duck portions,
pricking the skins with a fork. Fry them,
skin side down, for about 5 minutes,
until they give off fat. Turn them over
and fry on the other side more briefly.

2 Transfer the duck to an ovenproof
dish and drain off all but 15ml/1 tbsp
of the fat left in the pan.

3 Add the onion to the pan and fry for
5 minutes. Add the cinnamon, thyme
and stock and bring to the boil. Pour
over the duck, reserving a little of the
stock, and bake for 1¼ hours.

4 Make the *picada*. Heat the olive oil
in a frying pan and fry the bread over
a high heat. Drain on kitchen paper
and reserve. Briefly fry the garlic and
reserve with the bread.

5 Put all the nuts in a mortar and pound,
or reduce to a paste in a food processor
or blender. Add the bread, torn into
pieces, and the garlic, and reduce to a
thick, smooth paste with a little pan
stock. Add the parsley and seasoning.

COOK'S TIP

A good stock is essential for this dish.
Buy a large duck (plus two extra duck
breasts if you want the portions to be
generous) and joint it yourself, using
the giblets and carcass for stock.
Alternatively, buy duck portions and a
carton of chicken stock.

6 Peel, core and halve the pears. Fry
quickly in the oil in the frying pan until
beginning to colour on the cut sides.

7 Add the *picada* to the ovenproof dish
with the raisins and pears. Bake for a
further 15 minutes until the pears are
tender. Season to taste and garnish with
thyme or parsley. Serve with mashed
potatoes and vegetables, if you wish.

BRAISED QUAIL <u>WITH</u> WINTER VEGETABLES

QUAIL ARE BOTH PLENTIFUL AND VERY POPULAR IN SPAIN, ESPECIALLY DURING THE HUNTING SEASON, WHEN EVERY MAN TURNS OUT WITH A GUN, A DOG AND A KNAPSACK. ROASTING AND BRAISING ARE THE TWO CLASSIC TECHNIQUES FOR COOKING QUAIL. HERE, IN CORDONICES ESTOFADAS, THEY ARE COOKED AND SERVED IN A RED WINE SAUCE, THEN ELEGANTLY DISPLAYED ON CRISP CROÛTES.

4 Add more olive oil to the casserole with all the vegetables and shallots. Cook until just colouring. Return the quail to the casserole, breast-sides down, and pour in the red wine. Cover the casserole and transfer to the oven. Cook for about 30 minutes, or until the quail are tender.

5 Meanwhile, make the croûtes. Using a 10cm/4in plain cutter stamp out rounds from the bread. Heat the oil in a frying pan and cook the bread over a high heat until golden on both sides. Drain on kitchen paper and keep warm.

6 Place the croûtes on heated plates and set a quail on top of each one. Arrange the vegetables around the quail, cover and keep hot.

7 Boil the cooking juices hard until reduced to a syrupy consistency. Add the brandy and warm through, then season the sauce with salt and black pepper to taste. Drizzle the sauce over the quail and garnish with parsley, then serve immediately.

SERVES FOUR

INGREDIENTS
  4 quail, cleaned
  175g/6oz small carrots, scrubbed
  175g/6oz baby turnips
  60ml/4 tbsp olive oil
  4 shallots, halved
  450ml/¾ pint/scant 2 cups red wine
  30ml/2 tbsp Spanish brandy
  salt and ground black pepper
  fresh flat leaf parsley, to garnish
For the croûtes
  4 slices stale bread, crusts removed
  60ml/4 tbsp olive oil

1 Preheat the oven to 220°C/425°F/Gas 7. Season the quail with salt and freshly ground black pepper.

2 Using a sharp knife, cut the carrots and baby turnips into chunks. (If the carrots are very small, you can leave them whole if you prefer.)

3 Heat half the olive oil in a flameproof casserole and add the quail. Fry until browned all over, using two wooden spoons or a pair of tongs to turn the birds. Remove from the casserole and set aside.

MARINATED PIGEON IN RED WINE

GREAT CLOUDS OF MIGRATING PIGEONS FLY OVER THE MOUNTAINS OF SPAIN TWICE A YEAR, AND SHOOTING THEM IS A BIG SPORT. HERE THEY ARE MARINATED IN SPICED VINEGAR AND RED WINE, THEN COOKED IN THE MARINADE. REARED SQUAB CAN ALSO BE USED. CABBAGE IS A FAMILIAR PARTNER TO PIGEON, BUT PURÉED CELERIAC ALSO GOES VERY WELL.

SERVES FOUR

INGREDIENTS

    4 pigeons (squabs), each weighing
      about 225g/8oz, cleaned
    30ml/2 tbsp olive oil
    1 onion, roughly chopped
    225g/8oz/3 cups brown cap (cremini)
      mushrooms, sliced
    plain (all-purpose) flour, for dusting
    300ml/½ pint/1¼ cups beef or
      game stock
    30ml/2 tbsp chopped fresh parsley
    salt and ground black pepper
    fresh flat leaf parsley, to garnish
For the marinade
    15ml/1 tbsp olive oil
    1 onion, chopped
    1 carrot, chopped
    1 celery stick, chopped
    3 garlic cloves, sliced
    6 allspice berries, bruised
    2 bay leaves
    8 black peppercorns, bruised
    120ml/4fl oz/½ cup red wine vinegar
    150ml/¼ pint/⅔ cup red wine

1 Starting a day ahead, combine all the ingredients for the marinade in a large dish. Add the pigeons and turn them in the marinade, then cover and chill for 12 hours, turning occasionally.

VARIATION

If you are unable to buy pigeon, this recipe works equally well with rabbit or hare. Buy portions and make deep slashes in the flesh so that the marinade soaks in and flavours right to the centre.

2 Preheat the oven to 150°C/300°F/ Gas 2. Heat the oil in a large, flameproof casserole and cook the onion and mushrooms for about 5 minutes, until the onion has softened.

3 Meanwhile, remove the pigeons to a plate with a slotted spoon and strain the marinade into a bowl, then set both aside separately.

4 Sprinkle the flour on the pigeons and add them to the casserole, breast-sides down. Pour in the marinade and stock, and add the chopped parsley and seasoning. Cover and cook for 1½ hours or until tender.

5 Check the seasoning, then serve the pigeons on warmed plates with the sauce. Garnish with parsley.

PECHUGAS DE PICHONES CON SETAS

PIGEONS ARE CAUGHT IN NETS AS THEY COME SKIMMING THROUGH THE MOUNTAIN PASSES. THE SPORT COMBINES WELL WITH MUSHROOM PICKING — ANOTHER SPANISH DIVERSION. USE THE STRONGEST-FLAVOURED MUSHROOMS YOU CAN FIND. THE PIGEON BREASTS ARE COOKED IN THEIR OWN RICH SAUCE, THEN ELEGANTLY DISPLAYED ON THE SERVING DISH.

SERVES SIX

INGREDIENTS

6 pigeons (or squabs), cleaned
90ml/6 tbsp olive oil
1 large onion, chopped
2 garlic cloves, finely chopped
450g/1lb/6 cups brown cap (cremini)
   or small open cap field (portabello)
   mushrooms (use wild mushrooms,
   if possible)
150g/5oz Serrano or other
   ham, diced
150ml/¼ pint/⅔ cup red wine
salt and ground black pepper
60ml/4 tbsp chopped fresh parsley,
   to garnish
fried potatoes, to serve
For the stock
1 large onion, unpeeled,
   roughly chopped
2 carrots, roughly chopped
1 celery stick, roughly chopped
6 tough parsley stalks, snapped
   or bruised
1 bay leaf
1 garlic clove, unpeeled but smashed
4 sprigs of fresh thyme
12 black peppercorns, crushed

1 First prepare the pigeons. Find the wishbone by pushing your forefinger and thumb in the neck end. It runs up each side; snap it out. Once this is gone, it is easy to take off the breast portions. Cut down on one side of the breastbone with a large knife, then scrape along the rib cage, to get the breast meat off whole. Repeat this, and season the meat.

2 Cut the pigeon carcasses across the ribs and flatten them in a large pan. Add all the stock ingredients and just cover with water. Simmer gently for about 1½ hours to make a rich dark stock. Allow to cool slightly, then strain into a large bowl.

3 Heat 30ml/2 tbsp of the olive oil in a large shallow flameproof casserole and fry the onion and garlic gently for a few minutes, until soft. Meanwhile, pull the mushroom stalks out of the caps, then chop the stalks finely and add to the casserole, with the ham cubes. Fry briefly, stirring. Pour in the wine and 250ml/8fl oz/1 cup of the stock. Simmer gently to reduce a little.

COOK'S TIP
The Spanish definitely prefer wild birds — and they are available in abundance while they are in season. Squabs are the same family as pigeons, but are dovecote birds. They are plumper and slightly blander and benefit from this richly flavoured sauce.

4 Heat 30ml/2 tbsp oil in a large frying pan. Put the pigeon breasts in the pan, skin downward and fry for 2 minutes on each side. Remove to the casserole and simmer for 2–3 minutes.

5 Fry the mushroom caps, in 30ml/2 tbsp oil, in the same pan. Arrange the breasts in a ring on an oval platter. Pile the mushrooms in the centre. Spoon the ham and sauce over the pigeon, and sprinkle with parsley.

GUINEA FOWL WITH SAFFRON AND NUT SAUCE

THE ARABS INTRODUCED SAFFRON TO SPAIN AND THIS IS A MOORISH SAUCE, OF SAFFRON, TOASTED ALMONDS GROUND WITH PARSLEY AND SEVERAL SPICES. PEPITA IS THE SPANISH WORD FOR A SEED OR NUT, HENCE THE NAME PINTADA EN PEPITORIA. *SERVE WITH A RIOJA RESERVA, TO DRINK.*

3 Cut the bird into eight serving pieces, discarding the wing tips, backbone, breastbones and leg tips. This will give you two legs (split them at the joint), two wings with one-third of the breast attached, and two short breast pieces.

4 Heat the olive oil in a wide shallow flameproof casserole and fry the bread slice on both sides. Fry the garlic quickly, then remove both to a blender.

5 Season the poultry well and fry them, turning until golden on all sides. Add the remaining stock and the sherry to the pan, stirring to deglaze the pan. Add the bay leaf and thyme and cover. Cook gently for 10 minutes.

6 Grind together the bread, garlic and almonds. Add the parsley, saffron liquid, nutmeg and cloves, and purée. Stir into the poultry juices, add the lemon juice and paprika, season and serve.

SERVES FOUR

INGREDIENTS
25g/1oz/¼ cup blanched almonds
pinch of saffron threads (0.1g)
120ml/8 tbsp chicken stock
1.2–1.3kg/2½–3lb guinea fowl
60ml/4fl oz/½ cup olive oil
1 thick slice of bread, without crusts
2 garlic cloves, finely chopped
120ml/4fl oz/½ cup fino sherry
1 bay leaf, crumbled
4 thyme sprigs
15ml/1 tbsp finely chopped
  fresh parsley
pinch of freshly grated nutmeg
pinch of ground cloves
juice of ½ lemon
5ml/1 tsp paprika
salt and ground black pepper

1 Preheat the oven to 150°C/300°F/Gas 2. Spread the almonds on a baking sheet and toast in the oven for about 20 minutes until golden brown.

2 Crumble the saffron with your fingers into a jug (pitcher) or small bowl, pour over 30ml/2 tbsp hot chicken stock and leave to soak.

PERDICES CON UVAS

PARTRIDGES ARE SPAIN'S COMMONEST GAME BIRDS. THEY HAVE A NATURAL AFFINITY WITH GRAPES, AS WILD BIRDS OFTEN ATTACK THE HARVEST. GAME HENS OR ANY PLUMP SMALL BIRD CAN BE USED FOR THIS POT ROAST, WHERE GRAPES ARE USED FOR THE GARNISH AND THE SAUCE.

SERVES FOUR

INGREDIENTS

4 partridges, cleaned
500g/1¼lb red grapes, split and
   seeded, plus extra to garnish
45–60ml/3–4 tbsp olive oil
4 rashers (slices) smoked streaky
   (fatty) bacon, halved across
1 onion, chopped
2 garlic cloves, finely chopped
1 bay leaf
120ml/4fl oz/½ cup dry white wine
250ml/8fl oz/1 cup game or
   chicken stock
freshly grated nutmeg
salt and ground black pepper
30ml/2 tbsp chopped fresh parsley,
   to garnish

2 Fry the bacon until crisp, then reserve on a plate. Put the birds into the casserole breast sides down and fry until coloured. Turn them with two spoons, frying and turning until brown all over. Remove.

3 Fry the onion and garlic, adding a little more oil if needed, until softened.

4 Return the birds to the casserole and arrange two pieces of bacon on top of each. Push 125g/5oz grapes in round them, and add the bay leaf. Pour in the white wine and stock. Add plenty of black pepper. Simmer, covered, for 30 minutes.

5 Remove the birds and bacon to a plate. Spoon the casserole contents into a food processor, discarding the bay leaf, and purée. Add plenty of nutmeg and check the seasoning.

6 Return the birds to the pan, pour the sauce around them, and add 125g/5oz grapes. Heat through. Serve, garnished with extra grapes, crumbled bacon and a little parsley.

1 Season the birds inside and out, then stuff with 250g/9oz grapes. Put 45ml/ 3 tbsp oil in a flameproof casserole into which the birds will fit snugly.

MEAT AND FURRED GAME

*From beef with chocolate sauce to kidneys in sherry and the
ever-popular meatballs in tomato sauce, there are dishes for every
occasion. Try beef steaks with blue cheese sauce, a spring stew
of veal with young vegetables, a lamb dish with lemon,
a Pyrennean stew with fresh and dried peppers, or classic pulse
dishes such as fabada and cocido. Oxtail stewed is reminiscent
of the Spanish bulls, while rabbit in garlic sauce is a
recipe dating back to before Roman times.*

CHORIZO <u>WITH</u> CHESTNUTS

CHESTNUTS ARE NATIVE TO GALICIA AND ARE A POPULAR ADDITION TO A VARIETY OF DISHES.
CHORIZOS Y CASTANAS MAKES A GOOD SIDE DISH FOR ROAST TURKEY AND A POPULAR SUPPER DISH
SERVED ON ITS OWN. ADD A LITTLE CHILLI IF YOU LIKE THINGS HOT AND SPICY.

SERVES THREE TO SIX

INGREDIENTS
  15ml/1 tbsp olive oil
  4 red chorizo sausages, sliced
  200g/7oz/1¼ cups peeled
    cooked chestnuts
  15ml/1 tbsp paprika
  salt and ground black pepper
  crusty bread, to serve

COOK'S TIP
In Spain, chorizo for frying is sold as red
links. Both mild and spicy types are
available. Similar kinds of red sausage
are made in Italy and Mexico.

1 Heat the oil in a wide frying pan and
put in the chorizo slices in a single
layer. Cook the chorizo for 3–4 minutes,
turning frequently, until it starts to give
off its oil.

2 Tip in the peeled chestnuts and
toss until warm and covered with the
chorizo oil. Add the paprika and season
with salt and ground black pepper.
Serve hot with crusty bread.

ALBÓNDIGAS CON SALSA DE TOMATE

SPANISH MEN LIKE TO FIND TRADITIONAL DISHES IN THEIR FAVOURITE TAPAS BAR. THESE TASTY
MEATBALLS IN TOMATO SAUCE ARE USUALLY SERVED IN LITTLE BROWN, INDIVIDUAL CASSEROLE DISHES,
ACCOMPANIED BY CRUSTY BREAD. THEY MAKE A GOOD SUPPER, TOO, WITH A GREEN SALAD OR PASTA.

SERVES FOUR

INGREDIENTS
  225g/8oz minced (ground) beef
  4 spring onions (scallions),
    thinly sliced
  2 garlic cloves, finely chopped
  30ml/2 tbsp grated fresh
    Parmesan cheese
  10ml/2 tsp fresh thyme leaves
  15ml/1 tbsp olive oil
  3 tomatoes, chopped
  30ml/2 tbsp red or dry white wine
  10ml/2 tsp chopped fresh rosemary
  pinch of sugar
  salt and ground black pepper
  fresh thyme, to garnish

VARIATION
Albóndigas are equally good made of
half beef and half pork, or a mixture of
meats, including ham. In the sausage-
making areas, particularly Extremadura,
they may be made completely of pork.
Meatballs, called *la prueba* ("the try-
out"), are made to test the seasoning.

1 Put the minced beef in a bowl. Add
the spring onions, garlic, Parmesan and
thyme and plenty of salt and pepper.

2 Stir well to combine, then shape the
mixture into 12 small firm balls.

VARIATION
To make *biftek andaluz* (the nearest
thing Spain has to a beefburger), shape
the meat mixture into four wide patties
and fry. Serve the patties on a slice of
grilled (broiled) beefsteak tomato, or
surrounded by tomato sauce. Top with
a fried egg for decoration, if you like.

3 Heat the olive oil in a large, heavy
frying pan and cook the meatballs for
about 5 minutes, turning frequently,
until evenly browned all over.

4 Add the chopped tomatoes, wine,
rosemary and sugar to the pan, with
salt and ground black pepper to taste.

5 Cover the pan and cook gently for
about 15 minutes until the tomatoes are
pulpy and the meatballs are cooked
through. Check the sauce for seasoning
and serve the meatballs hot, garnished
with the thyme.

RIÑONES AL JEREZ

KIDNEYS COOKED IN SHERRY ARE EXTREMELY POPULAR IN TAPAS BARS, AND MAKE AN EXCELLENT FAMILY SUPPER. AS A FIRST COURSE, PARTNER THE DISH WITH FRIED TOAST TRIANGLES OR CRUSTY BREAD. A FINO MONTILLA WINE, LESS WELL KNOWN THAN SHERRY BUT WITH THE SAME DRY QUALITIES, COULD REPLACE THE SHERRY. C.B. MONTILLA IS OFTEN THE CHOICE IN ANDALUSIA FOR THIS DISH.

SERVES FOUR

INGREDIENTS

12 plump lamb's kidneys
60ml/4 tbsp olive oil
115g/4oz smoked bacon lardons,
  or diced pancetta
1 large onion, chopped
2 garlic cloves, finely chopped
30ml/2 tbsp plain (all-purpose) flour
150ml/¼ pint/⅔ cup fino sherry
  or C.B. Montilla wine
15ml/1 tbsp tomato purée (paste)
30ml/2 tbsp chopped fresh parsley
salt and ground black pepper
new potatoes, boiled and buttered,
  to serve (optional)

1 Halve and skin the kidneys, then remove the cores. Cut the kidneys into cubes. Heat half the oil in a large frying pan and fry the bacon or pancetta until the fat starts to run. Add the onion and garlic and fry until softened. Remove to a plate.

2 Add the remaining oil to the pan and divide the kidneys into four batches. Put in one handful, and stir-fry over a high heat until sealed. (They should not give off any juice.) Remove to a plate and repeat with a second handful and remove to the plate. Continue until they are all cooked.

3 Return the onion and bacon mixture to the pan. Sprinkle with flour and cook, stirring gently. Add the sherry or Montilla wine and stir until thickened. Add the tomato purée and parsley. Return the kidneys to the pan, and heat through. Season well and serve hot with buttered new potatoes, if you like.

LIVER AND BACON CASSEROLE

IN SPAIN, LIVER MEANS PIG'S LIVER, AND IS COOKED HERE IN A WELL-SEASONED SAUCE. LAMBS ARE KILLED WHEN THEY ARE VERY SMALL AND THE LIVER IS NOT MUCH OF A MEAL. THE PIG'S LIVER IS THE FIRST THING TO BE EATEN FROM THE NEW PIG, AND SO IS ASSOCIATED WITH ONE OF THE BIG FEASTS OF THE YEAR, MATANZA. YOU CAN SUBSTITUTE LAMB'S LIVER IF YOU PREFER.

SERVES THREE TO FOUR

INGREDIENTS

    450g/1lb pig's or lamb's liver,
        trimmed and sliced
    60ml/4 tbsp milk (for pig's liver)
    30ml/2 tbsp olive oil
    225g/8oz rindless smoked lean bacon
        rashers (strips), cut into pieces
    2 onions, halved and sliced
    175g/6oz/2¼ cups brown cap
        (cremini) mushrooms, halved
    25g/1oz/2 tbsp butter
    30ml/2 tbsp plain (all-purpose) flour
    150ml/¼ pint/⅔ cup hot
        chicken stock
    15ml/1 tbsp soy sauce
    5ml/1 tsp paprika
    salt and ground black pepper

1 If using pig's liver, soak it in the milk for 1 hour for a milder flavour, then blot dry with kitchen paper.

2 Heat the oil in a frying pan and stir-fry the bacon until crisp. Add the onion and cook, stirring, until softened. Add the mushrooms and fry for 1 minute.

3 Using a slotted spoon, remove the bacon and vegetables from the pan and keep warm. Add the liver to the fat remaining in the pan and cook over a high heat for 3–4 minutes, turning once to seal the slices on both sides. Remove from the pan and keep warm.

4 Melt the butter in the pan, sprinkle the flour over and cook briefly. Stir in the stock, soy sauce and paprika and bring to a simmer. Return the liver and vegetables. Simmer gently for 3–4 minutes. Check the seasoning.

VARIATION
Bread is the classic accompaniment to this dish, but macaroni or a choice of vegetables make equally good partners.

FABADA

This bean and sausage hotpot from the wild mountains of Asturias on the northern coast of Spain, has achieved world fame. It used to contain dried broad (fava) beans, which gave it the name, but when these old-fashioned beans were abandoned and modern fabes — white kidney beans — were adopted, it became a truly great dish. Cured sausages, a pork knuckle and belly pork lend the beans an incredible richness, which is enhanced by saffron and paprika. It is a good dish for winter evenings, served with glasses of cider.

SERVES EIGHT

INGREDIENTS

   500–800g/1¼–1¾lb belly pork,
     in thick slices
   1 smoked gammon (smoked or cured
     ham) knuckle, about 675g/1½lb,
     skin slashed
   800g/1¾lb dried cannellini beans,
     soaked overnight (see Cook's Tip)
   5ml/1 tsp black peppercorns, crushed
   15ml/1 tbsp paprika
   pinch of saffron threads (0.2g)
   1 bay leaf
   30ml/2 tbsp oil (optional)
   4 garlic cloves, chopped
   3 red chorizo sausages, thickly sliced
   175g/6oz *morcilla* or black
     pudding (blood sausage),
     thickly sliced
   ground black pepper (optional)

1 Using a very large stockpot (with a capacity of at least 6 litres/10 pints/ 25 cups), put the pork belly and knuckle into the pot with water to cover. Bring to the boil, then drain the meat and return it to the stockpot.

COOK'S TIP
The quality of the bean is a feature of the dish so try to use luxury Spanish beans, now widely exported. *Fabes* are like very large, white cannellini beans. If luxury Spanish beans are unavailable use *lingots* (the French *cassoulet* bean) or large white kidney bean.

2 Add the drained beans to the pot and pour over 2.3 litres/4 pints/10 cups water. Bring to the boil very slowly, then boil for 10 minutes. Reduce the heat and add the peppercorns, paprika, crumbled saffron and the bay leaf.

3 Simmer very gently over a very low heat for 2 hours. (It is best to put the pot over a small burner, turned low.) Check occasionally that the beans are still covered with liquid, but do not stir energetically or the beans will break up.

4 Remove the pork belly and knuckle and set them aside to cool. Strip off the skin and fat, and take 30ml/2 tbsp chopped fat for frying (or use oil). Heat this in a frying pan and cook the garlic lightly, then spoon it into the beans.

VARIATION
Most Spanish bean stews are flavoured with meat from the pig and are then enriched with pork fat. However, in the north, beans are cooked with clams.

5 Fry the chorizo and *morcilla* or black pudding lightly in the same pan. Gently stir into the bean pot.

6 Remove all the meat from the ham bone. Chop it with the pork and return to the stockpot. Simmer for a few minutes. Check the seasonings (there should be enough salt from the meat already) and serve.

BLACK BEAN STEW

TOLOSA IN THE BASQUE COUNTRY IS FAMOUS FOR ITS BLACK BEAN STEW — POTAJE DE ALUBIAS NEGRAS — MADE SPICY WITH VARIOUS SAUSAGES AND PICKLED PORK. HERE IS A SIMPLIFIED VERSION, WITH EXTRA FRESH VEGETABLES THAT ADD WONDERFULLY TO ITS FLAVOUR.

SERVES FIVE TO SIX

INGREDIENTS
275g/10oz/1½ cups black
   beans, soaked overnight
   in cold water
675g/1½lb boneless belly
   pork rashers (strips)
60ml/4 tbsp olive oil
350g/12oz baby (pearl) onions
2 celery sticks, thickly sliced
150g/5oz chorizo, cut
   into chunks
10ml/2 tsp paprika
600ml/1 pint/2½ cups light chicken
   or vegetable stock
2 green (bell) peppers, seeded
   and cut into large pieces
salt and ground black pepper

1 Drain the beans into a pan and cover with fresh water. Bring to the boil and boil rapidly for 10 minutes. Drain the beans and put in an ovenproof dish.

2 Preheat the oven to 160°C/325°F/ Gas 3. Cut away any rind from the pork, then cut it into large chunks.

3 Heat the oil in a large frying pan and fry the onions and celery for 3 minutes. Add the pork and fry for 10 minutes, or until the pork is browned.

4 Add the chorizo and fry for 2 minutes, then sprinkle in the paprika. Tip the mixture into the beans and mix well to combine thoroughly.

5 Add the stock to the pan and bring to the boil, then pour over the meat and beans. Cover and bake for 1 hour.

6 Stir the green peppers into the stew and return to the oven for a further 15 minutes. Season and serve hot.

VARIATION
This is the sort of stew to which you can add a variety of winter vegetables, such as chunks of leek, turnip and celeriac.

STUFFED ROAST LOIN OF PORK

PORK IS SPAIN'S MOST POPULAR MEAT, THE LOIN PARTICULARLY SO. FOR THIS DISH, LOMO DE CERDO RELLENO, YOU NEED THE WHOLE CUT WITH THE FLAP ON THE SIDE TO ENCLOSE THE STUFFING, WHICH IS RICHLY FLAVOURED WITH FIGS. MEAT AND FRUIT ARE A POPULAR CATALAN COMBINATION.

SERVES FOUR

INGREDIENTS
   60ml/4 tbsp olive oil
   1 onion, finely chopped
   2 garlic cloves, chopped
   75g/3oz/1½ cups stale breadcrumbs
   4 ready-to-eat dried figs, chopped
   8 pitted green olives, chopped
   25g/1oz/¼ cup flaked almonds
   15ml/1 tbsp lemon juice
   15ml/1 tbsp chopped fresh parsley
   1 egg yolk
   1kg/2¼lb boned loin of pork with
      the side flap attached
   salt, paprika and black pepper

1 Preheat the oven to 200°C/400°F/ Gas 6. Heat 45ml/3 tbsp of the oil in a pan, add the onion and garlic, and cook gently until softened. Remove the pan from the heat, and stir in the breadcrumbs, figs, olives, almonds, lemon juice, parsley and egg yolk. Season with salt, paprika and pepper.

2 Remove any string from the pork and unroll the belly flap, cutting away any excess fat or meat to enable you to do so. Spread half the stuffing over the flat piece and roll it up, starting from the thick side. Tie the joint at intervals with string to hold it together.

3 Pour the remaining oil into a small roasting pan and add the pork. Roast for 1¼ hours. Meanwhile, form the remaining stuffing mixture into balls and add to the pan, 15–20 minutes before the end of cooking time.

4 Remove the pork from the oven and leave it rest for 10 minutes. Carve into thick slices and serve with the stuffing balls and any juices from the pan. This dish is also good served cold.

PORK EMPANADA

THIS FLAT, TWO-CRUST GALICIAN PIE IS FAMOUS BECAUSE THERE IS NO OCCASION ON WHICH IT IS NOT SERVED. IT IS FESTIVAL FOOD; IT GREETS THE BOATS OF RETURNING FISHERMEN AND IT IS THE MEN'S LUNCHBOX STAPLE. FILLINGS VARY ENORMOUSLY, AND MAY INCLUDE FISH SUCH AS SARDINES, OR SCALLOPS FOR SPECIAL OCCASIONS. THESE PIES ARE GOOD HOT OR COLD.

SERVES EIGHT

INGREDIENTS
    75ml/5 tbsp olive oil
    2 onions, chopped
    4 garlic cloves, finely chopped
    1kg/2¼lb boned pork loin, diced
    175g/6oz smoked gammon (smoked
        or cured ham) or raw ham, diced
    3 red chorizo or other spicy sausages
        (about 300g/11oz)
    3 (bell) peppers (mixed colours),
        seeded and chopped
    175ml/6fl oz/¾ cup white wine
    200g/7oz can tomatoes
    pinch of saffron threads (0.1g)
    5ml/1 tsp paprika
    30ml/2 tbsp chopped fresh parsley
    salt and ground black pepper
For the corn meal dough
    250g/9oz corn meal
    7g/2 tsp easy-blend (rapid-rise)
        dried yeast
    5ml/1 tsp caster (superfine) sugar
    250g/9oz plain (all-purpose) flour,
        plus extra for dusting
    5ml/1 tsp salt
    200ml/7fl oz/scant 1 cup
        warm water
    30ml/2 tbsp oil
    2 eggs, beaten, plus 1 for the glaze

1 Make the filling. Heat 60ml/4 tbsp oil in a frying pan and fry the onions, adding the garlic when the onions begin to colour. Transfer to a flameproof casserole. Add the pork and gammon or ham to the pan, and fry until coloured, stirring. Transfer to the casserole.

2 Add 15ml/1 tbsp oil, the sausage and the peppers to the pan and fry. Transfer to the casserole. Deglaze the pan with the wine, allowing it to bubble and reduce. Pour into the casserole.

3 Add the tomatoes, saffron, paprika and parsley and season. Cook gently for 20–30 minutes. Leave to cool.

4 Meanwhile make the dough. Put the corn meal into a food processor. Add the dried yeast with the sugar. Gradually add the flour, salt, water, oil and 2 eggs and beat, to make a smooth soft dough.

5 Turn the dough into a clean bowl, cover with a dishtowel and leave in a warm place for 40–50 minutes, to rise.

6 Preheat the oven to 200°C/400°F/ Gas 6. Grease a shallow roasting pan or dish 30 × 20cm/12 × 8in. Halve the dough. Roll out one half on a floured surface, a little larger than the pan. Lift this in place, leaving the border hanging over the edge.

7 Spoon in the filling. Roll out the lid and lay it in place. Fold the outside edge over the lid (trimming as necessary) and press gently all round with a fork, to seal the pie. Prick the surface and brush with beaten egg.

8 Bake the pie for 30–35 minutes (covering the ends if they brown too much). Cut the pie into squares.

SKEWERED LAMB WITH RED ONION SALSA

THE MOORS FIRST INTRODUCED SKEWERED AND BARBECUED MEAT TO SPAIN, WHERE IT HAS BEEN POPULAR FOR OVER 1,500 YEARS. THESE SPICED SKEWERS ARE ACCOMPANIED BY A SIMPLE SALSA.

SERVES FOUR

INGREDIENTS
  500–675g/1¼–1½lb ready-trimmed,
    cubed lamb
  5ml/1 tsp ground cumin
  10ml/2 tsp paprika
  30ml/2 tbsp olive oil
  salt and ground black pepper
For the red onion salsa
  1 red onion, very thinly sliced
  1 large tomato, seeded
    and chopped
  15ml/1 tbsp red wine vinegar
  3–4 fresh basil or mint leaves,
    roughly torn

VARIATION
Skewer squares of (bell) pepper, and whole bay leaves between the cubes of spicy, marinated meat.

1 Season the lamb with the cumin, paprika, oil and black pepper. Toss well to coat. Leave in a cool place for several hours, or in the refrigerator overnight, so that the lamb absorbs all the spicy flavours.

2 Spear the cubes of lamb on four skewers, leaving one end of each of the skewers free for picking up.

3 To make the salsa, put the sliced onion, tomato, vinegar and basil or mint leaves in a small bowl and stir together. Season to taste with salt and pepper.

4 If cooking on a barbecue, the charcoal should be grey with no flames before you start cooking. Alternatively, preheat the grill (broiler) with the shelf about 15cm/6in from the heat source. Generously brush the grill pan with oil.

5 Season the lamb with salt and cook for 5–10 minutes, turning the skewers occasionally, until the lamb is well browned but still slightly pink in the centre. Serve hot, with the salsa.

COOK'S TIP
If using wooden skewers, soak them in cold water first, to prevent them burning.

COCHIFRITO

ARAGON AND NAVARRE IN THE PYRENEES ARE KNOWN FOR THEIR FINE INGREDIENTS – AND ALSO FOR THEIR SIMPLE COOKING. "IF THE QUALITY IS THERE, NO NEED TO EMPLOY TRICKS IN THE KITCHEN" RUNS THE SPANISH PROVERB. THE MEAT IS FRIED SIMPLY AND FLAVOURED WITH LEMON JUICE AND PAPRIKA IN THIS DISH. IT CAPTURES THE VERY ESSENCE OF LAMB.

SERVES FOUR

INGREDIENTS
  800g/1¾lb very well-trimmed,
    tender lamb (see Cook's Tip),
    in cubes or strips
  30ml/2 tbsp olive oil, plus extra
  1 onion, chopped
  2 garlic cloves, finely chopped
  5ml/1 tsp paprika
  juice of 2 lemons
  15ml/1 tbsp finely chopped
    fresh parsley
  salt and ground black pepper

COOK'S TIP
The sweetest lamb is cut from the shoulder. However, it also contains quite a lot of fat, often in layers through the meat, so allow extra weight, and cut it out.

1 Season the lamb with salt and ground black pepper. Heat the 30ml/2 tbsp olive oil in a large frying pan or casserole over a high heat and add the meat in handfuls. Add the onion at the same time, and keep pushing the meat around the pan with a spatula. Add more meat to the pan as each batch is sealed. Add the chopped garlic and a little more oil if necessary.

2 When the meat is golden and the onion soft, sprinkle with paprika and lemon juice. Cover and simmer for 15 minutes. Check the seasonings and add a dusting of parsley, then serve.

VARIATION
This dish may also be made using pork in place of the lamb – the name *cochifrito* means little pig, fried.

LAMB <u>WITH</u> RED PEPPERS <u>AND</u> RIOJA

WORLD-FAMOUS FOR ITS RED WINE, RIOJA ALSO PRODUCES EXCELLENT RED PEPPERS. IT EVEN HAS A RED PEPPER FAIR, AT LODOSO, EVERY YEAR. TOGETHER THEY GIVE THIS LAMB STEW A LOVELY RICH FLAVOUR. BOILED POTATOES MAKE A VERY GOOD ACCOMPANIMENT.

SERVES FOUR

INGREDIENTS

 15ml/1 tbsp plain (all-purpose) flour
 1kg/2¼lb lean lamb, cubed
 60ml/4 tbsp olive oil
 2 red onions, sliced
 4 garlic cloves, sliced
 10ml/2 tsp paprika
 1.5ml/¼ tsp ground cloves
 400ml/14fl oz/1⅔ cups red Rioja
 150ml/¼ pint/⅔ cup lamb stock
 2 bay leaves
 2 thyme sprigs
 3 red (bell) peppers, halved
  and seeded
 salt and ground black pepper
 bay leaves and thyme sprigs,
  to garnish (optional)

1 Preheat the oven to 160°C/325°F/ Gas 3. Season the flour, add the lamb and toss lightly to coat.

2 Heat the oil in a frying pan and fry the lamb until browned. Transfer to an ovenproof dish. Fry the onions and garlic until soft. Add to the meat.

3 Add the paprika, cloves, Rioja, lamb stock, bay leaves and thyme and bring the mixture to a gentle simmer. Add the halved red peppers. Cover the dish with a lid or foil and cook for about 30 minutes, or until the meat is tender. Garnish with more bay leaves and thyme sprigs, if you like.

VEAL CASSEROLE WITH BROAD BEANS

THIS DELICATE STEW, FLAVOURED WITH SHERRY AND PLENTY OF GARLIC, IS A SPRING DISH MADE WITH NEW VEGETABLES — MENESTRA DE TERNERA. FOR A DELICIOUS FLAVOUR BE SURE TO ADD PLENTY OF PARSLEY JUST BEFORE SERVING. LAMB IS EQUALLY GOOD COOKED IN THIS WAY.

SERVES SIX

INGREDIENTS
  45ml/3 tbsp olive oil
  1.3–1.6kg/3–3½lb veal, cut into
    5cm/2in cubes
  1 large onion, chopped
  6 large garlic cloves, unpeeled
  1 bay leaf
  5ml/1 tsp paprika
  240ml/8fl oz/1 cup fino sherry
  100g/4oz/scant 1 cup shelled,
    skinned broad (fava) beans
  60ml/4 tbsp chopped fresh flat
    leaf parsley
  salt and ground black pepper

1 Heat 30ml/2 tbsp oil in a large flameproof casserole. Add half the meat and brown well on all sides. Transfer to a plate. Brown the rest of the meat and remove from the pan.

2 Add the remaining oil to the pan and cook the onion until soft. Return the meat to the casserole and stir well to mix with the onion.

3 Add the garlic cloves, bay leaf, paprika and sherry. Season with salt and black pepper. Bring to simmering point, then cover and cook very gently for 30–40 minutes.

4 Add the broad beans to the casserole about 10 minutes before the end of the cooking time. Check the seasoning and stir in the chopped parsley just before serving.

COCIDO

The Spanish national dish, cocido is also Madrid's most famous stew. The name simply means "boiled dinner" and it used to be made more than once a week. A pot of fresh and salt meat with chicken and sausages is simmered with chickpeas and some fresh vegetables. The broth makes a soup course and then the rest is displayed on two splendid platters. Serve with a bottle of Viña Arana from La Rioja Alta or Bodegas Bilbainas Viña Pomal.

SERVES EIGHT

INGREDIENTS
500–800g/1¼–1¾lb cured brisket or silverside (pot roast)
250g/9oz smoked streaky (fatty) bacon, in one piece, or 250g/9oz belly pork
1 knuckle gammon (smoked or cured ham) bone, with some meat still attached
500–750g/1¼–1¾lb beef marrow bone, sawn through
1 pig's trotter (foot), sawn through
1 whole garlic bulb
2 bay leaves
5ml/1 tsp black peppercorns, lightly crushed
250g/9oz/1¼ cups dried chickpeas, soaked overnight and drained
2 quarters corn-fed chicken
1 small onion, studded with 2 or 3 cloves
2 large carrots, cut into big pieces
2 leeks, cut into chunks
500g/1¼lb small new potatoes, scrubbed
2 red chorizo sausages
1 *morcilla* or 250g/9oz black pudding (blood sausage)
30ml/2 tbsp long grain rice
1 small (bell) pepper, finely diced
salt

1 Put the salt meat – brisket or silverside, bacon or pork and knuckle – into a large pan and cover with water. Bring slowly to the boil, simmer for 5 minutes to remove excess salt, and drain.

VARIATIONS
The types of meat used in this hearty stew can be varied. Just make sure that you include a salty meat, a meat on the bone, a smoked meat, a piece of pork, a piece of beef and a piece of chicken – plus a paprika sausage.

2 Using a very large stockpot (with a capacity of at least 6 litres/10 pints/5 quarts), pack in all the meat, skin side down, with the marrowbone and trotter. Add the garlic bulb, bay leaves and peppercorns, with water to cover. Bring to simmering point, skimming off any scum, with a slotted spoon.

3 Add the drained chickpeas, cover and simmer on the lowest possible heat for 1½ hours, checking occasionally that there is enough liquid.

4 Add the chicken and onion to the pot. Cook until the chickpeas are done.

5 Start the vegetables. Put the carrots, leeks and potatoes into a large pan with the chorizo (but not the *morcilla* or black pudding). Cover with water and bring to the boil. Simmer for 25 minutes, until the potatoes are cooked. About 5 minutes before the end, add the *morcilla* or black pudding.

6 Strain off enough broth from the meat pot (about 1.2 litres/2 pints/5 cups) into a pan, for soup. Bring back to the boil, sprinkle in the rice and cook for 15 minutes. Add the diced pepper and cook for 2–3 minutes more. Serve the soup as the first course.

7 Drain the vegetables and sausages and arrange on a platter. Serve as a separate second course or as an accompaniment with the meat.

8 Slice the meats, removing the marrow from the bone and adding it to the chickpeas. Arrange with all the meats on a heated serving platter, moistening with a little broth.

ROPA VIEJA

THE NAME OF THIS DISH MEANS "OLD CLOTHES", WHICH SOUNDS A GOOD DEAL MORE ROMANTIC THAN LEFTOVERS. IT IS A DISH FOR USING UP MEATS FROM THE COCIDO, AND THE RECIPE SHOWS BOTH JEWISH AND ARAB INFLUENCES. IT IS NORMALLY MADE WITH COLD ROAST BEEF, BUT IT IS IDEAL FOR FINISHING UP COLD TURKEY AND OTHER CHRISTMAS MEATS AND EVEN STUFFING.

3 If using the fresh pepper, add it to the casserole and stir-fry until softened.

4 Add the tomatoes and the chopped baked pepper, if using, the meat stock, cumin, allspice, ground cloves and cayenne pepper. Season to taste. Add the cubed meat and simmer gently.

5 Heat 45ml/3 tbsp oil over a high heat in a large frying pan. Fry the aubergine cubes, in batches if necessary, until they are brown on all sides. (If you need to add more oil, add it to an empty pan, and reheat to a high heat, before adding more aubergine cubes.)

6 Add the aubergine and chickpeas to the casserole and bring to a simmer, adding a little more stock to cover, if necessary – the dish should be almost solid. Check the seasonings, garnish with mint, if using, and serve.

SERVES FOUR

INGREDIENTS
  2 small aubergines (eggplant)
  90ml/6 tbsp olive oil
  1 large onion, chopped
  3 garlic cloves, finely chopped
  1 fresh, or baked, red (bell) pepper,
    seeded and sliced (optional)
  400g/14oz can tomatoes
  250ml/8fl oz/1 cup meat stock
  2.5ml/½ tsp ground cumin
  2.5ml/½ tsp ground allspice
  pinch of ground cloves
  2.5ml/½ tsp cayenne pepper
  400g/14oz cooked beef, cubed
    (or mixed turkey, ham, etc)
  400g/14oz can chickpeas, drained
  salt and ground black pepper
  chopped fresh mint, to garnish
    (optional)

1 Cut the aubergines into cubes and put them into a colander. Sprinkle with 10ml/2 tsp salt, turning the cubes over with your hands. Leave to drain for about 1 hour. Rinse, then squeeze them dry using kitchen paper.

2 Meanwhile put 30ml/2 tbsp oil in a wide flameproof casserole and fry the onion and garlic until soft.

SOLOMILLO <u>WITH</u> CABRALES SAUCE

WELL-HUNG BEEF IS A FEATURE OF THE BASQUE COUNTRY, SERVED HERE WITH CABRALES, THE BLUE CHEESE FROM SPAIN'S NORTHERN MOUNTAINS. FRENCH ROQUEFORT IS ALSO EXTREMELY POPULAR, BECAUSE IT APPEALS TO THE SPANISH LOVE OF SALTY FLAVOURS. IN THIS RECIPE THE SALT AND BRANDY IN THE SAUCE ARE PERFECTLY BALANCED BY THE CREAM.

SERVES FOUR

INGREDIENTS
  25g/1oz/2 tbsp butter
  30ml/2 tbsp olive oil
  4 fillet steaks, cut 5cm/2in thick,
    about 150g/5oz each
  salt and coarsely ground black pepper
  fresh flat leaf parsley, to garnish
For the blue cheese sauce
  30ml/2 tbsp Spanish brandy
  150ml/5fl oz/⅔ cup double
    (heavy) cream
  75g/3oz *Cabrales* or Roquefort
    cheese, crumbled

COOK'S TIP
Cabrales is also known as *Picón* and *Treviso* and has a slightly more acidic flavour than Roquefort.

1 Heat the butter and oil together in a heavy frying pan, over a high heat. Season the steaks well. Fry them for 2 minutes on each side, to sear them.

2 Lower the heat slightly and cook for a further 2–3 minutes on each side, or according to your taste. Remove the steaks to a warm plate.

3 Reduce the heat and add the brandy, stirring to pick up the juices. Add the cream and boil to reduce a little.

4 Add the crumbled cheese and mash it into the sauce using a spoon. Taste for seasoning. Serve in a small sauce jug (pitcher), or poured over the steaks. Garnish the beef with parsley.

CARNE CON CHOCOLATE

CHOCOLATE CAME TO EUROPE VIA SPAIN. IT IS NOT NATURALLY SWEET AND SO CHOCOLATE SQUARES ARE USED IN SPAIN IN THE WAY THAT OTHER COUNTRIES USE GRAVY BROWNING. IT GIVES THIS STEW A RICH DARKNESS, WHICH IS ENHANCED BY THE BRANDY. SERVE WITH A RIOJA RESERVA.

SERVES SIX

INGREDIENTS
  60ml/4 tbsp olive oil
  1kg/2¼lb trimmed stewing beef
  5ml/1 tsp paprika
  150g/5oz smoked bacon lardons,
    or diced pancetta
  1 large Spanish onion, chopped
  4 carrots, sliced thickly
  1 large leek, white only, sliced
  6 garlic cloves
  225g/8oz brown cap (cremini)
    mushrooms, sliced
  4 tomatoes, peeled, seeded
    and chopped
  45ml/3 tbsp plain (all-purpose) flour
  12 peppercorns, crushed
  1 pig's trotter (foot), sawn through
  250ml/8fl oz/1 cup dry red wine
  1 bay leaf
  4 sprigs of thyme
  120ml/4fl oz/½ cup Spanish brandy
  300ml/10fl oz/1¼ cups meat stock
  450g/1lb small potatoes, peeled
  25g/1oz dark (bittersweet)
    chocolate, grated
  salt and ground black pepper
  45ml/3 tbsp chopped fresh parsley,
    to garnish

1 Preheat the oven to 180°C/350°F/ Gas 4. Heat 30ml/2 tbsp oil in a large frying pan. Season the cubed beef with paprika and fry in two batches, over a high heat, turning until browned on all sides. Reserve the first batch on a plate when done. Add a little more oil, if needed, and fry the second batch.

2 Meanwhile heat 15ml/1 tbsp oil in a large flameproof casserole and fry the bacon or pancetta. When the fat starts to run, add the onion, carrots and leek and cook gently until the onion softens.

3 Smash the garlic cloves with the flat of a knife and add them to the pan, with the mushrooms and tomatoes. Stir and cook gently, then sprinkle with the flour and cook briefly.

4 Add the meat, salt and peppercorns to the casserole. Tuck in the trotter. Add a little wine, stir to deglaze, then add all the wine, stirring well. Add the bay leaf and thyme. Pour in the brandy and stock to cover. Return to a simmer, then cover and cook in the oven for 1¼ hours.

5 Cook the potatoes in a pan of boiling water for 15 minutes. Add them to the casserole with the chocolate. Simmer for another 30 minutes. Remove the trotter, check the amount of liquid and taste for seasoning. Sprinkle with chopped parsley and serve.

RABO DE TORO

IN THE SPANISH KITCHEN, THE MOST FAMOUS PART OF THE BULL IS HIS TAIL — ALTHOUGH MOST PEOPLE ARE MORE LIKELY TO COOK WITH OXTAIL. EITHER MAKES A RICH, SUCCULENT MEAT STEW, WHICH CAN BE PREPARED SEVERAL DAYS AHEAD, AND TASTES EVEN BETTER REHEATED.

SERVES SIX

INGREDIENTS
  60ml/4 tbsp olive oil
  2 onions, chopped
  30ml/2 tbsp plain (all-purpose) flour
  1.6kg/3½lb oxtail, chopped across
  6 carrots
  2 large garlic cloves, smashed
  1 bay leaf
  2 thyme sprigs
  2 leeks, sliced thinly
  1 clove
  pinch of freshly grated nutmeg
  350ml/12fl oz/1½ cups red wine
  30ml/2 tbsp vinegar
  350ml/12fl oz/1½ cups stock
  30ml/2 tbsp fino sherry
  60ml/4 tbsp chopped fresh parsley
  salt, paprika and black pepper
  boiled potatoes, to serve

1 Starting a day ahead, preheat the oven to 150°C/300°F/Gas 2. Heat 30ml/2 tbsp oil in a large frying pan, add the onions and fry until softened. Remove to a casserole (in which the oxtail will fit in a single layer).

2 Season the flour with salt, paprika and pepper and dust the oxtail pieces all over. Add the remaining oil to the pan and put in the oxtail pieces, on their sides at first. Fry, turning them to brown all over, then fit them into the casserole, standing upright.

3 Cut the carrots into short lengths and push into the spaces between the pieces of oxtail in the casserole. Tuck in the garlic cloves, bay leaf and thyme sprigs and add the sliced leeks.

4 Add the clove, grated nutmeg and more black pepper. Pour in the wine, vinegar and just enough stock to cover. Bring to simmering point, then cover the casserole with a lid and put in the oven. Cook for about 3 hours, or until the meat is falling off the bones.

5 Skim the fat off the top of the stew. Spoon the larger meat pieces on to a plate and remove the bones and fat.

6 Push all the remaining oxtail and the carrots to one end of the pan and discard the bay leaf and thyme. Spoon the garlic and some of the soft vegetables into a food processor and purée with the sherry. Return the meat and purée to the casserole and heat through. Stir in the parsley, check the seasonings and serve with boiled potatoes.

VENISON CHOPS <u>WITH</u> ROMESCO SAUCE

ROMESCO IS THE CATALAN WORD FOR THE ÑORA CHILLI. IT LENDS A SPICY ROUNDNESS TO ONE OF SPAIN'S GREATEST SAUCES, FROM TARRAGONA. THE SAUCE ALSO CONTAINS GROUND TOASTED NUTS AND OFTEN ANOTHER FIERCER CHILLI. IT CAN BE SERVED COLD, AS A DIP FOR VEGETABLES, BUT THIS SPICY VERSION IS THE IDEAL PARTNER FOR GAME CHOPS — VENADO CON ROMESCO. BOAR CHOPS CAN ALSO BE USED BUT NEED LONGER COOKING. CHOOSE GRAN SANGRE DE TORO TO DRINK.

4 Add the soaked chillies and tomatoes to the processor or blender. Tip in the garlic, with the oil from the pan and blend the mixture to form a smooth paste.

5 With the motor running, gradually add the remaining olive oil and then the sherry and wine vinegars. When the sauce is smooth and well blended, scrape it into a bowl and season with salt and ground black pepper to taste. Cover with clear film (plastic wrap) and chill for 2 hours.

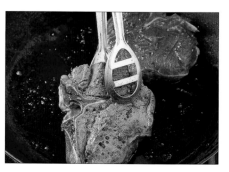

SERVES FOUR

INGREDIENTS

    4 venison chops, cut 2cm/¾in thick
      and about 175–200g/6–7oz each
    30ml/2 tbsp olive oil
    50g/2oz/4 tbsp butter
    braised Savoy cabbage, to serve
For the sauce
    3 *ñora* chillies
    1 hot dried chilli
    25g/1oz/¼ cup almonds
    150ml/¼ pint/⅔ cup olive oil
    1 slice stale bread, crusts removed
    3 garlic cloves, chopped
    3 tomatoes, peeled, seeded and
      roughly chopped
    60ml/4 tbsp sherry vinegar
    60ml/4 tbsp red wine vinegar
    salt and ground black pepper

1 To make the romesco sauce, slit the chillies and remove the seeds, then leave the chillies to soak in warm water for about 30 minutes until soft. Drain the chillies, dry them on kitchen paper and chop finely.

2 Dry-fry the almonds in a frying pan over a medium heat, shaking the pan occasionally, until the nuts are toasted evenly. Transfer the nuts to a food processor or blender.

3 Add 45ml/3 tbsp oil to the frying pan and fry the bread slice until golden on both sides. Lift it out with a slotted spoon and drain on kitchen paper. Tear the bread and add to the food processor or blender. Fry the chopped garlic in the oil remaining in the pan.

6 Season the chops with pepper. Heat the olive oil and butter in a heavy frying pan and fry the chops for about 5 minutes each side until golden brown and cooked through.

7 When the chops are almost cooked, transfer the romesco sauce to a pan and heat it gently. If it is too thick, stir in a little boiling water.

8 Serve the sauce with the chops, accompanied by braised cabbage.

RABBIT SALMOREJO

THE CARTHAGINIANS NAMED SPAIN "RABBIT LAND" AND THE ROMANS KEPT THE NAME, REFERRING TO THE COUNTRY AS HISPANIA. THE MODERN NAME, ESPAÑA, IS CLEARLY DERIVED FROM THIS OLD NAME AND SERVES TO REMIND US HOW COMMON RABBITS ARE THROUGHOUT SPAIN. THIS IS AN UPDATED VERSION OF ONE OF THE CLASSIC MEDITERRANEAN RABBIT STEWS. SALMOREJO INDICATES POUNDED GARLIC, BREAD AND VINEGAR, WHILE WINE IS A MODERN TOUCH.

SERVES FOUR

INGREDIENTS
675g/1½lb rabbit, jointed
300ml/½ pint/1¼ cups dry
  white wine
15ml/1 tbsp sherry vinegar
several oregano sprigs
2 bay leaves
30ml/2 tbsp plain (all-purpose) flour
90ml/6 tbsp olive oil
175g/6oz baby (pearl) onions,
  peeled and left whole
4 garlic cloves, sliced
150ml/¼ pint/⅔ cup chicken stock
1 dried chilli, seeded and
  finely chopped
10ml/2 tsp paprika
salt and ground black pepper
fresh flat leaf parsley sprigs,
  to garnish (optional)

1 Put the rabbit in a bowl. Add the wine, vinegar, oregano and bay leaves and toss together. Marinate for several hours or overnight in the refrigerator.

2 Drain the rabbit, reserving the marinade, and pat it dry with kitchen paper. Season the flour and use to dust the marinated rabbit.

3 Heat the oil in a large, wide flameproof casserole or frying pan. Fry the rabbit pieces until golden on all sides, then remove them and set aside. Fry the onions until they are beginning to colour, then reserve on a separate plate.

4 Add the garlic to the pan and fry, then add the strained marinade, with the chicken stock, chilli and paprika.

5 Return the rabbit and the reserved onions to the pan. Bring to a simmer, then cover and simmer gently for about 45 minutes until the rabbit is tender. Check the seasoning, adding more vinegar and paprika if necessary. Serve the dish garnished with a few sprigs of flat leaf parsley, if you like.

COOK'S TIP
If wished, rather than cooking on the stove, transfer the stew to an ovenproof dish and bake in the oven at 180°C/ 350°F/Gas 4 for about 50 minutes.

DESSERTS AND BAKING

Iced desserts were introduced to Spain by the Moors, who also created luxurious dishes of fruit in syrups. Caramel is a much-loved flavour and is used in a winter fruit salad of oranges and a drunken cake soaked in brandy. Custards are also popular and come with a crisp caramel topping or baked with a caramel syrup. As well as desserts there are delicious pastries and cookies, light breakfast rolls and solid, satisfying loaves baked with barley and brown flour.

RUM AND RAISIN ICE CREAM

HELADO CON RON Y PASAS IS AN ICE CREAM WITH A LONG TRADITION IN SPAIN. DARK RUM COMES FROM THE FORMER SPANISH ISLAND OF CUBA, WHILE THE MALAGA REGION PRODUCES SOME OF THE BEST MUSCATEL RAISINS IN THE WORLD, HUGE AND BLACK — THOUGH FROM A WHITE GRAPE.

SERVES FOUR TO SIX

INGREDIENTS

150g/5oz/1 cup large Muscatel raisins, Malagan if possible
60ml/4 tbsp dark rum
4 egg yolks
75g/3oz/6 tbsp light brown sugar
5ml/1 tsp cornflour (cornstarch)
300ml/½ pint/1¼ cups full-fat (whole) milk
300ml/½ pint/1¼ cups whipping cream
wafers or biscuits (cookies), to serve

1 Put the raisins in a bowl, add the rum and mix well. Cover and leave to soak for 3–4 hours or overnight.

2 Whisk together the egg yolks, sugar and cornflour in a large bowl until the mixture is thick and foamy. Heat the milk in a large heavy pan to just below boiling point.

3 Whisk the milk into the eggs, then pour back into the pan. Cook over a gentle heat, stirring with a wooden spoon, until the custard thickens and is smooth. Leave to cool.

4 Whip the cream until it is just thick but still falls from a spoon, then fold it into the cold custard. If you have an ice cream maker, pour the mixture into the machine tub, then churn until thick. Transfer to a freezerproof container. Working by hand, pour the mixture into a plastic tub or similar freezerproof container. Freeze for 4 hours, beating once in a food processor after 2 hours, then beat again after 4 hours.

5 Fold the soaked raisins into the soft ice cream, then cover and freeze for 2–3 hours, or until it is firm enough to scoop. Serve in bowls or tall glasses, with wafers or dessert biscuits.

SORBETE DE LIMÓN

THE MOORS INTRODUCED ICES TO ANDALUCIA A THOUSAND YEARS AGO. EATING THIS SMOOTH, TANGY SORBET, YOU CAN IMAGINE YOURSELF IN A PALACE LIKE THE ONE AT GRANADA, LOUNGING ON SILKEN CUSHIONS, WITH THE STARS ABOVE, NIGHTINGALES SINGING AND THE FOUNTAINS TINKLING.

SERVES SIX

INGREDIENTS

200g/7oz/1 cup caster
  (superfine) sugar
300ml/¼l pint/1¼ cups water
4 lemons, washed
1 large (US extra large) egg white
a little granulated sugar,
  for sprinkling

1 Put the sugar and water into a heavy pan and bring slowly to the boil, stirring occasionally, until the sugar has just dissolved.

2 Using a swivel vegetable peeler, pare the rind thinly from two of the lemons directly into the pan. Simmer for about 2 minutes without stirring, then remove the pan from the heat. Leave the syrup to cool, then chill.

3 Squeeze the juice from all the lemons and carefully strain it into the syrup, making sure all the pips are removed. Take the lemon rind out of the syrup and set it aside until you make the garnish.

4 If you have an ice cream maker, strain the syrup into the machine tub and churn for 10 minutes until thickening.

5 Lightly whisk the egg white with a fork and pour it into the machine. Continue to churn for 10–15 minutes, until firm enough to scoop.

6 Working by hand, strain the syrup into a plastic tub or a similar shallow freezerproof container and freeze for 4 hours, until the mixture is mushy.

7 Scoop the mushy mixture into a food processor and beat until smooth. Lightly whisk the egg white with a fork until it is just frothy. Spoon the sorbet back into its container and beat in the egg white. Return to the freezer for 1 hour.

8 To make the sugared rind garnish, use the blanched rind from step 2. Cut into very thin strips and sprinkle with granulated sugar on a plate. Scoop the sorbet into bowls or glasses and decorate with sugared lemon rind.

VARIATION
Sorbet (sherbet) can be made from any citrus fruit. As a guide, you will need 300ml/½ pint/1¼ cups of fresh fruit juice and the pared rind of half the squeezed fruits. For example, use four oranges or two oranges and two lemons, or, to make a grapefruit sorbet, use the rind of one ruby grapefruit and the juice of two.

HONEY-BAKED FIGS WITH HAZELNUT ICE CREAM

Two wild ingredients – figs and hazelnuts – are used to make this delectable dessert, higos con helado de avellana. Fresh figs are baked in a lightly spiced lemon and honey syrup and are served with home-made roasted hazelnut ice cream.

SERVES FOUR

INGREDIENTS
  finely pared rind of 1 lemon
  1 cinnamon stick, roughly broken
  60ml/4 tbsp clear honey
  8 large figs
For the hazelnut ice cream
  450ml/¾ pint/scant 2 cups double
    (heavy) cream
  50g/2oz/¼ cup caster
    (superfine) sugar
  3 large (US extra large) egg yolks
  1.5ml/¼ tsp vanilla essence (extract)
  75g/3oz/¾ cup hazelnuts

1 Make the ice cream. Gently heat the cream in a pan until almost boiling. Meanwhile, beat the sugar and egg yolks in a bowl until creamy.

2 Pour a little hot cream into the egg yolk mixture and stir with a wooden spoon. Pour back into the pan and mix well. Cook over a low heat, stirring constantly, until the mixture thickens slightly and lightly coats the back of the spoon – do not allow it to boil.

3 Pour the custard into a bowl, stir in the vanilla essence and leave to cool.

4 Preheat the oven to 180°C/350°F/ Gas 4. Place the hazelnuts on a baking sheet and roast for 10–12 minutes, or until golden. Leave the nuts to cool, then grind them in a food processor.

5 If you have an ice cream machine, pour in the cold custard and churn until half set. Add the ground hazelnuts and continue to churn until the ice cream is thick. Freeze until firm.

6 Working by hand, pour the custard into a freezerproof container and freeze for 2 hours, or until the custard feels firm around the edges. Turn into a bowl and beat with an electric whisk or turn into a food processor and beat until smooth. Stir in the hazelnuts and freeze until half set. Beat once more, then freeze until firm.

7 Preheat the oven to 200°C/400°F/ Gas 6. Remove the ice cream from the freezer and allow to soften slightly.

8 To make the syrup, put the lemon rind, cinnamon stick, honey and 200ml/ 7fl oz/scant 1 cup water in a small pan and heat slowly until boiling. Simmer the mixture for 5 minutes, then leave to stand for 15 minutes.

9 Using a sharp knife, cut the figs almost into quarters but leaving the figs still attached at the base. Pack them into a casserole, in a single layer, and pour the honey syrup round and over them. Cover the dish tightly with foil and bake for 10 minutes.

10 Arrange the figs on small serving plates, with the cooking syrup poured round them. Serve accompanied by a scoop or two of the ice cream.

COOK'S TIPS
• When toasting the hazelnuts, keep a close eye on them because they can scorch very quickly, spoiling the flavour of the ice cream.
• In southern Spain, red-fleshed figs with a wonderfully sweet flavour grow wild in the scrub.

BITTER CHOCOLATE MOUSSES

THE SPANISH INTRODUCED CHOCOLATE TO EUROPE, AND CHOCOLATE MOUSSE REMAINS A FAVOURITE DESSERT IN A COUNTRY THAT USUALLY FAVOURS CUSTARDS AND FRESH FRUIT. THESE DELICIOUS CREMAS DE CHOCOLATE ARE RICH WITH CHOCOLATE, WITH A HINT OF ORANGE LENT BY THE LIQUEUR.

2 Whip the cream until soft peaks form, then stir a spoonful into the chocolate mixture to lighten it. Gently fold in the remaining whipped cream.

3 In a clean, grease-free bowl, use an electric mixer to slowly whisk the egg whites until frothy. Increase the speed and continue until the egg whites form soft peaks. Gradually sprinkle the sugar over the egg whites and continue beating until the whites are stiff and glossy. (Be careful not to over-whisk the eggs.)

4 Using a rubber spatula or large metal spoon, stir a quarter of the egg whites into the chocolate mixture to lighten it, then gently fold in the remaining whites, cutting down to the bottom of the bowl, along the sides and up to the top in a semicircular motion until they are just combined. Don't worry about a few white streaks.

SERVES EIGHT

INGREDIENTS
　225g/8oz dark (bittersweet)
　　chocolate, chopped
　30ml/2 tbsp orange liqueur or a good
　　Spanish brandy such as Torres
　50g/2oz/¼ cup unsalted (sweet)
　　butter, cut into small pieces
　4 large (US extra large)
　　eggs, separated
　90ml/6 tbsp whipping cream
　45ml/3 tbsp caster (superfine) sugar

COOK'S TIP
The addition of 1.5ml/¼ tsp cream of tartar to the egg whites helps them to stabilize and hold the volume.

1 Place the chocolate and 60ml/4 tbsp water in a heavy pan. Melt over a low heat, stirring. Off the heat whisk in the orange liqueur or brandy and butter. Beat the egg yolks until thick and creamy, then slowly beat into the melted chocolate until well blended.

5 Gently spoon the mixture into eight individual dishes or a 2 litre/3½ pint/ 8 cup bowl. Chill for at least 2 hours until set before serving.

FLAN

THESE LITTLE BAKED CARAMEL CUSTARDS, MADE IN BUCKET-SHAPED MOULDS, ARE THE BEST-KNOWN AND MOST POPULAR OF ALL SPANISH DESSERTS. IF YOU DON'T OWN SMALL MOULDS, YOU CAN MAKE ONE LARGE FLAN INSTEAD BUT IT WILL NEED TO BE COOKED FOR A LITTLE LONGER.

SERVES EIGHT

INGREDIENTS
   250g/9oz/1¼ cups granulated sugar
   1 vanilla pod (bean) or 10ml/2 tsp
   vanilla essence (extract)
   400ml/14fl oz/1⅔ cups milk
   250ml/8fl oz/1 cup whipping cream
   5 large (US extra large) eggs
   2 egg yolks

1 Select your moulds – eight metal dariole moulds, about 120ml/4fl oz/ ½ cup each, or a soufflé dish 1 litre/ 1¾ pints/4 cups in capacity. Arrange in a roasting pan.

2 Put 175g/6oz/⅞ cup of the sugar in a small heavy pan with 60ml/4 tbsp water. Bring to the boil over a high heat, swirling the pan to dissolve the sugar. Boil, without stirring, for about 5 minutes until the syrup turns a dark caramel colour.

3 If using individual moulds, pour a little caramel into each one. If using a single mould, lift it with oven gloves and quickly swirl the dish to coat the base with the caramel. (The caramel will harden quickly as it cools.)

4 Preheat the oven to 160°C/325°F/ Gas 3. If using, split the vanilla pod lengthways and scrape out the seeds. Pour the milk and cream into a pan, add the vanilla seeds or essence and bring the mixture close to the boil, stirring. Remove from the heat and allow to stand for 15–20 minutes.

5 In a bowl, whisk the eggs and extra yolks with the remaining sugar for 2–3 minutes until creamy. Whisk in the warm milk and cream mixture, and then strain it into the caramel-lined mould(s). Cover with foil.

6 Pour boiling water into the pan, to come halfway up the sides of the mould(s). Bake until the custard is just set (20–25 minutes for small moulds; about 40 minutes for a large one. A knife inserted to test should come out clean.) Remove from the water, leave to cool, then chill overnight.

7 To turn out, run a palette knife around the custard(s). Cover a large mould with a serving dish and, holding tightly, invert the dish and plate together. Lift one edge of the mould, waiting for the caramel to run down, then remove the mould. Cover the small moulds with saucers and invert them to serve.

CREMA CATALANA

THIS FABULOUS SPANISH DESSERT OF CREAMY CUSTARD TOPPED WITH A NET OF BRITTLE SUGAR, MAY WELL BE THE ORIGINAL OF ALL CRÈME BRÛLÉES. CREMAT IS THE CATALAN WORD FOR "BURNT", AND THIS WAS PROBABLY PART OF ITS ORIGINAL NAME.

SERVES FOUR

INGREDIENTS
475ml/16fl oz/2 cups milk
pared rind of ½ lemon
1 cinnamon stick
4 large egg yolks
105ml/7 tbsp caster
 (superfine) sugar
25ml/1½ tbsp cornflour (cornstarch)
ground nutmeg, for sprinkling

COOK'S TIP
A special tool known as a *quemadora* is sold to caramelize the top of this dessert. A metal disc on a wooden handle is heated like a hot poker, then held over the sugar crust.

1 Put the milk in a pan with the lemon rind and cinnamon stick. Bring to the boil, then simmer for 10 minutes. Remove the lemon rind and cinnamon. Put the egg yolks and 45ml/3 tbsp sugar in a bowl, and whisk until pale yellow. Add the cornflour and mix well.

2 Stir a few tablespoons of the hot milk into the egg yolk mixture, then tip back into the remaining milk. Return to the heat and cook gently, stirring, for about 5 minutes, until thickened and smooth. Do not boil.

3 Pour the custard into four shallow ovenproof dishes, about 13cm/5in in diameter. Leave to cool, then chill for a few hours, or overnight, until firm.

4 No more than 30 minutes before serving, sprinkle each dessert with 15ml/1 tbsp of the sugar and a little nutmeg. Preheat the grill (broiler) to high. Place the dishes under the grill, on the highest shelf, and cook until the sugar caramelizes. This will only take a few seconds and it will caramelize unevenly. Leave the custards to cool for a few minutes before serving.

ARROPE

This is an old Arab recipe whose name means "syrup"; this version comes from the Pyrenees region. In southern Spain, grapes, quince and melon might be used. Arrope starts as a lovely fruit compote and ends up as a syrupy jam, to be scooped up with bread.

SERVES TEN

INGREDIENTS

  3 firm peaches, unpeeled
  1kg/2¼lb/5 cups granulated sugar
  3 large eating apples
  finely grated rind of 1 lemon
  3 firm pears
  finely grated rind of 1 orange
  1 small sweet potato, 150g/5oz
    prepared weight
  200g/7oz butternut squash, peeled
    and prepared weight
  250ml/8fl oz/1 cup dark rum
  30ml/2 tbsp clear honey

1 Cut the peaches into eighths, without peeling them, and place in the bottom of a large flameproof casserole. Sprinkle with 15ml/1 tbsp of the sugar.

2 Peel and core the apples and cut them into 16 segments, then arrange on top of the peaches. Sprinkle the lemon rind over the top, along with 15ml/ 1 tbsp of the sugar. Prepare the pears in the same way as the apples, place in the casserole, then sprinkle over the orange rind, followed by 15ml/1 tbsp of the sugar.

3 Slice the sweet potato into pieces half the size of the pears and spread them over the top. Prepare the squash in the same way, layering it on top. Sprinkle about 15ml/1 tbsp of the sugar. Cover with a plate that fits inside the rim, and weigh down with a couple of cans. Stand for a minimum of 2 hours (maximum 12) for juice to form.

4 Remove the cans and plate, put the casserole over a fairly low heat and bring to a simmer. Cook and soften the fruit for 20 minutes, stirring once or twice to prevent sticking.

5 Add the remaining sugar, in three or four batches, stirring to dissolve each batch before adding the next. Bring the mixture up to a rolling boil, over a medium high heat, and boil very steadily for 45 minutes. Stir and lift off any scum.

6 The syrup should be considerably reduced. Test by pouring a spoonful on a plate. It should wrinkle when a spoon is pulled across (like jam in the early stages, before a full set is achieved).

7 Off the heat, add the rum and honey and stir well to combine. Return the casserole to a moderate heat and cook for a further 10 minutes, stirring frequently to prevent the fruit sticking to the base of the pan. The colour will deepen to russet brown. Remove the pan from the heat and set aside to cool.

8 If the resulting compote is a little too stiff, then stir in some more rum before serving.

COOK'S TIP
Arrope is immensely rich, so portions should be small. By the time you reach the bottom of the pot it becomes very thick and sticky, and is best scooped up on bits of bread.

ORANGES WITH CARAMEL WIGS

NARANJAS CON PELUCAS IS A PRETTY VARIATION ON THE NORMAL ORANGE SALAD. THE SLIGHTLY BITTER, CARAMELIZED ORANGE RIND AND SYRUP HAS A WONDERFUL FLAVOUR AND TEXTURE THAT SITS IN PERFECT CONTRAST TO THE SWEET, JUICY ORANGES.

5 Put half the sugar into a small pan and add 15ml/1 tbsp water. Heat gently until the mixture caramelizes, shaking the pan a little if one side starts to brown too fast. As soon as the mixture colours, dip the bottom of the pan into cold water. Add 30ml/2 tbsp hot water and the orange rind to the caramel, then stir until the caramel dissolves. Turn the rind on to a plate, to cool.

6 Make a caramel syrup for serving. Put the remaining sugar in a small pan with 15ml/1 tbsp water, and make caramel as before. When it has coloured nicely, stand well back, pour in the boiling water and stir with a wooden spoon to dissolve. Add the reserved juices and pour into a serving jug (pitcher).

7 To serve, arrange the orange strips in a criss-cross pattern on top of each orange. Remove the cocktail sticks and pour a little caramel syrup round the base of each orange.

SERVES SIX

INGREDIENTS
  6 oranges
  120g/4oz/generous ½ cup caster
   (superfine) sugar
  120ml/4fl oz/½ cup boiling water
  cocktail sticks (toothpicks)

1 Using a vegetable peeler, thinly pare the rind off a few of the oranges to make 12 long strips.

2 Using a sharp knife, peel all the oranges, reserving the rind and discarding the pith. Reserve the juice and freeze the oranges separately for 30 minutes.

3 Slice the oranges, reform and secure with a cocktail stick (toothpick). Chill.

4 To make the wigs, simmer the rind for about 5 minutes, drain, rinse, and then repeat. Trim with scissors.

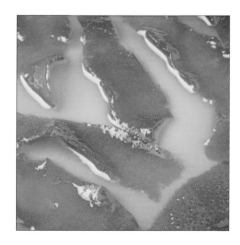

HAZELNUT MERINGUES <u>WITH</u> NECTARINES

MERINGUES GO BACK TO MOORISH TIMES, AND HAZELNUTS, FROM THE WOODED PYRENEES, ARE A POPULAR FLAVOURING. SERVE THEM AS AN ACCOMPANIMENT TO PEACHES IN SYRUP, OR TRY THEM WITH CREAM WHIPPED WITH MALAGA'S DESSERT WINE, AND STUFFED WITH FRESH NECTARINES.

SERVES FIVE

INGREDIENTS

   3 large (US extra large) egg whites
   175g/6oz/generous ¾ cup caster
    (superfine) sugar
   50g/2oz/½ cup chopped
    hazelnuts, toasted
   300ml/½ pint/1¼ cups double
    (heavy) cream
   60ml/4 tbsp sweet Malaga
    dessert wine
   2 nectarines, stoned (pitted)
    and sliced
   fresh mint sprigs, to decorate

COOK'S TIP
Peaches can be used in place of the nectarines, but are better peeled. To remove the skins, place the peaches in a bowl and pour over boiling water to cover. Leave to stand for a few minutes, then drain. The skins should peel off very easily.

1 Preheat the oven to 140°C/275°F/ Gas 1. Line two large baking sheets with baking parchment.

2 Whisk the egg whites in a grease-free bowl until they form stiff peaks when the whisks are lifted. Gradually whisk in the caster sugar a spoonful at a time, until a stiff, glossy meringue forms.

3 Using a large metal spoon, gently fold two-thirds of the chopped toasted hazelnuts into the whisked egg whites.

4 Divide the meringue mixture between the baking sheets, spooning five ovals on to each one. Scatter the remaining toasted hazelnuts over the meringues on one baking sheet, then flatten the tops of the others using the back of a spoon.

5 Bake the meringues for 1–1¼ hours until crisp and dry, then lift them off the baking parchment and leave to cool.

6 Put the cream and dessert wine in a bowl and whisk to form soft peaks. Spoon some of the cream on to each of the plain meringues. Arrange a few nectarine slices on each.

7 Put one cream-topped meringue and one nut-topped meringue on each dessert plate. Garnish with fresh mint and serve immediately.

APPLE-STUFFED CRÊPES

SPAIN'S DAIRY COUNTRY LIES ALONG THE COOLER NORTHERN COAST AND CRÊPES ARE EXTREMELY POPULAR THERE. THE ASTURIAS, WHICH RUN EAST TO WEST ALONG THE COAST, ARE APPLE AND CIDER COUNTRY, TOO, AND CRÊPES, WHICH ARE KNOWN AS FRISUELOS, ARE MADE WITH A VARIETY OF SWEET FILLINGS, SUCH AS THIS SUCCULENT APPLE ONE.

SERVES FOUR

INGREDIENTS

   115g/4oz/1 cup plain
    (all-purpose) flour
   pinch of salt
   2 large (US extra large) eggs
   175ml/6fl oz/¾ cup milk
   120ml/4fl oz/½ cup sweet cider
   butter, for frying
   4 eating apples
   60ml/4 tbsp caster (superfine) sugar
   120ml/8 tbsp clear honey, and
    150ml/¼ pint/⅔ cup double (heavy)
    cream, to serve

COOK'S TIP
For the best results, use full-fat (whole) milk in the batter.

1 Make the batter. Sift the flour and salt into a large bowl. Add the eggs and milk and beat until smooth. Stir in the cider. Leave to stand for 30 minutes.

2 Heat a small heavy non-stick frying pan. Add a little butter and ladle in enough batter to coat the pan thinly.

3 Cook the crêpe for about 1 minute until it is golden underneath, then flip it over and cook the other side until golden. Slide the crêpe on to a plate, then repeat with the remaining batter to make seven more. Set the crêpes aside and keep warm.

4 Make the apple filling. Core the apples and cut them into thick slices. Heat 15g/½oz butter in a large frying pan. Add the apples to the pan and cook until golden on both sides. Transfer the slices to a bowl with a slotted spoon and sprinkle with sugar.

5 Fold each pancake in half, then fold in half again to form a cone. Fill each with some of the fried apples. Place two filled pancakes on each dessert plate. Drizzle with a little honey and serve at once, accompanied by cream.

TORRIJAS

TRANSLATED AS "POOR KNIGHTS", THESE SUGARED TOASTS ARE PERFECT FOR ALMOST EVERY OCCASION. THEY MAKE A GOOD TEA-TIME SNACK FOR CHILDREN, OR TO ACCOMPANY A CUP OF HOT CHOCOLATE. AS A PARTY DESSERT THEY ARE THE EQUIVALENT OF FRANCE'S TOASTED BRIOCHE — AN ACCOMPANIMENT TO ICE CREAM, OR TO ANY BAKED FRUIT. THEY ARE ALSO VERY POPULAR BY THEMSELVES.

SERVES FOUR

INGREDIENTS
   120ml/4fl oz/½ cup white wine
   2 large eggs
   12 thick rounds of stale
   French bread
   60–90ml/4–6 tbsp sunflower oil
   ground cinnamon, and caster
   (superfine) sugar, for dusting

COOK'S TIP
These toasts are often enjoyed at festivals and are a typical dish from Madrid (although variations can be found all over Europe). Milk can be used in place of white wine, if liked, making them suitable for children.

1 Pour the wine into a shallow dish and dip the bread rounds into it.

2 Beat the eggs together in another shallow dish. Dip half the bread rounds into the beaten egg on each side so that they are completely covered.

3 Heat 60ml/4 tbsp oil in a pan until very hot and fry the bread rounds for about 1 minute on each side until crisp and golden. Reserve on kitchen paper, then dip and fry the rest, adding more oil if necessary. Serve hot, sprinkled with cinnamon and sugar.

LECHE FRITA <u>WITH</u> BLACK FRUIT SAUCE

THE NAME OF THIS DESSERT MEANS "FRIED MILK", BUT IT IS REALLY CUSTARD SQUARES. IT IS VERY POPULAR IN THE BASQUE COUNTRY, AND HAS A MELTING, CREAMY CENTRE AND CRUNCHY, GOLDEN COATING. HERE, IT IS SERVED HOT WITH A DARK FRUIT SAUCE, BUT IT IS ALSO GOOD COLD.

SERVES SIX TO EIGHT

INGREDIENTS
550ml/18fl oz/2½ cups full-fat
(whole) milk
3 finely pared strips of lemon rind
½ cinnamon stick
90g/3½oz/½ cup caster (superfine)
sugar, plus extra for sprinkling
60ml/4 tbsp cornflour (cornstarch)
30ml/2 tbsp plain (all-purpose) flour
3 large (US extra large) egg yolks
2 large (US extra large) eggs
90–120ml/6–8 tbsp stale
breadcrumbs or dried crumbs
sunflower oil, for frying
ground cinnamon, for dusting
For the sauce
450g/1lb blackcurrants
or blackberries
90g/3½oz/½ cup granulated sugar,
plus extra for dusting

1 Put the milk, lemon rind, cinnamon stick and sugar in a pan and bring to the boil, stirring gently. Cover and leave to infuse for 20 minutes.

2 Put the cornflour and flour in a bowl and beat in the egg yolks with a wooden spoon. Add a little of the milk and beat to make a smooth batter.

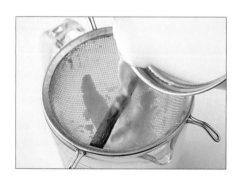

3 Strain the remaining hot milk into the batter, then pour back into the pan. Cook over a low heat, stirring constantly. (The mixture won't curdle, but it will thicken unevenly if you let it.) Cook for a couple of minutes, until it thickens and separates from the side of the pan.

4 Beat the mixture hard with the spoon to ensure a really smooth consistency. Pour into an 18–20cm/7–8in, 1cm/½in-deep rectangular dish, and smooth the top. Cool, then chill until firm.

5 Make the fruit sauce. Cook the blackcurrants or blackberries with the sugar and a little water for about 10 minutes until soft.

6 Reserve 30–45ml/2–3 tbsp whole currants or berries, then put the rest in a food processor and blend to make a smooth purée. Return the purée and berries to the pan.

7 Cut the chilled custard into eight or twelve squares. Beat the eggs in a shallow dish and spread out the breadcrumbs on a plate. Lift half of the squares with a metal spatula into the egg. Coat on both sides, then lift into the crumbs and cover all over. Repeat with the second batch of squares.

8 Pour about 1cm/½in oil into a deep frying pan and heat until very hot.

9 Lift two or three coated squares with a palette knife (metal spatula) into the oil and fry for a couple of minutes, shaking or spooning the oil over the top, until golden. Reserve on kitchen paper, while frying the other batches.

10 To serve, arrange the custard squares on plates and sprinkle with sugar and cinnamon. Pour a circle of warm sauce round the squares, distributing the whole berries evenly.

COOK'S TIP
In Spain, milk is usually drunk at breakfast or used for cheese. In northern Spain, the milk has a wonderful quality and has been given special status as a dessert ingredient. Most popular of all the milk desserts are *leche frita*, *flan* and *filloas* (thin pancakes).

GUIRLACHE

This is an Arab sweetmeat from the Pyrenees, combining toasted nuts and caramel to produce a crisp nut brittle — a forerunner of some familiar chocolate bar fillings. It is less well known than turrón, *the Spanish Christmas nougat, which is made with similar ingredients and is widely available commercially.*

MAKES ABOUT 24 PIECES

INGREDIENTS
    115g/4oz/1 cup almonds, half
      blanched, half unblanched
    115g/4oz/1 cup hazelnuts, half
      blanched, half unblanched
    5ml/1 tsp almond oil or
      a flavourless oil
    200g/7oz/1 cup granulated sugar
    15ml/1 tbsp lemon juice

COOK'S TIP
Guirlache may be served as an after-
dinner treat. It is also very good
pulverized and used as a topping for
mousses and whipped cream. It also
makes wonderful ice cream.

1 Preheat the oven to 150°C/300°F/
Gas 2. Scatter the nuts on a baking
sheet and toast for about 30 minutes,
shaking the sheet occasionally. The nuts
should smell pleasant and have turned
brown and be very dry.

2 Coarsely chop the toasted nuts or
crush them roughly with a rolling pin.
Cover another baking tray with foil
and grease it generously with the oil.

3 Put the sugar in a pile in a small pan
and pour the lemon juice round it. Cook
over a high heat, shaking the pan, until
the sugar turns a coffee colour. (As it
cooks, the pile of sugar will melt and
collapse into caramel.)

4 Immediately tip in the nuts and stir
once, then pour the mixture on to the
foil and spread out into a thin, even
layer. Leave the mixture to harden.

5 Once set, break up the caramel into
pieces and store in an airtight tin.

PANELLETS

The Catalan name for these nutty festival cakes means "little bread", but they are, in fact, much closer to marzipan, with a slightly soft centre that is produced by their secret ingredient — sweet potato. Patisseries make hundreds of these little cakes for All Saints' Day, on 1st November, when families take flowers to the graveyards.

MAKES ABOUT 24

INGREDIENTS
   115g/4oz sweet potato
   butter, for greasing
   1 large (US extra large) egg,
      separated
   225g/8oz/2 cups ground almonds
   200g/7oz/1 cup caster (superfine)
      sugar, plus extra for sprinkling
   finely grated rind of 1 small lemon
   7.5ml/1½ tsp vanilla essence
      (extract)
   60ml/4 tbsp pine nuts
   60ml/4 tbsp pistachio nuts, chopped

1 Dice the sweet potato, and cook it in a pan of boiling water for 15 minutes, or until soft. Drain and leave to cool.

2 Preheat the oven to 200°C/400°F/ Gas 6. Line one or two baking sheets with foil and grease well with butter.

3 Put the cooled sweet potato in a food processor and process to make a smooth purée, then work in the egg yolk, ground almonds, sugar, lemon rind and vanilla essence to make a soft dough. Transfer the dough to a bowl and chill for 30 minutes.

4 Spoon walnut-sized balls of dough on to the foil, spacing them about 2.5cm/ 1in apart, then flatten them out slightly.

5 Lightly beat the egg white and brush over the cakes. Sprinkle half the cakes with pine nuts, slightly less than 5ml/ 1 tsp each, and half with pistachio nuts. Sprinkle lightly with sugar and bake for 10 minutes, or until lightly browned.

6 Leave to cool on the foil, then lift off with a metal spatula.

PESTIÑOS

THE ARABS INVENTED ALL SORTS OF SWEET BITES, TO EAT AFTER THE MAIN COURSE OR WITH DRINKS. BATHED IN SCENTED HONEY SYRUP, PESTIÑOS WERE OFTEN DEEP-FRIED AND KNOWN AS DULCES DE SÁRTEN, WHICH MEANS "SWEETS FROM THE FRYING PAN". HOWEVER, AT HOME IT IS A GOOD DEAL EASIER TO BAKE THEM AND THEY PUFF BEAUTIFULLY IN THE OVEN.

MAKES ABOUT THIRTY

INGREDIENTS
    225g/8oz/2 cups plain (all-purpose)
      flour, plus extra for dusting
    60ml/4 tbsp sunflower oil
    15ml/1 tbsp aniseed, lightly crushed
    45ml/3 tbsp caster (superfine) sugar
    250ml/8fl oz/1 cup water
    60ml/4 tbsp anisette
    3 small (US medium) eggs
For the anis syrup
    60ml/4 tbsp clear honey
    60ml/4 tbsp anisette

1 Preheat the oven to 190°C/375°F/ Gas 5. Sift the flour on to a sheet of baking parchment. Heat the oil in a small pan with the crushed aniseed, until the aniseed releases its aroma. Strain the oil into a larger pan and add the sugar, water and anisette. Heat to a rolling boil.

2 Remove the pan from the heat and add the sifted flour, all in one go. Beat vigorously with a wooden spoon until the mixture leaves the sides of the pan clean. Leave to cool.

3 Meanwhile lightly beat the eggs. Gradually incorporate the egg into the dough mixture, beating hard. You may not need to use all the egg – the paste should be soft but not sloppy. Reserve any remaining beaten egg.

4 Grease and flour two baking sheets. Fit a plain nozzle to a piping (pastry) bag and pipe small rounds of dough about 2.5cm/1in across on the sheets, spacing them about 2.5cm/1in apart. Brush with the remaining beaten egg.

5 Bake for about 30 minutes, or until lightly brown and an even texture right through. (Lift one off the sheet to test.)

6 Melt the honey in a small pan and stir in the anisette. Just before serving, use a slotted spoon to dunk the *pestiños* into the syrup.

COOK'S TIP
Anisette is a sweet aniseed liqueur that gives the syrup a wonderful flavour. If you cannot find anisette, use another anis spirit such as Ricard instead.

CHURROS

This Spanish breakfast doughnut is sold in all tapas bars, which so conveniently transform into cafés in the morning. Freshly fried, churros accompany a cup of hot chocolate or coffee. They are also served as festival fare, piped into great vats of oil, cut into loops, then tied with grass string and sold to eat while walking along.

MAKES TWELVE TO FIFTEEN

INGREDIENTS
  200g/7oz/1¾ cups plain
    (all-purpose) flour
  1.5ml/¼ tsp salt
  30ml/2 tbsp caster
    (superfine) sugar
  250ml/8fl oz/1 cup water
  60ml/4 tbsp olive or
    sunflower oil
  1 egg, beaten
  caster (superfine) sugar and ground
    cinnamon, for dusting
  oil, for deep-frying

1 Sift the flour, salt and sugar on to a plate or piece of baking parchment. Put the water and oil in a pan and bring to the boil.

2 Tip the flour mixture into the pan and beat with a wooden spoon until the mixture forms a stiff paste. Leave to cool for 2 minutes, then gradually beat in the egg to make a smooth dough.

3 Oil a large baking sheet. Sprinkle plenty of sugar on to a plate and stir in a little cinnamon.

4 Spoon the dough into a large piping (pastry) bag fitted with a 1cm/½in plain piping nozzle. Pipe little coils or "S" shapes on to the baking sheet.

5 Heat 5cm/2in of oil in a large pan to 168ºC/336ºF, or until a little piece of dough dropped into the oil sizzles on the surface.

6 Using an oiled metal spatula, lower several of the piped shapes into the oil and fry for about 2 minutes until light golden.

7 Drain the churros on kitchen paper, then dip them into the sugar and cinnamon mixture, to coat. Cook the remaining churros in the same way and serve immediately.

BASQUE APPLE TART

TARTA DE MANZANA OR PASTEL VASCO, AS IT IS ALSO KNOWN, IS MADE WITH A HEAVY SWEET PASTRY, WHICH HAS THE TEXTURE AND TASTE OF CAKE. IT OFTEN HAS A CUSTARD CENTRE. THIS ONE HAS AN APPLE FILLING, BUT OTHER FRESH FRUIT, SUCH AS APRICOTS OR PLUMS, WORK JUST AS WELL.

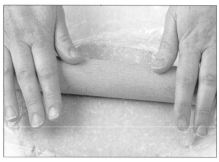

4 Place the larger piece of dough on a lightly floured piece of clear film (plastic wrap) and cover with another piece of film. Roll out to a 25cm/10in round. Remove the top layer of film and lift up the dough on the second film. Place the dough face down in the tin and peel off the film. Press into the tin so that it stands just clear of the top.

5 Pack the tin with the apples and sprinkle with cinnamon. Roll out the second piece of dough in the same way, to exactly the same size as the tin. Lay the dough on top of the apples and fold the overlapping edges of the bottom piece of dough inward. Gently press the edges together with a fork, to seal.

SERVES SIX

INGREDIENTS
   215g/7½oz/scant 2 cups plain (all-
      purpose) flour, plus extra for rolling
   5ml/1 tsp baking powder
   pinch of salt
   115g/4oz/½ cup cold unsalted
      (sweet) butter, cubed
   finely grated rind of ½ lemon
   75g/3oz/scant ½ cup caster
      (superfine) sugar, plus extra
      for sprinkling
   2 small (US medium) eggs
   3 eating apples, peeled, cored
      and cubed
   ground cinnamon, for sprinkling
   whipped cream, to serve

1 Sift the flour, baking powder and salt into a food processor. Add the butter and grated lemon rind and process briefly to combine, then add the sugar, 1 whole egg and the yolk of the second egg to the flour mixture and process to make a soft dough.

2 Divide the dough into two pieces, one portion nearly double the size of the other. Pat the dough into two flat cakes. Wrap tightly in clear film (plastic wrap) and chill for at least 2 hours until firm.

3 Preheat the oven to 180°C/350°F/ Gas 4. Place a baking sheet in the oven and grease a 20cm/8in loose-based flan tin (tart pan).

6 Prick the dough a few times, brush with egg white and sprinkle with sugar. Place on the hot baking sheet and bake for 20 minutes, then reduce the temperature to 160°C/325°F/Gas 3 for a further 25–30 minutes until golden.

7 Leave the tart to cool in the tin for 30 minutes, then unmould and cool on a wire rack. Serve with whipped cream.

BISCOCHO BORRACHO

THE NAME OF THIS MOIST, NUTTY DESSERT TRANSLATES AS "DRUNKEN CAKE", INDICATING THAT IT IS SOAKED IN BRANDY-FLAVOURED SYRUP. THE CAKE CAN BE LAYERED WITH CREAM, BUT THIS VERSION IS MADE IN A MOULD, THEN TURNED OUT. PIPE WITH WHIPPED CREAM IF YOU LIKE.

SERVES SIX TO EIGHT

INGREDIENTS
    butter, for greasing
    90g/3½oz/¾ cup plain
      (all-purpose) flour
    6 large (US extra large) eggs
    90g/3½oz/½ cup caster
      (superfine) sugar
    finely grated rind of 1 lemon
    90ml/6 tbsp toasted flaked
      almonds
    250ml/8fl oz/1 cup whipping
      cream, to serve
For the syrup
    115g/4oz/generous ½ cup caster
      (superfine) sugar
    120ml/4fl oz/½ cup boiling water
    105ml/7 tbsp Spanish brandy

1 Starting 1–2 days ahead, preheat the oven to 200°C/400°F/Gas 6. Butter a shallow tin (pan), about 28 × 18cm/ 11 × 7in. Line the tin with baking parchment and butter well.

2 Sift the flour a couple of times into a bowl. Separate the eggs, putting the whites into a large bowl. Put the yolks in a food processor with the sugar and lemon rind and beat until light. Whisk the whites to soft peaks, then work a little white into the yolk mixture.

3 Dribble two spoonfuls of the yolk mixture across the whites, sift some flour over the top and cut in gently with a large spoon. Continue folding together in this way until all the egg yolk mixture and flour have been incorporated.

4 Turn the mixture into the prepared tin and smooth over. Bake for 12 minutes. Leave the cake to set for 5 minutes, then turn out on to a wire rack. Peel off the paper and leave to cool completely.

5 Make the syrup. Place 50g/2oz/¼ cup sugar into a small pan and add 15ml/ 1 tbsp water. Heat until it caramelizes, shaking the pan a little if one side starts to brown too fast. As soon as it colours, dip the base of the pan into a bowl of cold water. Add the remaining sugar and pour in the boiling water. Bring back to a simmer, stirring until the sugar has dissolved. Pour into a jug (pitcher) and add the brandy.

6 Put the cake back into the tin and drizzle half the syrup over it. Choose a 700ml/1½ pint/3 cup capacity mould or tin; cut the cake into scallops with a spoon and layer half into the bottom of it. Scatter 30ml/2 tbsp almonds over the top, and push them down the cracks. Top with the remaining cake and nuts.

7 Pour the remaining syrup over the cake, cover with foil and weight down the top. Chill until ready to serve.

8 To serve, whip the cream. Run a knife round the mould and turn the cake out on to a long dish. Scatter with almonds and serve with the cream.

BREAKFAST ENSAIMADAS

ORIGINALLY FROM MAJORCA THESE SNAIL-SHAPED BUNS, MADE OF THE LIGHTEST POSSIBLE DOUGH, ARE A DELICIOUS TRADITIONAL TREAT. THEY ARE NOW EATEN IN MADRID AND THROUGHOUT SOUTHERN AND EASTERN SPAIN FOR BREAKFAST. TRADITIONALLY LARD OR SAIM, AS IT IS KNOWN IN SPAIN, WAS USED TO BRUSH OVER THE TOPS, BUT NOWADAYS BUTTER IS USED AND ADDS A DELICIOUS RICHNESS.

MAKES SIXTEEN ROLLS

INGREDIENTS
  225g/8oz/2 cups unbleached strong
    white bread flour
  2.5ml/½ tsp salt
  50g/2oz/¼ cup caster
    (superfine) sugar
  15g/½oz fresh yeast
  75ml/5 tbsp lukewarm milk
  1 egg
  30ml/2 tbsp sunflower oil
  50g/2oz/¼ cup butter, melted
  icing (confectioners') sugar,
    for dusting

COOK'S TIP
Coating the dough with butter helps
to separate the coils as they expand.

1 Lightly grease two baking sheets. Sift the flour and salt together in a large mixing bowl and add the sugar.

2 In a small bowl, cream the yeast and lukewarm milk together. Pour the mixture into the centre of the flour, then sprinkle a little of the flour evenly over the top of the liquid. Leave in a warm place for about 15 minutes until frothy.

3 Turn the mixture into a food processor and process briefly to combine. In a small bowl, beat together the egg and sunflower oil, then pour the mixture into the food processor and work to a smooth dough. Process the dough for several minutes, until it becomes smooth and elastic.

4 Put the dough in a lightly oiled bowl, cover with clear film (plastic wrap) and leave to rise, in a warm place, for 1 hour, or until doubled in size.

5 Put the dough in the food processor and use the pulse button to work until smooth. Turn out on to a lightly floured surface and divide into 16 equal pieces.

6 Shape each piece of dough into a thin rope about 38cm/15in long. Pour the melted butter on to a plate and dip each piece of dough into it to coat.

7 On the baking sheets, curl each rope into a loose spiral, spacing them well apart. Tuck the ends under to seal. Cover with clear film and leave to rise, in a warm place, for about 45 minutes, or until doubled in size.

8 Preheat the oven to 190°C/375°F/ Gas 5. Brush the rolls with water and dust with icing sugar. Bake for about 10 minutes, or until light golden brown. Cool on a wire rack. Dust again with icing sugar and serve warm.

TWELFTH NIGHT BREAD

JANUARY 6TH, EPIPHANY, CELEBRATES THE ARRIVAL OF THE THREE KINGS AT CHRIST'S MANGER AND IN SPAIN, IT IS THE DAY FOR EXCHANGING CHRISTMAS GIFTS. THIS ROSCON DE REYES *— THE KINGS' RING — IS SPECIALLY BAKED FOR THE OCCASION. TRADITIONALLY IT CONTAINS A BEAN, A TINY CHINA BABY OR A SILVER COIN, AND THE LUCKY PERSON TO FIND IT IS DECLARED KING OF THE PARTY.*

SERVES TWELVE

INGREDIENTS
  450g/1lb/4 cups unbleached strong
    white bread flour
  2.5ml/½ tsp salt
  25g/1oz fresh yeast
  140ml/scant ¼ pint/scant ⅔ cup
    mixed lukewarm milk and water
  75g/3oz/6 tbsp butter
  75g/3oz/6 tbsp caster
    (superfine) sugar
  10ml/2 tsp finely grated lemon rind
  10ml/2 tsp finely grated orange rind
  2 eggs
  15ml/1 tbsp brandy
  15ml/1 tbsp orange flower water
  silver coin or dried bean (optional)
  1 egg white, lightly beaten,
    for glazing
For the decoration
  a mixture of glacé (candied)
    fruit slices
  flaked almonds

1 Lightly grease a large baking sheet. Sift together the flour and salt into a large bowl. Make a well in the centre.

2 In a bowl, mix the yeast with the milk and water until the yeast has dissolved. Pour into the centre of the flour and stir in enough of the flour from around the sides of the bowl to make a thick batter.

3 Sprinkle a little of the remaining flour over the top of the batter and leave to turn spongy, in a warm place, for about 15 minutes or until frothy.

4 Using an electric whisk or a wooden spoon, beat together the butter and sugar in a bowl until soft and creamy.

5 Add the citrus rinds, eggs, brandy and orange flower water to the flour mixture and mix to a sticky dough.

6 Beat the mixture until it forms a fairly smooth dough. Gradually beat in the butter mixture and beat for a few minutes until the dough is smooth and elastic. Cover with lightly oiled clear film (plastic wrap) and leave to rise, in a warm place, for about 1½ hours, or until doubled in size.

7 Punch the dough down and turn out on to a lightly floured surface. Gently knead for 2 or 3 minutes, incorporating the lucky coin or bean, if using.

8 Using a rolling pin, roll out the dough into a long strip measuring about 65 × 13cm/26 × 5in.

9 Roll up the dough from one long side like a Swiss roll (jelly roll) to make a long sausage shape. Place seam side down on the prepared baking sheet and seal the ends together. Cover with lightly oiled clear film and leave to rise, in a warm place, for 1–1½ hours, or until doubled in size.

10 Preheat the oven to 180°C/350°F/ Gas 4. Brush the dough ring with lightly beaten egg white and decorate with glacé fruit slices, pushing them slightly into the dough. Sprinkle with flaked almonds and bake for 30–35 minutes, or until risen and golden. Turn out on to a wire rack to cool.

PAN DE CEBADA

GALICIA IS KNOWN FOR ITS COUNTRY BREADS, WHICH OFTEN INCLUDE FLOURS OTHER THAN WHEAT.
MAIZE GROWS IN NORTHERN SPAIN AND IS USED TO MAKE COARSE CORN MEAL; CEBADA MEANS BARLEY.
TOGETHER BARLEY AND MAIZE FLOURS GIVE THIS BREAD A CLOSE, HEAVY TEXTURE AND A RICH TASTE.

3 Return the starter to the bowl, cover with clear film (plastic wrap) and leave in a warm place for 36 hours.

4 To make the dough, put the yeast and water in a small bowl and cream together. Return the sourdough starter to the food processor, pour in the yeast mixture and process to combine well. Gradually add the wholemeal flour, with the salt, and work the whole dough until it becomes smooth and elastic.

5 Transfer the dough to a lightly oiled bowl, cover with clear film and leave, in a warm place, for 1½–2 hours until nearly doubled in size.

6 Return the dough to the food processor and use the pulse button to work it to a smooth dough. Dust a baking sheet with corn meal, and shape the dough on it to a plump round. Sprinkle with a little corn meal. Cover with a large upturned bowl. Leave to rise, in a warm place, for about 1 hour, or until nearly doubled in size.

MAKES ONE LARGE LOAF

INGREDIENTS
corn meal, for dusting
For the sourdough starter
175g/6oz/1½ cups corn meal
225g/8oz/2 cups strong wholemeal
(whole-wheat) bread flour
75g/3oz/⅔ cup barley flour
For the dough
20g/¾oz fresh yeast
45ml/3 tbsp lukewarm water
225g/8oz/2 cups strong wholemeal
bread flour
15ml/1 tbsp salt

COOK'S TIP
Allow 2 days to make the bread. It keeps very well and, once baked, will last for a week or more – if you haven't eaten it long before then.

1 Make the starter. In a pan, mix the corn meal with 300ml/½ pint/1¼ cups water, then blend in another 300ml/½ pint/1¼ cups of water. Cook over a gentle heat, stirring, until thickened. Transfer to a large bowl and cool.

2 Put the mixture into a food processor. Work in the wholemeal and barley flours and process thoroughly.

7 Preheat the oven to 220°C/425°F/Gas 7 and place an empty roasting pan in the bottom of the oven.

8 Pour 300ml/½ pint/1¼ cups cold water into the roasting pan. Lift the bowl off the risen loaf and put the baking sheet in the oven. Bake the bread for 10 minutes. Remove the pan of water, reduce the oven temperature to 190°C/375°F/Gas 5 and bake for about 20 minutes. Cool on a wire rack.

PAN GALLEGO

THIS GALICIAN BREAD IS DISTINGUISHED BY ITS PRETTY TWISTED TOP. THE OLIVE OIL GIVES IT A SOFT CRUMB AND THE MILLET, PUMPKIN AND SUNFLOWER SEEDS SCATTERED THROUGH THE LOAF PROVIDE AN INTERESTING COMBINATION OF TEXTURES.

MAKES ONE LARGE LOAF

INGREDIENTS

   corn meal, for dusting
   350g/12oz/3 cups unbleached strong
     white bread flour
   115g/4oz/1 cup strong wholemeal
     (whole-wheat) bread flour
   10ml/2 tsp salt
   20g/¾oz fresh yeast
   275ml/9fl oz/generous 1 cup
     lukewarm water
   30ml/2 tbsp olive oil or melted lard
   30ml/2 tbsp pumpkin seeds
   30ml/2 tbsp sunflower seeds
   15ml/1 tbsp millet

1 Sprinkle a baking sheet with corn meal. Put the flours and salt together in a food processor and process to mix.

2 In a small bowl, mix the yeast with the water. Add to the flours with the olive oil or melted lard and process to make a firm dough. Continue until the dough is smooth and elastic.

3 Place the dough in a lightly oiled bowl, then cover it with clear film (plastic wrap) and leave to rise, in a warm place, for about 1½–2 hours, or until doubled in size.

4 Return the dough to the processor and use the pulse button to work the dough smooth. Turn out on a lightly floured surface and gently knead in the pumpkin seeds, sunflower seeds and millet. Cover the dough again and leave to rest for 5 minutes.

5 Shape the dough into a round ball and twist the centre to make a cap. Transfer to the prepared baking sheet and dust with corn meal. Cover with a large upturned bowl and leave to rise, in a warm place, for 45 minutes, or until doubled in size.

6 Meanwhile, place an empty roasting pan in the bottom of the oven. Preheat the oven to 220°C/425°F/Gas 7.

7 Pour about 300ml/½ pint/1¼ cups cold water into the roasting pan. Remove the bowl from on top of the loaf and place the loaf (still on the baking sheet) in the oven, on the shelf above the roasting pan. Bake for 10 minutes.

8 Remove the pan of water from the oven and bake the bread for a further 25–30 minutes, or until it is well browned and sounds hollow when tapped on the base. Transfer the bread to a wire rack to cool.

SHOPPING AND FURTHER INFORMATION

AUSTRALIA

**Anna's Continental
Fine Foods**
3/86 Scarborough Beach Road
Mount Hawthorn
Tel: (08) 9443 1508

Casa Iberica
25 Johnston Street
Fitzroy
Melbourne VIC
Tel: (03) 9419 4420

**Torres Spanish Cellars
& Delicatessen**
75 Liverpool Street
Sydney NSW
Tel: (02) 9264 6862

Viva Spain
315 Victoria Street
Melbourne VIC
Tel: (03) 9329 0485

NEW ZEALAND

**Bel Mondo Italian
Mediterranean Foods**
68 St John
St Tauranga
Tel: (07) 579 0968

Mediterranean Foods Ltd
42 Constable Street
Newtown
Wellington
Tel: (04) 939 8100

UNITED KINGDOM

Bridisa
Borough Market
London SE1
Tel: 020 7403 6932

Casa Pepe
89 High Road
London N2
Tel: 020 8444 9098

La Coruna
103 Newington Butts
London SE1
Tel: 020 7703 3165

Garcia & Sons
248–250 Portobello Road
London W11
Tel: 020 7221 6119

The Grapevine Delicatessen
77 High Street
Odiham
Hampshire RG29
Tel: 01256 701900

Laymont & Shaw
The Old Chapel
Millpool
Truro
Cornwall TR1
Tel: 01872 270545

Lupe Pinto's Deli
24 Levan Street
Edinburgh EH3
Tel: 0131 228 6241

Maison Bouquillon
41 Moscow Road
London W2
Tel: 020 7229 2107

**Moreno Wine Importers
Co Limited**
11 Marylands Road
London W1
Tel: 020 7286 9678

P de la Fuente
288 Portobello Road
London W10
Tel: 020 7960 5687

Paris and Rios
93 Columbia Road
London E2
Tel: 020 7729 1147

Products from Spain
89 Charlotte Street
London W1
Tel: 020 7580 2905

Rias Altas
97 Frampton Street
London NW8
Tel: 020 7262 4340

UNITED STATES

Dean and Deluca
560 Broadway
New York NY 10012
Tel: (212) 226 6800

Deli Iberico
739 North LaSalle Drive
Chicago IL 60610
Tel: (312) 573 1510

New York Wine Warehouse
8-05 43rd Avenue
Long Island City
New York NY 11101
Tel: (718) 784 8776

Michael Skurnik Wines
575 Underhill Boulevard
Suite 216
Syosset NY 11791
Tel: (516) 677 9300

The Spanish Table
1427 Western Avenue
Seattle WA 98101
Tel: (206) 682 2827
also at:
1814 San Pablo Avenue
Berkley CA 94792
Tel: (510) 548 1383
also at:
109 North Guadalupe Street
Santa Fe NM 87501
Tel: (505) 986 0243

Spectrum Ingredients
5341 Old Redwood Highway
Petaluma CA 94954
Tel: (707) 778 8900

www.chefshop.com
A wide selection of mail order
Spanish ingredients and foods.

www.cmccompany.com
A wide selection of mail order
Spanish ingredients and foods.

www.ethnicgrocer.com
A wide selection of mail order
Spanish ingredients and foods.

www.spanish-gourmet.com
Information about Spanish
ingredients and foods.

ACKNOWLEDGEMENTS

The publisher would like to thank the following photographers and picture agencies for use of their images in this book:
Ian Aitken – pages 13 (top), 14, 15 (top left and right) and 26 (bottom); Anthony Blake Photo Library – page 21 (top); Cephas Picture Library – pages 11 (top) and 13 (bottom); Powerstock – pages 10, 11 (bottom), 15 (bottom), 16 (top and bottom), 17 (top and bottom) and 19 (top and bottom), 23 (bottom) and 27 (top); Travel Ink – pages 18 (top and bottom) and 20 (top and bottom); and Peter Wilson – pages 12 (top and bottom), 22 (top and bottom), 23 (top), 24, 25 (top and bottom), 26 (top) and 27 (bottom).

INDEX

A

albóndigas con salsa de tomate, 204
Alicante crusted rice, 143
allioli, 33
    calderete of rice with, 148
    salt cod fritters with, 162
almonds, 41
    avocado, orange and almond salad, 118
    biscocho borracho, 247
    chilled almond soup with grapes, 96
    guinea fowl with saffron and nut sauce, 200
    sherried onion soup with saffron, 97
    tapas of almonds, olives and cheese, 72
amanida, 122
America, foods from, 8
anchovies, 45, 47
    coca with onion and anchovy topping, 78
    marinated anchovies, 80
    olive and anchovy bites, 70
Andalusia, 10–11
andrajos, 152
anis: fideos con almejas, 150
    lentils with mushrooms and anis, 135
apples, 60
    apple-stuffed crêpes, 238
    Basque apple tart, 246
Aragón, 17
arrope, 235
arroz con pollo, 187
artichokes, 36
    artichoke rice cakes with Manchego, 139
    charred with lemon oil dip, 120

asparagus, 36
    scrambled eggs with spring asparagus, 108
Asturias, 15
Atlantic Ocean, 9
aubergines, 36
    stewed aubergine, 129
avocados: avocado, orange and almond salad, 118
    chilled avocado soup with cumin, 95

B

bacalao, 46
    in spicy tomato with potatoes, 169
bacon: broad beans with bacon, 134
    liver and bacon casserole, 207
    pollo a la Española, 186
Balearic Islands, 19
bananas: Cuban-style rice, 142
banderillas, 78
barbecued mini ribs, 91
Basque apple tart, 246
Basque Country, 16–17
bass, 44
    sea bass in a salt crust, 168
bay leaves 41
    grilled red mullet with, 166
beans, 9, 39
    caldo Gallego, 103
    fabada, 208
    see also black beans; broad beans
beef, 50, 51
    albóndigas con salsa de tomate, 204
    carne con chocolate, 222
    rabo de toro, 223
    solomillo with Cabrales sauce, 221

beetroot: sweet and salty vegetable crisps, 71
bell peppers *see* peppers
biscocho borracho, 247
biscuits, 63
bitter chocolate mousses, 232
black beans, 39
    black bean stew, 210
    Moors and Christians, 141
black fruit sauce, leche frita with, 240
black pudding, 42, 54
    fried black pudding, 90
    roast turkey with black fruit stuffing, 192
blood sausage
    see black pudding
brandy, 66
    biscocho borracho, 247
bread, 62
    pan de cebada, 250
    pan Gallego, 251
    Twelfth Night bread, 249
breakfast ensaimadas, 248
broad beans, 37
    broad beans with bacon, 134
    Catalan broad bean and potato soup, 98
    mushroom, bean and chorizo salad, 118
    tortilla with beans, 105
    veal casserole with broad beans, 217
broccoli: caldo Gallego, 103
buñuelos, 74
butter, 35
butterflied prawns in chocolate sauce, 83

C

cabbage, 37
    braised with chorizo, 124
cakes & buns, 63
    biscocho borracho, 247
    breakfast ensaimadas, 248
    panellets, 243
calamares rellenos, 175
calderete of rice with allioli, 148
caldo Gallego, 103
Canary Islands, 19
capers, 37
    mixed salad with olives and, 116
    pan-fried sole with lemon and, 167
Cantabria, 15

caramel: oranges with caramel wigs, 236
carne con chocolate, 222
carnivals, 24–27
Castile, 12–13
Catalan broad bean and potato soup, 98
Catalonia, 18
Catholicism, 7
central Spain, 12–13
cheese, 34–5
    artichoke rice cakes with Manchego, 139
    buñuelos, 74
    mussels with a parsley crust, 86
    solomillo with Cabrales sauce, 221
    spicy sausage and cheese tortilla, 106
    tapas of almonds, olives and, 72
chestnuts: chorizo with, 204
chicharrones, 74
chicken, 57
    arroz con pollo, 187
    chicken casserole with spiced figs, 191
    chicken chilindrón, 190
    chicken croquettes, 88
    chicken with lemon and garlic, 184
    chicken livers in sherry, 182
    crumbed chicken with green mayonnaise, 185
    orange chicken salad, 183
    pollo a la Española, 186
    pollo con langostinos, 188
chickpeas, 37
chillies, 9, 38–9
    patatas bravas, 126
    venison chops with romesco sauce, 224

chocolate, 9
  bitter chocolate
    mousses, 232
  butterflied prawns in
    chocolate sauce, 83
  carne con chocolate, 222
chorizo, 54–5
  black bean stew, 210
  braised cabbage with, 124
  chorizo with chestnuts, 204
  mushroom, bean and
    chorizo salad, 118
  spicy sausage and cheese
    tortilla, 106
Christmas, 24
churros, 245
cider, 67
clams, 48
  fideos con almejas, 150
  hake and clams with salsa
    verde, 172
  spiced, 85
coca with onion and anchovy
  topping, 78
cochofrito, 214
cocido, 7, 218
convents, 8
cookies see biscuits
coriander, 41
  Catalan broad bean and
    potato soup, 98
crema catalana, 234
crêpes, apple-stuffed, 238
crisps, sweet and salty
  vegetable, 71
croquettes: chicken, 88
Cuban-style rice, 142
cumin: chilled avocado soup
  with, 95
  orange and red onion salad
    with, 116

D
desserts, 61, 228–40, 246–7
drinks, 66–7
  see also wine
duck, 57
  spiced duck with pears, 194

E
eating & drinking, 20–1
eggs, 34
  Alicante crusted rice, 143
  Cuban-style rice, 142
  flamenco eggs, 110
  pan-fried ham and
    vegetables with, 111
  piperada sandwich, 107

  potato tortilla, 104
  scrambled eggs with
    prawns, 109
  scrambled eggs with spring
    asparagus, 108
  spicy sausage and cheese
    tortilla, 106
  tortilla with beans, 105
eggplant see aubergines
empanada, pork, 212
empanadillas, spinach, 77
ensaimadas, breakfast, 248
ensaladilla, 115
equipment, kitchen, 30–1, 42
escalivada, 133
Extremadura, 13

F
fabada, 208
fava beans see broad beans
feast days & fiestas, 24–7
fideos con almejas, 150
figs, 60
  chicken casserole with
    spiced, 191
  honey-baked figs with
    hazelnut ice cream, 230
  stuffed roast loin of
    pork, 211
fish: fresh, 44–5
  preserved, 46–7
  calderete of rice with
    allioli, 148
  fish soup with orange, 102
  marmitako, 177
  surtido de pescado, 159
  zarzuela, 178
  see also individual types
    of fish
flamenco eggs, 110
flans, 233
fritters, 63
fruit, 60
  arrope, 235

  leche frita with black fruit
    sauce, 240
  see also individual types
    of fruit

G
Galicia, 14
game, 58–9
garlic, 36
  chicken with lemon
    and, 184
  flash-fried squid with
    paprika and, 81
  sizzling prawns, 84
  sopa Castiliana, 99
gazpacho, 94
grapes, 60
  chilled almond soup with
    grapes, 96
  perdices con uvas, 201
guinea fowl, 57
  guinea fowl with saffron and
    nut sauce, 200
guirlache, 242
gypsies, 8

H
hake, 44–5
  and clams with salsa
    verde, 172
ham, 56
  calamares rellenos, 175
  pan-fried ham and
    vegetables with eggs, 111
  truchas a la Navarra, 165
hare, 59
  andrajos, 152
hazelnuts, 41
  hazelnut meringues with
    nectarines, 237
  honey-baked figs with
    hazelnut ice cream, 230
herbs, 41
honey, 61

I
ice cream: honey-baked
  figs with hazelnut
  ice cream, 230
  rum and raisin, 228

J
jamón serrano, 56

K
kidneys: riñones al Jerez, 206
king prawns in crispy
  batter, 82

L
la calçotada, 125
La Mancha, 13
lamb, 51
  cochofrito, 214
  lamb with red peppers and
    Rioja, 216
  skewered lamb with red
    onion salsa, 214
leche frita with black fruit
  sauce, 240
lemons, 60
  charred artichokes with
    lemon oil dip, 120
  chicken with lemon and
    garlic, 184
  mackerel in lemon
    samfaina, 170
  pan-fried sole with lemon
    and capers, 167
  sorbete de limón, 229
lentils, 37
  lentils with mushrooms and
    anis, 135
León, 12
Levante, 19
liver and bacon casserole, 207

M
mackerel, 44
  in lemon samfaina, 170
Madrid, 12
Manchego cheese, 35
  artichoke rice cakes
    with, 139
mangetout: scrambled eggs
  with spring asparagus, 108
Manual de Cocina, 21
mariscos, sopa des, 100
marmitako, 177
matanza, 27
mayonnaise: crumbed chicken
  with green mayonnaise, 185
Mediterranean Sea, 9

menestra, 130
meringues: hazelnut, with
    nectarines, 237
milk, 35
mixed salad with olives and
    capers, 116
mojete, 127
monkfish, 44
    with pimiento and cream
    sauce, 171
Moorish influence, 6
Moors and Christians, 141
mousses, bitter chocolate, 232
Murcia, 11
mushrooms, 37
    andrajos, 152
    lentils with mushrooms and
        anis, 135
    marinated mushrooms, 114
    mushroom, bean and
        chorizo salad, 118
    pechugas de pichones con
        setas, 198
mussels, 48
    mussels with a parsley
        crust, 86
    potato, mussel and
        watercress salad, 157

N

nectarines: hazelnut
    meringues with, 237
Nevarra, 17
New Year, 24
nuts: baked trout with rice,
    tomatoes and, 164
    guirlache, 242
    panellets, 243
    see also almonds; hazelnuts

O

octopus, 49
    octopus stew, 176
olive oil, 32; sauces, 33

olives, 32, 33
    mixed salad with olives and
        capers, 116
    olive and anchovy bites, 70
    tapas of almonds, olives and
        cheese, 72
onions, 36
    coca with onion and
        anchovy topping, 78
    orange and red onion salad
        with cumin, 116
    sherried onion soup with
        saffron, 97
    skewered lamb with red
        onion salsa, 214
oranges, 9, 60, 61
    avocado, orange and
        almond salad, 118
    fish soup with orange, 102
    orange chicken salad, 183
    orange and red onion salad
        with cumin, 116
    oranges with caramel
        wigs, 236
outdoor cooking, 20

P

paella, 43
    Alicante crusted rice, 143
    paella Valenciana, 144
    seafood paella, 146
pan de cebada, 250
panellets, 243
pan Gallego, 251
paprika, 40
    flash-fried squid with
        paprika and garlic, 81
parsley, 41
    hake and clams with salsa
        verde, 172
    lentils with mushrooms and
        anis, 135
    mussels with a parsley
        crust, 86

partridges: perdices con
    uvas, 201
pasta, 43
    andrajos, 152
    fideos con almejas, 50
    San Esteban canelones, 151
patatas bravas, 126
patronal festivals, 25
pears: spiced duck with, 194
pechugas de pichones con
    setas, 198
peppers, 38
    chicken chilindrón, 190
    lamb with red peppers and
        Rioja, 216
    marmitako, 177
    monkfish with pimiento and
        cream sauce, 171
    pimiento tartlets, 76
    stuffed tomatoes and
        peppers, 128
perdices con uvas, 201
pestiños, 244
picadas: pollo con
    langostinos, 188
    spiced duck with pears, 194
pigeon, 58
    marinated pigeon in red
        wine, 197
    pechugas de pichones con
        setas, 198
pilgrims, 8
pimiento tartlets, 76
pinchitos moruños, 89
pine nuts, 41
    spinach with raisins and
        pine nuts, 121
piperada sandwich, 107
pisto Manchego, 132
pollo con langostinos, 188
pollo a la Española, 186
pork, 7, 52–3
    barbecued mini ribs, 91
    black bean stew, 210
    caldo Gallego, 103
    chicharrones, 74
    fabada, 208
    pinchitos moruños, 89
    pork empanada, 212
    stuffed roast loin of, 211
potatoes, 39
    bacalao in spicy tomato
        with potatoes, 169
    Catalan broad bean and
        potato soup, 98
    patatas bravas, 126
    potato, mussel and
        watercress salad, 157

    potato tortilla, 104
    salt cod fritters with
        allioli, 162
    tortilla with beans, 105
prawns, 48–9
    butterflied prawns in
        chocolate sauce, 83
    king prawns in crispy
        batter, 82
    pollo con langostinos, 188
    scrambled eggs with
        prawns, 109
    sizzling prawns, 84
Pyrenees, 16–17

Q

quail, 58
    braised with winter
        vegetables, 196

R

rabbit, 59
    rabbit salmorejo, 225
rabo de toro, 223
raisins: calamares
    rellenos, 175
    rum and raisin ice
        cream, 228
    spinach with raisins and
        pine nuts, 121
red mullet, 45
    grilled red mullet with bay
        leaves, 166
red wine: braised quail with
    winter vegetables, 196
    lamb with red peppers and
        Rioja, 216
    pigeon marinated in red
        wine, 197
    stewed aubergine, 129
religion, 7–8
regions of Spain, 18–27
restaurants, 20–21
rice, 42

Alicante crusted rice, 143
arroz con pollo, 187
artichoke rice cakes with
　Manchego, 139
baked trout with rice,
　tomatoes and nuts, 164
calderete of rice with
　allioli, 148
Cuban-style rice, 142
Moors and Christians, 141
orange chicken salad, 183
paella Valenciana, 144
rice tortitas, 138
simple rice salad, 140
stuffed tomatoes and
　peppers, 128
vegetable rice pot, 147
riñones al Jerez, 206
romesco sauce: venison chops
　with, 224
ropa vieja, 220
rum and raisin ice cream, 228

S
saffron, 40
　guinea fowl with saffron and
　　nut sauce, 200
　paella Valenciana, 144
　sherried onion soup with, 97
salads: amanida, 122
　avocado, orange and
　　almond salad, 118
　ensaladilla, 115
　mixed salad with olives and
　　capers, 116
　mushroom, bean and
　　chorizo, 118
　orange chicken salad, 183
　orange and red onion salad
　　with cumin, 116
　potato, mussel and
　　watercress, 157
　seafood, 156
　simple rice, 140

skate with bitter salad
　leaves, 158
salt, 40
salt cod, 7, 44, 46
　bacalao in spicy tomato with
　　potatoes, 169
　salt cod fritters with
　　allioli, 162
San Esteban canelones, 151
sardines, 44, 47
　sardines en escabeche, 160
sausages, 54–5
　sausage and cheese tortilla,
　　spicy, 106
scallions see spring onions
scallops, 48
　vieiras de Santiago, 173
scrambled eggs: with
　prawns, 109
　with spring asparagus, 108
Semana Santa, 24
Sephardim, 7
shellfish, 47, 48–9
　seafood paella, 146
　seafood salad, 156
　sopa des mariscos, 100
sherry, 65
　barbecued mini ribs, 91
　chicken livers in sherry, 182
　fried whitebait with sherry
　　salsa, 161
　marinated mushrooms, 114
　riñones al Jerez, 206
　sherried onion soup with
　　saffron, 97
　sherry vinegar, 41
shrimp see prawns
skate with bitter salad
　leaves, 158
social life, 20
sole, 44
　pan-fried with lemon and
　　capers, 167
solomillo with Cabrales
　sauce, 221
sorbets: sorbete de limón, 229
soups, 94–103
　caldo Gallego, 103
　Catalan broad bean and
　　potato soup, 98
　chilled almond soup with
　　grapes, 96
　chilled avocado soup with
　　cumin, 95
　fish soup with orange, 102
　gazpacho, 94
　sherried onion soup with
　　saffron, 97

sopa Castiliana, 99
sopa des mariscos, 100
spices, 40
spinach, 36
　spinach empanadillas, 77
　spinach with raisins and
　　pine nuts, 121
spring onions:
　la calçotada, 125
squid, 49
　calamares rellenos, 175
　char-grilled, 174
　flash-fried with paprika and
　　garlic, 81
stews, types of, 51
surtido de pescado, 159
sweetmeats, 8, 61
　guirlache, 242
　pestinos, 244
sweet potatoes, 39
　panellets, 243

T
tapas, 22–3, 70–91
　tapas of almonds, olives
　　and cheese, 72
　see also individual tapas
　　dishes
tomatoes, 9, 38
　albóndigas con salsa de
　　tomate, 204
　bacalao in spicy tomato with
　　potatoes, 169
　baked trout with rice,
　　tomatoes and nuts, 164
　stuffed tomatoes and
　　peppers, 128
　vieiras de Santiago, 173
torrijas, 239
tortillas: potato tortilla, 104
　spicy sausage and cheese
　　tortilla, 106
　tortilla with beans, 105
trout, 45

baked with rice, tomatoes
　and nuts, 164
truchas a la Navarra, 165
tuna, 45, 47
　marmitako, 177
turkey, 57
　roast with black fruit
　　stuffing, 192
Twelfth Night bread, 249

V
veal, 50
　veal casserole with broad
　　beans, 217
vegetables, 36–9
　braised quail with winter
　　vegetables, 196
　escalivada, 133
　menestra, 130
　mojete, 127
　pan-fried ham and
　　vegetables with eggs, 111
　pisto Manchego, 132
　sweet and salty vegetable
　　crisps, 71
　vegetable rice pot, 147
　see also individual
　　vegetables
venison, 58–9
　venison chops with romesco
　　sauce, 224
vieiras de Santiago, 173

W
watercress: potato, mussel and
　watercress salad, 157
whitebait, 45
　fried with sherry salsa, 161
wild ingredients, 37, 59
wine, 64–5, 66
　see also red wine

Z
zarzuela, 178